KEIO ARCHITECTURE Year Book

2018 - 2019

The corporate vision of Sogo Shikaku is to contribute to development of a safe and secure society by fostering skilled engineers with a sense of ethics. Sogo Shikaku Gakuin has provided educational services mainly for professionals in architecture since its foundation. With the aging and declining population and surfacing environmental issues, to create a resilient and sustainable society is an urgent task in Japan. We consider it our mission to train engineers who can tackle the issues and are helping to prepare themselves to become qualified professionals including licensed architects. As a part of our mission, we support exhibitions and laboratory activities of architectural students as well as establish scholarships and fund lectures with the hope of encouraging students to pursue their dreams in architectural professions.

The idea of Keio Architecture aiming at an international design research and educational hub by a joint effort of the Faculty of Science and Technology and SFC has much in common with Sogo Shikaku's vision. We admire the achievements of the faculty and decided to support the publishment of the Year Book. The book introduces the activities of Keio Architecture in 2018 and 2019 and the works of the students as well as it records the lectures of three renowned architects, Professor Fumihiko Maki, Professor Kengo Kuma and Professor Shigeru Ban who have helped development of architectural education at Keio over the years. It is written in both Japanese and English to serve as the global platform in architecture, which marks one of the greatest characteristics of the book.

We sincerely hope that the book will not only contribute to further development of Keio Architecture but attract interests of various communities of architecture especially young generations who aspire to become successful engineers in the global architectural industry.

SOGO-SHIKAKU-GAKUIN Dean Takashi Kishi

ハイレベルなスキルと高い倫理観を持つ技術者の育成を通じ、安心・安全な社会づくりに貢献する──、それを企業理念として、私たち総合資格学院は創業以来、建築関係を中心とした資格スクールを運営してきました。近年、人口減少と高齢化社会の進行、そして環境問題のひずみが顕著に表れ始め、レジリエントで持続可能な社会をつくることが日本の喫緊の課題となっています。そういった課題に応えられる技術者を育てることが当学院の使命であると考え、建築士をはじめとした有資格者の育成に日々努めています。

その一環として、建築の世界を志す学生の方々が夢を持って志望の道に進めるよう、学生設計展への協賛や研究室の活動費の支援、そして大学単位では奨学金の創設や講演会のサポートなどを行っています。

慶應義塾大学の理工学部とSFCを結び、国際的なデザイン・リサーチ・教育センターを目指す「慶應アーキテクチャ」のお話をお伺いした際も、当学院の理念と共通する点を多く感じ、「イヤーブック」の制作・発行においてご協力させていただきました。

本書は2018年と2019年の「慶應アーキテクチャ」の活動、そして学生の提案をまとめるとともに、慶應義塾大学における建築教育の発展を後押しされてきた槇文彦先生や隈研吾先生、坂茂先生の講演を収録しております。全文、日本語と英語を併記しており、国際化を見据えて編集している点も特徴です。

本書が「慶應アーキテクチャ」のさらなる発展に寄与することはもちろんのこと、慶應義塾大学の関係者、さらには広く多くの建築関係者、特に建築の道を志す若い方々にご覧いただき、彼らが国内のみならず世界で活躍する技術者となることを期待しております。

総合資格学院　学院長　岸 隆司

Keio Architecture Yearbook 2018-19 presents a selection of undergraduate and graduate projects from architecture and urban design studios conducted at Keio University in 2018 and 2019.

Keio, the oldest University in Japan, still does not have a dedicated School of Architecture and Urban Design. Its twelve laboratories operating in the fields focusing at production of space are based within multidisciplinary schools which are located at distant campuses - Faculty of Science and Technology at Yagami, and Graduate School of Media and Governance at Shonan Fujisawa. Thus conceived, Keio Architecture functions as an international and collaborative Research, Design-Research and Education Hub, co-organized by participating laboratories, with an overarching aim to advance Architectural and Urban Design at Keio and within its international networks.

Architecture was introduced to Keio Faculty of Science and Technology in 2000, with inauguration of Kazuyo Sejima's and Kengo Kuma's laboratories. The next critical step was in 2010, with establishment of a semi-formal institutional framework of IKI - International Keio Institute for Architecture and Urbanism. Imagined and initiated by Darko Radović, Kazuyo Sejima (Yagami) and Hiroto Kobayashi (SFC), IKI was launched at Architecture Biennale in Venice in 2010. Since that, it served as a platform for international research and design activities, involving professionals from Keio, various Japanese and international institutions of renown and global prestige.

In 2018, Keio Architecture (following an advice by Fumihiko Maki) was announced, with a launch of the architecture.keio.ac.jp web site and introduction of the key project - Comprehensive Design Workshop for the Athletic and Recreational Facilities of the Hiyoshi, Shimoda, and Yagami Campuses – CDW. The Workshop, initiated by Dean of the Faculty of Science and Technology Kohei Itoh has evolved into a complex, heuristic design-research exercise in rethinking both those facilities and the broader quality of life and well-being within the Campuses and their neighbouring areas.

This Yearbook presents work produced within CDW in studios coordinated by Professors (in alphabetic order) Darko Radović, Hiroto Kobayashi, Jorge Almazán, Shigeru Ban and Tatsuya Kishimoto; Visiting Studio Professors Katsuhito Komatsu, Motoo Chiba, Satoshi Sano, Takumi Saikawa and Tatsuo Kondo; and a number of Guests, from the world-known and up-and-coming academics. Reflecting the spirit of emerging Keio Architecture, not only the material presented here but the book itself, generously supported by SOGO Shikakugaku, was entirely designed and developed by our students.

CDW and this book are part of celebrations of the 80th Anniversary of the Faculty of Science and Technology at Keio University.

慶應アーキテクチャイヤーブック2018-2019は、慶應義塾大学で建築・都市デザインに関わるさまざまな研究室に所属する学部生と修士生の作品を数多く掲載しています。

日本最古の大学である慶應義塾大学には、いまだ建築・都市デザインに特化した学部がありません。空間の生産性について研究・調査する12の研究室は幅広い学問領域の中に位置づけられており、物理的に離れた2つのキャンパス（理工学部が活動する矢上キャンパスと政策メディア研究科が拠点とする湘南藤沢キャンパス）に分かれて活動しています。それ故に、慶應アーキテクチャは国際的、学際的、そしてコラボレーティブなデザイン・リサーチ・教育として機能しており、慶應の建築・都市デザインの発展を目指し、数多くの研究室が国際的ネットワークを駆使して、共同で管理しています。

建築が慶應の理工学部に導入されたのは2000年、妹島和世氏と隈研吾氏が研究室を持つところから始まりました。2010年には、ダルコ・ラドヴィッチ教授、妹島和世教授（矢上）と小林博人教授（湘南藤沢）によって構想・始動したIKI（国際慶應建築・都市研究所）がベネチアのビエンナーレで発足。現在に至るまで、IKIは国際的リサーチ・教育のプラットフォーム・デザインとリサーチ活動の場として活躍し、慶應に所属する多くの学者や専門家、世界的にも有名な日本・海外の機関と関わってきました。

2018年に慶應アーキテクチャ（日本の建築界を代表する槇文彦氏のアドバイスのもと名づけられました）が発表され、architecture.keio.ac.jpという公式サイトと合わせて、キープロジェクトであるCDW（日吉・下田・矢上キャンパスにおけるスポーツとレクリエーション施設の包括的デザインワークショップ）が始動しました。CDWプロジェクトに関しては、理工学部長を勤めた伊藤公平教授の提案もあり、スポーツとレクリエーション施設の設計だけにとどまらず、キャンパスと近隣住民のQOLと福祉について再考していく、実に複雑でヒューリスティックな課題へと進化を遂げました。

この慶應アーキテクチャイヤーブック2018-2019には、CDWプロジェクトにまつわる作品を多く載せてあります。この場を借りて、ご協力いただきましたスタジオのコーディネーターであるダルコ・ラドヴィッチ、小林博人、ホルヘ・アルマザン、坂茂と岸本達也、加えて客員教授の小松克人、千葉元生、佐野哲史、齋川拓未、近藤哲雄（英語における名前順）、そして世に名を馳せる先生方から今後の建築界を担う若手の建築家までを含むゲスト講演者や学者の皆様にお礼申し上げます。慶應アーキテクチャの発展を願う精神に基づき、本書に掲載されているマテリアルはもちろん、出版も総合資格学院様の寛大なるサポートのもと、全て学生の手によって行われています。

またCDWと本書は慶應義塾大学理工学部80周年記念行事の一環として取り上げられております。

2   Preface by the Publsiher
    Sogoshikaku

3   Introduction of Keio Architecture Year Book
    Darko Radović

4   Index

7   Chapter 1 : Introduction

    10   Introduction
         Akira Haseyama, Eiji Okada, Kohei Ito, Darko Radović, Hiroto Kobayashi

    14   Discussion
         Darko Radović, Hiroto Kobayashi

    Column 1   The snapshots from production of Keio Architecture   LOGO

—2018—

21 Chapter 2 : Studio B

    25   Overview of the Studio B

    26   Interview
         Takumi Saikawa, Tetsuo Kondo

    34   Student Works
         Yumi Ishii, Yusuke Ono, Takuomi Samejima, Yuichi Tatsumi, Itaru Iwasaki
         Keitaro Onishi, Xuang Yang, Kyoko Suganuma, Manon Ellie

    Column 2   The snapshots from production of Keio Architecture   POSTER 1
    Column 3   The snapshots from production of Keio Architecture   MODEL 1

45 Chapter 3 : Seizu 3

    49   Overview of the Seizu 3

    50   Interview
         Hiroyuki Ito, Motoo Chiba

    54   Student Works
         Kyoko Ito, Hiroki Shigemura, Yoshihisa Moriya, Motomi Matsubara
         Junpei Kawamoto, Amami Iwata, Shinichi Nishibori, Kousuke Miyano
         Akari Hara, Yuki Wada

    Column 4   The snapshots from production of Keio Architecture   PAVILION 1

61 Chapter 4 : Exhibition

    64   Exhibition Appearance

    68   Lecture
         Kengo Kuma, Fumihiko Maki, Shigeru Ban

    Column 5   The snapshots from production of Keio Architecture   ROOM 1

—2019—

81 Overview 5 : Studio A

    85   Outline of the Studio A

    86   Interview
         Satoshi Sano, Katsuhito Komatsu, Motoo Chiba

    98   Student Works
         Norimi Kinoshita, Hiroki Shigemura, Shohei Yamashita, Zan Krivec, Gabriel Chatel
         Shinichi Nishibori, Junpei Kawamoto, Manca Kosir, Francisco Javier Celaya Moron
         Amami Iwata, Shun Kato, Sanja Zonja, Yuki Wada

    Column 6   The snapshots from production of Keio Architecture   POSTER 2

115 Chapter 6 : Seizu 3

    119 Overview of the Seizu 3

    120 Interview
         Takashi Suo, Takumi Saikawa

    124 Student Works
         Shunsuke Shimizu, Ryota Ibaraki, Koki Suzuki, Yuki Mori, Muxi Yang
         Daiki Sekiguchi, Maroya Harigaya, Yoshitomo Yonamoto

    Column 7   The snapshots from production of Keio Architecture   MODEL 2

131 Chapter 7 : SFC Studio

    135 Overview of the SFC Studio

    136 Student Works
         Ilham Ras, Gabriel Chatel, Yusuke Nakagawa, Deric Low Seong Hee
         Francisco Javier Celaya Moron, Ayano Yasunaga,Hiroshi Ohara
         Daiki Sekiguchi, Mayu Masuda,Yuko Yamashita

    Column 8   The snapshots from production of Keio Architecture   PAVILION 2
    Column 9   The snapshots from production of Keio Architecture   STAMP

141 Chapter 8 : Exhibition

    144 Exhibition Appearance

    148 Symposium
         Sakai Toshiaki, Yamashita Shohei, Renan Prandini Tan, Olena Kopytina
         Monya Kazuma, Waki Narumi, Neno Kezic, Gabriele Masera, Tadej Glažar,
         Estanislau Roca

    152 Lecture
         Kengo Kuma, Fumihiko Maki, Yoshio Taniguchi

    Column 10   The snapshots from production of Keio Architecture   FURNITURE1

—Lecture—

161 Chapter 9 : Lecture Series

    164 List of Lecturers

    166 Lecture
         Gabriele Masera, Leonardo Chiesi, Manuela Grecchi, Matteo Ruta
         Vladimir Lojanica, Ray Lucas, Ronan Paddison, Alison Young
         Haide Imai, Vuk Radović, Davisi Boontharm, Akitaka Suzuki

    Column 11   The snapshots from production of Keio Architecture   FURNITURE 2

179 Chapter 10 : Profile

2 慶應アーキテクチャ KA Book の出版にあたって
総合資格学院

3 慶應アーキテクチャ KA Book のイントロダクション
ダルコ・ラドヴィッチ

4 目次

7 第 1 章：序章
10 イントロダクション
長谷山彰、岡田英史、伊藤公平、ダルコ・ラドヴィッチ、小林博人
14 ディスカッション
ダルコ・ラドヴィッチ、小林博人
コラム 1 慶應アーキテクチャ　プロジェクトのスナップショット　ロゴ

—2018—

21 第 2 章：スタジオ B
25 スタジオ B の課題概要
26 インタビュー
齋川拓未、近藤哲雄
34 生徒の作品
石井結実、小野裕介、鮫島卓臣、巽祐一、岩崎達
大西慶太郎、楊宣、菅沼響子、マノン・エリー
コラム 2 慶應アーキテクチャ　プロジェクトのスナップショット　ポスター 1
コラム 3 慶應アーキテクチャ　プロジェクトのスナップショット　模型 1

45 第 3 章：製図 3
49 製図 3 の課題概要
50 インタビュー
伊藤博之、千葉元生
54 生徒の作品
伊藤京子、重村浩槻、守屋嘉久、松原元実
川本純平、岩田あま美、西堀槙一、宮野公輔
原明里、和田雄樹
コラム 4 慶應アーキテクチャ　プロジェクトのスナップショット　パビリオン 1

61 第 4 章：展示会
64 展示会風景
68 レクチャー
隈研吾、槇文彦、坂茂
コラム 5 慶應アーキテクチャ　プロジェクトのスナップショット　まむし部屋 1

—2019—

81 第 5 章：スタジオ A
85 スタジオ A の課題概要
86 インタビュー
佐野哲史、小松克仁、千葉元生
98 生徒の作品
木下規海、重村浩槻、山下翔平、ジャン・クレヴィック、ガブリエル・チャテル
西堀槙　、川本純平、マンカ・コシ　ル、フランシスコ・ハヴィエ　ル・セレヤ・モロン
岩田あま美、加藤旬、サーニャ・ゾーニャ、和田雄樹
コラム 6 慶應アーキテクチャ　プロジェクトのスナップショット　ポスター 2

115 第 6 章：製図 3
119 製図 3 の課題概要
120 インタビュー
周防貴之、齋川拓未
124 生徒の作品
清水俊祐、茨城亮太、鈴木浩貴、森祐樹、楊沐渓
関口大樹、針谷円、要名本義明
コラム 7 慶應アーキテクチャ　プロジェクトのスナップショット　模型 2

131 第 7 章：湘南藤沢スタジオ
135 SFC スタジオの課題概要
136 生徒の作品
イルハム・ラス、ガブリエル・チャテル、中川雄介、デレク・ロウ・セオン・ヒー、
フランシスコ・ハヴィエール・セレヤ・モロン、安永彩乃、
小原寛史、関口大樹、増田真由、山下裕子
コラム 8 慶應アーキテクチャ　プロジェクトのスナップショット　パビリオン 2
コラム 9 慶應アーキテクチャ　プロジェクトのスナップショット　スタンプ

141 第 8 章：展示会
144 展示会風景
148 シンポジウム
坂井利彰、山下翔平、レナン・ブランディーニタン、エレーナ・コピティーナ、
門矢和真、脇成実、丸山優佑、ネノ・ケジック、ガブリエル・マゼーラ、
タディ・グラザール、エスタニスラウ・ロカ
152 レクチャー
隈研吾、槇文彦、谷口吉生
コラム 10 慶應アーキテクチャ　プロジェクトのスナップショット　家具 1

—講義—

161 第 9 章：レクチャーシリーズ
164 講演者リスト
166 レクチャー
ガブリエル・マゼーラ、レオナルド・キエーゼ、マニュエラ・グリッチ、
マッテオ・ルタ、ブラディミル・ロジャニカ、レイ・ルーカス、
ローナン・パディソン、アリソン・ヤング、ハイデ・イマイ、
ヴック・ラドヴィッチ、ダビシ・ブンタム、鈴木瑛貴
コラム 11 慶應アーキテクチャ　プロジェクトのスナップショット　家具 2

179 第 10 章：プロフィール

第 1 章　イントロダクション

Keio Architecture is both a reality and a dream. Keio Architecture is reality, because none less than twelve research laboratories at Keio University deal with production of space. At the same time, Keio Architecture as a discrete, concentrated programme focused at the fields of architecture and urbanism in the oldest university in Japan is still only a dream. Over the last two decades, an awareness about the possibility that Keio University could offer what research and education in these fields in Japan need has been informally conceptualised. In 2018-19 the generous framework of Comprehensive Design Workshop, provided by the Faculty of Science and Technology has provided all of those who believe in Keio Architecture with a worthy project that is presented in this volume. The key inspiration and support to Keio Architecture CDW was provided by Professor Kohei Itoh, Dean in 2018, who has initiated CDW in 2018. Professor Eiji Okada (Dean in 2019) guided the project to become an important part of the 80th Anniversary Celebrations of the Faculty of Science and Technology. Professor Akira Haseyama, President of Keio University, has elevated the opening of CDW 2019 to the University level.

　慶應アーキテクチャは現実のものであり、また我々の夢でもあります。現に慶應塾大学では 12 を超える研究室が、空間の生産性について日々調査・研究を行っております。同時に、日本最古の大学において、建築・都市の分野に特化・集中したプログラムとして慶應アーキテクチャが動き始めるには、まだまだ乗り越えなけらばならない課題が多くあります。この 20 年の間に、日本の建築・都市におけるリサーチと教育に求められているものを、慶應義塾大学が提供できる可能性が内々で認知されてきました。2018 － 2019 年、理工学部によってこれだけ大きく成長した CDW の枠組みは、慶應アーキテクチャを信じる全ての人々にとって有意義なプロジェクトとなったことでしょう。2018 年度に理工学部長をお勤めになられて伊藤公平先生によって動き始めた慶應アーキテクチャは、2019 年度、岡田英史先生（2019 年度理工学部長）によって、慶応義塾大学理工学部 80 周年の重要イベントの一つとして取り上げられました。また長谷山彰塾長によって、2019 年度 CDW は大学レベルのイベントにまで発展していきました。

Akira Haseyama　　長谷山彰

Congratulation for the success of the CDW project, which is one of the main projects of Keio Architecture.

I attended the special lecture "Keio Architecture and its Trajectories", the conversation between two famous architects Mr. Fumihiko Maki and Mr. Yoshio Taniguchi, held in Kyosei Building Hiyoshi Campus. I was happy to hear all the interesting stories about the history of Keio Architecture, starting from Mr. Tomoo Maki Standing Director (Mr. Fumihiko's Father) and Mr. Yoshiro Taniguchi (Mr. Yoshio's Father). Both lecturers have designed several buildings that exist in Keio. Mr. Maki has designed the new library in Mita Campus, the library in Hiyoshi Campus, and the entire SFC Campus. Mr. Taniguchi has designed the new gymnasium for Keio Yochisha Primary School and the buildings for SFC Secondary School. I was surprised to hear how much effort the two architects, who have a strong connection between Keio, have put in order to design these buildings, taking so much care of the space where the young generation grows. Thank you very much for planning such a grand project.

And finally, taking the success of this workshop, I hope for the future development of Keio Architecture and all of those who took part in this wonderful project.

慶應アーキテクチャプロジェクトの一環である、「Comprehensive Design Workshop（CDW）2019」の成功を心よりお慶び申し上げます。

私は、日吉キャンパス協生館藤原洋記念ホールにて行われた、建築家の槇文彦氏と谷口吉生氏による対談「慶應建築の系譜」を聴講いたしました。そこで、戦前の槇智雄常任理事（文彦氏の叔父）と谷口吉郎氏（吉生氏の父）から始まる慶應建築の歴史に関する数々の証言に触れることができました。講師の槇氏は、慶應義塾の図書館新館や日吉図書館、湘南藤沢キャンパスの設計を手掛けられ、同じく谷口氏は、幼稚舎の新体育館や湘南藤沢中・高等部の校舎を設計されており、ともに義塾に大変ゆかりのあるお二人の建築家が、若者の成長を見守る空間を意識して設計に力を尽くされたことに感銘を受けました。両氏による大変貴重な対談を企画いただきまして、厚く御礼申し上げます。

最後になりましたが、本ワークショップを機に、慶應アーキテクチャがますますご発展されますこと、そして関係のすべての皆様の更なるご活躍とご健勝をお祈りいたします。

Eiji Okada　　岡田英史

"Center of Space and Environment Design Engineering" of Science and Technology, Graduate School of Keio University was established on 2000, as an important key area in the organizational change of the graduate school. With this establishment, the systematic education of architecture has started in the department of Science and Technology, and 20 years is trying to pass. During these years, as the base of the education and studies of the faculty has been established, the education and research system of Keio architecture and urban design has also developed as "Keio Architecture", with the cooperation of the professors teaching architecture in SFC campus.

2019 is the year of the 80th anniversary of the faculty of Science and Technology, and also celebrates the 150th birth of Ginjiro Fujiwara, who is the founder of Fujiwara Institute of Technology, later known as our faculty. As one event to commemorate these, "CDW Comprehensive Design Workshop 2019" was held in Hiyoshi campus by the professors of Keio Architecture, lead by Professor Darko Radović (Faculty of Science and Technology) and Professor Hiroto Kobayashi (Faculty of Environment and Information), with the collaboration of the Institute of Physical Education. As one program of this workshop, there was an open talk between Mr. Fumihiko Maki and Mr. Yoshio Taniguchi titled "Keio Architecture and its Trajectories". Mr. Fumihiko Maki designed the new library of Mita campus, the library in Hiyoshi campus, and the entire campus of SFC. Mr. Yoshio Taniguchi designed the new gymnasium of Yochisha primary school, 21 wing new building, and the school building of Syonan-Fujisawa junior and senior high school. The two have also graduated from the faculty of Technology before architecture education has started in Keio University, and is a big senior for us. There was also a special lecture titled "Architecture and City after Olympics" by Mr. Kengo Kuma, who has put a lot of effort in establishing the architecture education in the faculty of Science and Technology. Many architects and professors of architecture and urban design from overseas took part in this workshop too. Keio Architecture is building its international network steadily. Everyone before Keio Architecture, everyone who created the organization, and the everyone who has been brought up by Keio Architecture gathered up with this workshop, so it has become a wonderful opportunity for us to look at the future of architecture and urban design of Keio University. I hope Keio Architecture spreads its network and develops further on.

應義塾大学大学院理工学研究科の「空間・環境デザイン工学分野」は、大学院の組織改革における重点領域の一つとして2000年に新たに創設されました。これに伴い、理工学部で建築に関する系統的な教育が開始されてから、20年が経過しようとしています。この間、理工学部における教育・研究の基盤を確立するとともに、湘南藤沢キャンパスの建築系教員と連携し、「慶應アーキテクチャ」として慶應義塾の建築・都市デザインの教育・研究体制を発展させてきました。

2019年は、理工学部創立80年、また、理工学部の前身である藤原工業大学を設立した藤原銀次郎翁の生誕150年にあたります。これらを記念するイベントの一つとして、ダルコ・ラドヴィッチ教授（理工学部）と小林博人教授（環境情報学部）を中心とした慶應アーキテクチャの教員による"CDW COMPREHENSIVE DESIGN WORKSHOP 2019"が、体育研究所などの協力をいただいて、日吉キャンパスにおいて開催されました。このワークショップでは、三田キャンパスの図書館新館、日吉図書館の設計や湘南藤沢キャンパスのグランドデザインを手がけた槇文彦氏、幼稚舎の新体育館、新館21や湘南藤沢中等部・高等部の校舎を設計された谷口吉生氏による対談「慶應建築の系譜」が行われました。お二人は、建築教育が始まる前の慶應義塾大学工学部にて学ばれた先輩でもあります。さらに、理工学部における建築教育の立ち上げに多大なご

尽力をいただいた隈研吾氏による特別講演「Architecture and City after Olympics」が行われました。また、ワークショップには、海外からも多くの建築・都市デザインの教授、建築家に参加いただき、慶應アーキテクチャが着実に国際的なネットワーク構築を進めていることが示されました。今回のワークショップは、慶應アーキテクチャ以前の人々、慶應アーキテクチャによる建築・都市デザインの組織体制を作り上げてきた人々、慶應アーキテクチャに育てられた人々が一同に会することで、慶應義塾における建築・都市デザインの今後を展望する良い機会となりました。慶應アーキテクチャがネットワークを広げ、さらに発展することを期待しております。

Kohei Ito　　伊藤公平

　I was happy and grateful to see the wonderful success of this workshop, which was one of the main projects of the 80th anniversary of Keio University Science and Technology (Rikou-gaku), as one audience and also as the former Deen of the department of Rikou-gaku. I would like to thank all teachers of Rikou-gaku, led by Professor Darko Radović, teachers of SFC led by Professor Hiroto Kobayashi, teachers of the Institute of Physical Education, staff and students. Most of the events held in Rikou-gaku tend to be opened only to students studying in the same field, ending up with a closed atmosphere. On the other hand, this attempt of this event was to contribute to social development from a broader scale, by designing sports facilities in Hiyoshi Campus from scratch with the fresh minds of the students. Such a nice theme was selected, since the team of Great Britain has chosen Hiyoshi Campus as their main camp for the 2020 Olympics, and the planning of a campus considering health with sports is also becoming an important goal for us. Students studying in Rikou-gaku and SFC responded to this new challenge, and came up with new ideas under the guidance of the Professors from Rikou-gaku, SFC, and the Institute of Physical Education. All the achievements (drawings and models and etc…) were presented at the exhibition. World-famous architects, Mr. Fumihiko Maki, Mr. Yoshio Taniguchi, Ms. Kazuyo Sejima, and Mr. Kengo Kuma also visited the exhibition and kindly gave passionate advice to the students. There were also special lectures by Mr. Fumihiko Maki, Mr. Yoshio Taniguchi, and Mr. Kengo Kuma as one part of the workshop. It is the proof of the ability and power to make things done of Keio Architecture Team, that we were able to open the lectures as the Distinguished Lecture Series of Rikou-gaku widely to the public. I would like to show my best respect and appreciation to those who took part in these events.

　慶應義塾大学理工学部創立80年記念事業の柱のひとつとして企画された Keio Architecture: Comprehensive Design Workshop が、ダルコ・ラドヴィッチ教授率いる理工学部教員・スタッフ・学生、小林博人教授率いる SFC 教員・スタッフ・学生、体育研究所の教員の皆さんの尽力で大成功をおさめたことは、前理工学部長として、また、Workshop に参加したひとりの聴衆として感謝感激の一言でした。一般的な理工系のイベントは、理工系の理工系による理工系のための企画として閉じる傾向があります。一方、当事業では広く社会発展に貢献するための試行として、日吉キャンパスを中心としたスポーツ施設を学生の自由な発想でゼロから設計することをテーマに掲げました。2020年東京オリンピックでは英国チームが日吉キャンパスをキャンプ地に選んだこと、そして、スポーツに加えて健康を意識したキャンパス計画が今後ますます重要となることから、このような企画が広く社会的にアピールできると考えたからです。この新しい挑戦に理工学部と SFC の学生が呼応し、理工学部・SFC・体育研究所教員の指導のもとでさまざまな創造的なアイデアを生み出し、その設計図やモデルをエキシビションにて発表しました。そこには槇文彦氏、谷口吉生氏、妹島和世氏、隈研吾氏という世界を代表する建築家が訪れ、学生達の作品を熱心に鑑賞しアドバイスを寄せてくださいました。さらには、槇文彦氏、谷口吉生氏、隈研吾氏による講演会が Workshop の一環として開催され、理工学部の Distinguished Lecture Series としても広く一般公開できたことは、Keio Architecture Team の実力と実行力の証でありました。関係した皆さま全員に敬意と謝意を表します。

Akira Haseyama

Graduated Keio University faculty of Law in 1975, and faculty of literature in 1979. Doctor of Law in 1988. Professor of faculty of literature in 1997. Became the head of Keio University in 2017, after serving the deen and standing director of literature. Also served as the president of Japan Federation of Private Universities. Specialty is legal history and ancient history of Japan.

長谷山彰

1975 年慶應義塾大学法学部卒業、1979 年同文学部卒業。1988 年法学博士。1997 年文学部教授。文学部長、常任理事を経て 2017 年慶應義塾長。日本私立大学連盟会長なども務める。専門は法制史・日本古代史。

Eiji Okada

Graduated from the faculty of electrical engineering of Keio University in 1986. Completed doctoral course at Keio University Graduate School of Science and Technology in 1990. Employed by Keio University since 1991, and now is a professor of Department of Electronic Engineering, faculty of Science and Engineering. Specialize in biomedical optical engineering, biological function measurement by near infrared spectroscopy. Serving as the dean of the faculty of Science and Technology and the chair of the graduate school of Science and Engineering.

岡田英史

1986 年慶應義塾大学理工学部電気工学科卒業。1990 年慶應義塾大学大学院理工学研究科後期博士課程修了。1991 年より慶應義塾大学に任用され、現在、理工学部電子工学科教授。専門分野は、生体医用光工学、近赤外分光法による生体機能計測。2019 年 4 月から理工学部長、理工学研究科委員長。

Kohei Ito

Professor of Rikou-gaku, Kieo University. Served as deen of Rikou-gaku and the chairman of the graduate school of Science and Technology since 2017 to 2019. Currently, the representative of AI / Advanced Programing Consortium of Keio University. The founder of IBM Ouantum Computer Network Hub of Keio University.

伊藤公平

慶應義塾大学理工学部教授。2017 年より 2019 年は理工学部長・理工学研究科委員長を務め、現在は慶應義塾 AI・高度プログラミングコンソーシアム代表。慶應義塾における IBM Quantum Computer Network Hub ファウンダー。

The first phase of CDW was conducted in 2017-18. The opening explored a wide variety of imaginative, hypothetical spatial and programmatic transformations of Hiyoshi, Shimoda, and Yagami Campuses and the adjoining areas. These ideas were exhibited at the Raiosha Centre in July 2018. The events included numerous lectures, delivered, among others, by Fumihiko Maki, Kengo Kuma, Shigeru Ban.

That provided solid basis for the second phase in 2018-19. While in 2018 CDW aimed to communicate with the immediately involved communities, the final CDW Exhibition, Symposium and Lectures were presented to the broadest public. In July 2019, Keio Architecture joined celebrations of the 80th Anniversary of the Faculty of Science and Technology. Three intensive days of events included:

• CDW Keio Architecture and Urban Design Competitions, with awards decided by an International Jury comprised of Darko Radović (Coordinator), Kazuyo Sejima (President), Kohei Itoh (CDW Initiator), Akira Mita (Keio), Davisi Boontharm (Meiji University), Gabriele Masera (Politecnico di Milano), Estanislau Roca (UPC Barcelona), Neno Kezić (University of Split), Tadej Glažar (University of Ljubljana), Takashi Suo (Suo Architects), Takumi Saikawa (TSA).

• 80th Distinguished Keio Science and Technology Lectures

-Fumihiko Maki and Yoshio Taniguchi: Keio Architecture and its Trajectories (Introduced by President Akira Haseyama, and Deans Eiji Okada, Jun Murai; Chair Hiroto Kobayashi)

-Kengo Kuma: Architecture and City after Olympics (Introduced by Dean Eiji Okada; Chair Darko Radović)

•Keio Architecture 2019 Symposium - Sports, Bodies and Spaces: (Chairs Toshiaki Sakai, Darko Radović, Masahito Motoyama)

-Keio research student presentations Physical Education Institute and Keio Architecture

Neno Kezić: Small Sport facilities of Global Standard

Gabriele Masera: Sustainable Campus and Recreation

Tadej Glažar: Sport in Architectural Education

Estanislau Roca: Sport Events and Quality of Public Space

All that, and more, is presented in this volume.

This book celebrates the enthusiasm of all participants in CDW and, in particular, co+labo radović. Keio Architecture 2018-19 is a testimony of an energy and intoxicating optimism of everyone involved, fueled by belief that we all are making an important step in the history of the oldest university in Japan - making of a much needed, unique, international, interdisciplinary programme which would bring the spirit of the founder of Keio, Yukichi Fukuzawa into the fields of architecture and urbanism and into the 21st century.

CDWの最初の段階は2017から2018年に実施されました。日吉・下田・矢上キャンパスとその周辺における仮説的な空間とプログラムの変換をさまざまな視点から行いました。建築・都市を専攻するさまざまなスタジオで生み出された作品は、2018年6月に慶應日吉キャンパスにある来往舎で展示され、槇文彦氏・隈研吾氏・坂茂氏による講演も設けられました。

この第1段階で行われた取り組みは、2018年から2019年に行われた第2段階の大きな基盤となりました。2018年度は、主に関連コミュニティーに向けて発信されたのに対し、最後のCDW展示会、シンポジウムとレクチャーは、より幅広く公衆に向けて公開されました。2019年の6月に開催された慶應アーキテクチャのイベントは理工学部創立80周年記念の一環として取り上げられ、展示会が行われた3日間には以下のプログラムが用意されました。

・CDW慶應建築・都市デザインコンペティション
審査員：Darko Radović（コーディネーター）、妹島和世（名誉称号）、伊藤公平（CDW創始者）、三田彰（慶應）、Davisi Boontharm（明治大学）、Gabriele Masera（ミラノ工科大学）、Estanislau Roca（UPCバルセロナ）、Neno Kezić（スプリット大学）、Tadej Glažar（リュブリャナ大学）、周防貴之（SUO）、齋川拓未（TSA）.
・理工学部80周年記念特別講演
‐槇文彦氏と谷口吉生氏の対談：慶應建築の系譜
（挨拶：長谷山彰塾長、岡田英史理工学部長、村井純教授
司会：小林博人教授）
‐隈研吾氏：オリンピック後の建築と都市
（挨拶：岡田英史理工学部長　司会：Darko Radović教授
質疑応答：Estanislau Roca教授）
・慶應アーキテクチャ2019年シンポジウム　‐スポーツ、体と空間：日々の生活と非日常的体験‐
（司会：坂井利彰、Darko Radović教授、元山雅仁）
‐慶應学生によるリサーチプレゼンテーション
体育研究所,
慶應アーキテクチャ
Neno Kezić: 世界標準の小さなスポーツ施設
Gabriele Masera: サステナブルなキャンパス
Tadej Glažar: 建築教育におけるスポーツ
Estanislau Roca: スポーツイベントと公共空間の質
これら、そしてより多くの内容が本書に掲載されております。
この本はCDWに参加した皆さんの熱意を祝うものでもあり、私ダルコ・ラドヴィッチ個人としまして慶應アーキテクチャ2018-2019は、CDWに関わったすべての人々のエネルギーとオプチミズムの証です。日本最古の大学、その歴史の重要なステップに貢献し、ユニークで国際的、学際的で重要なプログラムを創っているという皆の想いは、慶應義塾大学の創始者である福沢諭吉先生の精神を建築と都市、そして21世紀へといざなうものになるでしょう。

Hiroto Kobayashi
慶應アーキテクチャが目指すもの
小林博人

The future of our world seems increasingly complex, and therefore unpredictable. However, in order to cope with the unknown situations that will arise, we must embrace the complexity of this environment.

Keio Architecture does just that by welcoming diverse approaches to design and offering students a unique collection of experiences through workshops, research, courses, and internship programs. Keio University's vast network extends throughout the sciences and the humanities, and between the government and the civil society. We believe that cross-disciplinary interaction enhances education and brings architecture down to earth.

Architecture, for us, means a collaborative practice of problem solving with the goal of making the world a better place. We aim to send graduates out into society whose skills and minds are adaptive and flexible enough to respond the complex questions we face and, crucially, who approach their work in a spirit of good will toward fellow humans.

世界の未来は複雑化しており、それ故これから何が起きるかを予測することは難しくなってきています。しかし、予知できない、そしていつか実現するその状況に対応していくために、私たちは複雑な世界を受け入れていかなくてはなりません。

慶應アーキテクチャは、多様なデザインへのアプローチを受け入れ、学生にワークショップやリサーチ、授業、インターンシッププログラムといったユニークな体験を提供することで、これを実現していきます。慶應義塾大学の有する広いネットワークは、科学とヒューマニティの分野に渡り、行政や市民社会にも浸透しています。私たちはこの分野の横断的な交わりが、教育をより豊かで、慶應建築を地に足の着いたものにしてくれると考えています。

私たちの言うアーキテクチャとは、世界をより良い場所にするための問題解決を目指す共同実践を指します。慶應アーキテクチャの卒業生が、我々が直面する複雑な問題を受け入れ、柔軟に対応できる技能を持ち、それらに対して人としての良心を持って答えていくよう願っています。

Hiroto Kobayashi

Hiroto Kobayashi was born in Tokyo, Japan in 1961, and has studied at the Kyoto University and Graduate School of Design, Harvard University. He has worked for Nikken Sekkei, Norman Foster.
In 2003, Kobayashi founds Kobayashi Maki Design Workshop togather with Naomi Maki and has worked as the Principal. Since 2003 Kobayashi has taught at Keio University, and since 2012 is a Professor at Graduate School of Media and Governance.

小林博人

1961 年東京生まれ。京都大学、ハーバード大学大学院デザインスクール (GSD) で、建築設計・都市デザインを学び、その後日建設計東京、ノーマン・フォスター事務所フランクフルト事務所で設計の実務を行う。2003 年、槇直美と共に小林・槇デザインワークショップを設立、代表を務める。慶應義塾大学では 2003 年より講師を務め、2012 年より慶應義塾大学大学院政策・メディア研究科教授。

Discussion
Darko Radović / Hiroto Kobayashi   Conversation
ディスカッション
ダルコ・ラドヴィッチ / 小林博人 対談

Hopes for Keio Architecture
慶應アーキテクチャに望むこと

An active talk was held between two professors, Drako Radovic (Keio Hiyoshi Campus) and Hiroto Kobayashi (Keio Shonan Fujisawa Campus), who played the key roles in establishing Keio Architecture. The discussion was wide ranging, covering a variety of issues – such as the background of Keio Architecture, the links between Shonan Fujisawa and Hiyoshi Campus, and the place of Keio students and graduates in a changing society.

慶應アーキテクチャの設立にあたってその中核を担ったダルコ・ラドヴィッチ教授（日吉キャンパス）と小林博人教授（湘南藤沢キャンパス）の両氏に対談をお願いした。慶應アーキテクチャの設立に至った経緯や、湘南藤沢キャンパスと日吉キャンパスの繋がり、変化を続ける社会の中で慶應の学生に求めるものなど、多岐にわたって熱い議論が交わされた。

Hiroto Kobayashi (H) : So, Darko-san. I will start with the history of Keio, Keio architecture. It was amazing that Darko-san, before you started to talk about the collaborative work in 2010, I never thought about working with Rikogakubu even I knew that Rikogakubu has established architecture education and Sejima-san, Kuma-san those sort of familiar people, famous people and also Ikaga-san who I use to work with in Nikken Sekkei. When I entered SFC, there was this competing, sort of disconnected atmosphere was already established. So, I really could not imagine that we could work together, but it was sensational for me that you proposed the idea, "Why don't we do something together". So, Ok. (was my answer).

小林博人 (H): まずは慶應と慶應アーキテクチャの経緯から話を始めましょう。ダルコさんが 2010 年にコラボレーションをしようという話を始める前は、理工学部で妹島さんや隈さん、日建設計で共に働いたことのある伊香賀さんをはじめとする著名な先生方が建築教育を行っていることは知っていましたが、実は理工学部と共にプロジェクトを進めるなど考えてもいませんでした。私が SFC に入ったときには既にお互いが競い合い、切り離されたような雰囲気や関係性がありました。そのため、一緒に働くことができるとは想像もできませんでしたが、何かを一緒にやろうとダルコさんが提案してくれたのは私にとってとてもセンセーショナルな出来事であり、ならばいっしょにやりましょうというのが私の答えでした。

Darko Radović (D) :   When I joined Keio, I was also surprised to learn that SFC had its own rich base in architecture, but completely separated from the Faculty I was working in. I started thinking and discussing with you and others how to connect those, only geographically distant parts. That seemed impossible. At old university such as those where I taught before, the change tends to be incremental and slow – and I do not mind that. Universities need gravitas, but that makes radical changes at old universities difficult to make. So, soon after joining Keio I came up with this proposal to establish IKI – International Keio Institute for Architecture and Urbanism and start working together, which even to me seemed a little bit too ambitious. But, suddenly, you and Sejima-san were keen to join that effort. She responded by proposing the exact time and date to launch IKI at the Biennale of Architecture in Venice – and our dream started to become the reality.

ダルコ・
ラドヴィッチ (D):   博人さんが言うように、SFC と矢上キャンパスにはたくさんのつながりがあり、厳密には建築家ではないものの、建築と関係を持ったエンジニアやその他のフィールドのバックグラウンドを持った人たちがたくさんいて、フレームワークを除いてすべてが準備されているような状態でした。そこでフレームワークがなかった状態に対して IKI(International Keio Institute for Architecture Urbanism) は 1 つの発明でした。それができた時、私にとってそれはまるで 1 つの舞台のようであったことを覚えています。私たちはその光がより強く灯り、灯り続けることを願いました。そして、IKI は実際にその願いを叶えました。私にとって慶應アーキテクチャはその灯り続けた明かりのようなものです。IKI は慶應アーキテクチャとなり、そしてある時点で私たちはその光を灯し続けることに成功したのです。

(H) :   It was very nice, and Sejima-san was very positive and also all of a sudden many people got interested and joined from all over the world.

(H):   それはとても良い事でした。妹島さんはとても肯定的に考えてくれて、すぐに世界からたくさんの人が興味をもって参加してくれました。

An important step towards Keio architecture – the foundation of IKI – International Keio Institute of Architecture and Urban Design in Venice, at Architecture Biennale, August 29, 2010.
Picture, from left to right: Hitoshi Abe (UCLA), Yasushi Ikeda (SFC/Keio), Wang Shu (China Academy of Arts), Heinrich Wolf (Wolf Architects, South Africa), Shun Kanda (MIT) Kazuyo Sejima (SANAA; IKI Design Director/Keio), Hiroto Kobayashi (IKI Managing Director/Keio), Darko Radovic (IKI Director International/Keio)

慶應建築に向けて IKI(International Keio Institute for Architecture Urbanism) が設立された。2010 年 8 月 29 日第 12 回ヴェネチア・ビエンナーレ建築展にて阿部仁史 (UCLA)、池田靖史 (SFC/ 慶應義塾大学)、王澍 (中国美術学院)、ハインヒッリ・ウォルフ (南アフリカ)、神田駿 (MIT)、妹島和世 (IKI デザインディレクター / 慶應義塾大学)、小林博人 (IKI マネージングディレクター / 慶應義塾大学)、ダルコ・ラドヴィッチ (IKI ディレクターインターナショナル / 慶應義塾大学)

(D) :   So many potential links between SFC and Yagami were already there, as you said, both architects and many other colleagues, who are engineers and of other profiles, but with related careers and research interests. It was like everything was ready, except the framework. Then IKI came about, as a kind of framework. The idea was that only when we have a joint project, an event, IKI acts as a stage: the flashlights go on. And collaboration unfolds; when there is nothing, IKI stays dormant. But the hope was that the projects will start getting more and more frequent, and one day the lights will, simply, stay on. To me, Keio architecture is that – a stage which became life. IKI now becomes Keio Architecture. From one moment soon, I think, we Keio have the lights of architecture and urban design studies on, forever.

(D) :   SFC と矢上キャンパスには既にたくさんの繋がりがありました。あなたが言うように、建築家はもちろん、エンジニアや他分野であっても建築関係のキャリアやリサーチに興味を持っている人々がたくさんいました。まさにフレームワークを除いてすべてが整っていました。そこで IKI(International Keio Institute for Architecture Urbanism) がフレームワークとして現れたのです。初めの内は IKI を、共同プロジェクトやイベントがあるときに機能する舞台として、そして何もない時には活動しない機関として考えていました。そしてどこかで、次第にプロジェクトの回数が増えて行き、ついには活動し続ける存在になることを願っていました。私にとってまさに慶應アーキテクチャがこの存在となったのです。IKI は今慶應アーキテクチャとなり、そして近い将来、慶應で建築・都市デザインの研究が続けられることになるでしょう。

(H) :   Right.

(H) :   その通りですね。

(D) :   So, you mentioned the keywords; thinking across scales, diversity of thinking… In that sense, even the dreaded remoteness of the two campuses, somehow, helps. Distance can facilitate diversity.

(D) :   ちなみにあなたは、自由・スケールを超えた思考・思考の多様性というキーワードを掲げました。その観点からすると、2 つのキャンパスが物理的に離れているという事実も、なんだかんだプラスにはたらきます。距離が多様性を生む可能性もありますから。

(H) :   Right. The beauty of the SFC, they say it as a sort of a weakness, is the distance, but I believe that the distance is the strength because we can be independent and free because people see that we are separate form Mita and other campuses. And so, we tried to have a train connection form Shonandai and Yokohama but then personally I think it is okay to not have any trains. People can start something new. Nowadays we have new faculty members, Matsukawa-san (with his) computational design, Narukawa-san, originally a structure engineer – he designed many interesting things – Ishikawa Hajime-san is a landscape architect, and Shirai-san is mainly focusing on forestry, wooden architecture. So, those new members are very interesting, and we would like to work together. Engineering is more oriented in Riko-gaku and many different fields work together. So I think, the students have the possibility to enjoy both campuses. At the same time maybe, we can establish some common place, like a third place. That must be very interesting, and which must be related to urbanism, people and the real city. That's what I hope.

(H): その通りです。時に弱みと人に言われることもありますが、SFC の良さはその距離にあります。三田といった他キャンパスから離れていることから、私たちは独立して自由に活動することができます。湘南台と横浜の間に電車を通そうという話が出たこともありましたが、個人的にはなくてよいと思っています。SFC は何か新しい事を始められる環境が整っています。最近では、コンピューテーショナルデザインの松川さん、もともと構造エンジニアで数多くの設計経験がある鳴川さん、ランドスケープアーキテクトの石川さん、そして林業と木造建築を専攻する白井さんなど、新しい仲間がいて、皆面白い人たちばかりなので是非一緒に活動したいと思っています。理工学部ではエンジニアリングやデザイン思考が強いですし、さまざまな分野が独立しながらも同じ環境で研究をしています。学生達も 2 つのキャンパスを股にかけて楽しめる可能性があります。サードプレイスとでもいうようなコモンスペースを設立してもいいかもしれませんね。もし実現すれば間違いなく面白いものになるし、アーバニズムと人と実際の都市とを深く結び付ける存在になるでしょう。

(D): And that is a fascinating potential, there is such a strong educational message for students of architecture and urban design in that. It is so much better (to know) how much deeper your design needs to be when you can visit the site, touch, and know the site.

(D): それは非常に可能性を秘めていて、建築・都市デザインを学ぶ学生に対して強い教育的メッセージを投げかけるでしょう。自分のデザインがいかに深いものでなければならないか、実際に敷地を訪れ、触れたりしながらその場所をよく知ることで体感する方がよっぽどいいですから。

(H): We had a very good opening last month on May 21st. Ban-san who teaches in SFC has this concern about architecture education in Japan and said he wanted to have a lecture about it, so we combined his lecture and the launch of Keio Architecture. For doing that we produced a website Keio Architecture, took about 9 months but that was very nice, at least we could work together and start some things. We hope that everybody will look at the website, Keio Architecture. So, we now started, then how to keep on doing that is of course the interesting but difficult (task) but we are really hoping for that.

(H): 5 月 21 日には、慶應アーキテクチャの素晴らしいオープニングを迎えることができました。SFC で教鞭をとっている坂茂さんは日本の建築教育に大変関心があり、そのことに関してレクチャーを開きたいということでした。彼の講演会と慶應アーキテクチャの発足を組み合わせて、たくさんの人に来場していただきましたね。これに合わせて、慶應のウェブサイトも立ち上げました。作成に 9 ヶ月もの月日を要しましたが、少なくとも共に何かをはじめ、進めていく環境がそろったのではないかと思っています。多くの人に慶應アーキテクチャのウェブサイトを見てほしいです。慶應アーキテクチャはまだ始まったばかりで、どのように活動をつづけていくか探し求めている最中です。難しい課題ではありますが、同時に興味深い問題ですね。

(D) :   Great, because that was a very interesting moment. The hall was full and the audience was very interesting. Many of representatives of various corporations which you mentioned before were at the lecture. There is a lot of good will to collaborate, to think about the future with an open mind⋯ Keio architecture as a program can serve as a kind of bridge, a catalyst to create and channel positive energy between those big corporations, and our young students and academics, where there are no limits, where the blue sky is the "limit". And we can, maybe, help (this sounds preposterous, but it should be possible) and navigate these corporations in direction of a better world. Big corporations, of course, work with big business but, as you have mentioned in Ban-san's case, that should be balanced with an equally strong emphasis on powerless people, on people who have lost everything. Our program might, among other things, be program which seeks such links and connects people who make things happen and those who are deprived of the very basics. At this moment, we are in the middle of the semester, and our students have already heard ten or more lectures, some of which documented in this book, delivered by the colleagues from SFC and Yagami, Florence and Milano, Meiji University, Kuma-san from Tokyo University. Keio Architecture is already a kind of a microcosm of people who can contribute to the diversity of ideas and projects. Last year we had our first Keio Architecture book published. The project presented there was an imaginary Keio Graduate School of Design, Keio GSD. Maki-sensei and you gave introductory lectures, and I wrote a brief note, saying that in that project Keio students dream about their house. Their intellectual home. This year, I believe, this dream is, maybe, coming true, Keio Architecture as a dream as a dream come true.

(D):   ホールは満員となり、いろいろな方々に聴きに来ていただきました。空間を扱う名だたる企業の代表者もいらしていました。慶應アーキテクチャはあるプログラムとして、ある種確立された枠組みの中にいる大企業達と、果てしなく広がる青空のように広い可能性をもつ若い学生との間をつなぐ架け橋のような役割を果たすことができると考えます。そして、（これは途方もない事のように聞こえるかもしれませんが）そのような企業がより良い世界を作るようナビゲートしてくれることがあるかもしれません。もちろん大企業はビッグビジネスを対象に仕事をしていますが、小林さんが坂さんの件に関しても述べたように、強い権力を持たない人々やすべて失ってしまった人々に対しても同様に目を向けるべきです。そのため、我々のプログラムは、何かを成せる人と生活の基盤を奪われてしまったような人々とを繋ぐものであってほしい。そしてまた多様なものでもあってほしい。現在学期の半ばでありますが、この本に収められているように SFC や矢上、イタリア、明治大学、東京大学の隈研吾さんをはじめとして慶應でも 10 近いレクチャーが行われています。慶應アーキテクチャはすでに多方面で活躍する人々が集まる小宇宙のようなものになりつつあります。

(D) :   That is fascinating thought, but we should stay sober. We should be working with big corporations, which always were friends and power behind Keio – but our academic integrity should never stop encouraging Keio students to dream. To me, Keio Architecture should always be a dream. Not a year at Keio Architecture should be the same as previous one, because every year new students and new ideas come. Besides that, what we haven't mentioned yet, because we take it for granted but is of critical importance – both you and my laboratories are decidedly international. Keio Architecture should operate as an international graduate school, enriched by the constant flow of people from all over the world. Yes, of course, Keio Architecture has to stay Japanese to the core, but we also have to have that flow of fresh blood and ideas from all over the world coming to Keio – very much in the way we have already established. Yukichi Fukuzawa would know very well what we are talking about here.

(D):   昨年、私たちは初めて慶應アーキテクチャイヤーブックを出版しました。その本には、学生たちが考えた想像上の Keio Graduate School of Design, Keio GSD を載せました。その授業の最初のレクチャーを槙文彦先生とあなたに開いていただきました。その講義の際に私は、慶應義塾の生徒が自身の家のようなものを求めている、とメモした記憶があります。学問的な学び舎としての家です。今年、私はこの夢が、慶應アーキテクチャという夢が本当に実現するのではないかと考えています。しかし、冷静さを失ってはなりません。慶應義塾を支えてくださっているような大きな企業とも協力していかなければなりません。そして生徒たちが夢見続けることができるように促さなければならない。我々は毎年新たな生徒やアイデアを迎えいれるので、慶應義塾で過ごす 1 年は昨年と同様であってはならないのです。
私たち二人が当たり前に思いすぎて、今まで話に上がってきませんでしたが、私の研究室と博人さんの研究室はとても国際的な研究室です。慶應アーキテクチャも世界中からコンスタントに人を呼びこむ国際的な大学院として機能していかなくてはなりません。もちろんその中心は日本でなければなりませんが、我々がすでに取り組んできたように世界中からフレッシュな考えを取り入れることは大切です。福沢諭吉先生も我々のことをすぐに理解してくれることでしょう。

(H) : That's very important. So, we have many chances to go to America and south-east Asia and then we found that many interesting people and also very serious issues related to us and not related at all but⋯ so we have to open our eyes to everywhere in the world. And then maybe in terms of internationality, we should open our eyes to worldwide issues, and then we have many changes of inviting many students from several universities. We tend to see inside but as I mentioned, now the world is changing also, so I think we should really be careful about what's happening outside of Japan too. If we have many kinds of people, we can really open our eyes to those issues, otherwise it's easy for us to close and be internal. But I hope that the students, especially younger generations, open their eyes.

(H): それはとても重要なことです。私たちの研究会はアメリカや東南アジアに行く機会が多いのですが、私たちに関係していることも関係していないことも含めて、興味深い人々や深刻な問題をたくさん目の当たりにします。ですので、我々は世界のあらゆる場所に目を向けなければなりません。国際性の観点からも、世界各国の問題に目を向けていく必要がありますし、そうすることでいろいろな大学から生徒を招き入れることもできるでしょう。私たちはどうしても身内のことに関心を向けがちですが、世界は常に変化しているので、日本の外で起きていることに敏感になることも大切です。色々な人との関わりがあれば、そのような問題に目を向けることができます。逆にしなければ内向的になり、すぐ内に閉じこもってしまう。生徒達、得に若い世代の人達には、常に外に目を向けてほしいです。

(D) : I really believe in that what you stressed second time and third time, Hiroto-san. The world is changing. So, the main point is that if we allow young people to dream, then the key question is, why wouldn't that change be for the better? There is, somehow, always an assumption that when the world is changing that is dangerous and unpredictable. But, why the change would not be for the better? Young people, who have their lives and careers in front of them, have an interest in making a better world. I think that Keio Architecture should provide – in our field of course – such opportunities. But, the key should be in drawing upon what Keio already has – which is unique and powerful. Much of what we research and teach happens in real space. Hospitals are real spaces, science and technology products are operating in real spaces. Law gets implemented or shapes real spaces and – architecture and urban design are about making real space. I think that there is a fantastic integrative role within the studies and practice of architecture and urban design, and Keio Architecture should capitalize upon that⋯

(D): 私も同感です。博人さんが何度も繰り返しおっしゃっているように世界は変化しています。我々が若者に対して夢見られる環境を提供したら、世界がより良い方向に変わっていく可能性もあるのです。世界が変化するときはいつも、危険で予測不能であると思われがちですが、良い方向に変化することだってあるのです。これから世の中に出ていく若者は、より良い世界を作ってくことに対して関心を持っています。私は慶應アーキテクチャこそが、その機会を提供すべきであると考えています。でももちろんこれは、慶應が既に持っている独特で強力な力を引き出すことによって行わなければなりません。理工学部や法学、医学など慶應ではさまざまな分野が現実世界でその力を発揮しています。建築と都市デザインにおいてもそれは同様です。建築と都市デザインの研究と実践には、さまざまな分野を統合する力があって、私は慶應アーキテクチャこそ、その役割を担うべきであると思っています。

L

The snapshots from production of
Keio Architecture
LOGO
Logo design for CDW project
CDW ロゴ

What was needed to hold the CDW was the design of the logo symbolizing this workshop. The visual identity team focuses on designing from the features of the site and the goals we have anticipated.

CDWの開催に際し必要となったのが、このワークショップを象徴するロゴのデザインであった。ヴィジュアルアイデンティティーチームが中心となり、敷地の特徴や見据えたゴールなどからインスパイヤーされたデザインを検討中である。

1. This design is too simple, so you can use it, easily. シンプルに文字だけにすることで汎用性を高くした。
2. Using 'Keio color', mainly, so this design show Keio spirits. 慶應カラーを用いて慶應義塾の精神性を示した。
3. Everybody can read 'mamushi' by the snake and initials. 頭文字と蛇の絵で「まむし」と誰でも読める。
4. M shape created by wonderful sky and mountain. 山と空と谷を表現しながら、まむし谷のMをかたどった。
5. Images that blur the boundary and penetrate around. 境界をぼやかして周りに浸透していくイメージ。
6. The topography would work as joint for various elements. 蝮谷の地形から着想し、点在する要素をゆるやかに繋ぐ。
7. Represent the topography of the Mamushi Valley with its initial. 蝮谷の地形を表現しつつ、蝮谷めイニシャルで表現した。
8. Simple design considering the stamp production. シンプルでスタンプにできるようなデザインにした。
9. Represent the topography of the Mamushi Valley by initial M. 蝮谷の地形をイニシャルMの字とそこに道を書き込み表現した。
10. Hiragana represents the Japaneseness. ひらがなによる日本らしさの演出。
11. Layering residents and sports facilities in Hiyoshi. 住民とスポーツ施設の重なりで新たな色をつくる。
12. Represent the topography of the Mamushi Valley by initial M and Keio facilities. 蝮谷の地形をイニシャルMの字と慶應の校舎建築物を表現した。
13. M as in mountain. 頭文字Mをモチーフに。
14. Initial of Mamushi would be expressed in Keio colors. 蝮谷（Mamushi Dani / Mamushi Valley）の頭文字を慶應義塾の3色で表現する。
15. Diamond shape based design which can extend to several direction. ひし形をベースにフレキシブルなデザインが可能な案。
16. This is the topography of Mamushi Valley. 蝮谷の起伏をモチーフに。

1

9

2

10

3

11

4

12

5

13

6
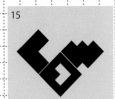

14

7

15

8

16

Chapter 2
Studio B 2018
Designing of Mamushi Center

第 2 章　2018 年度　スタジオ B　慶應義塾大学まむし谷センターの設計

The task for the studio B 2018 was to design the master plan of the entire valley called Mamushi-Valley and a hub "Mamushi-Valley Center". For the first half, students discussed the tasks and problems about the current situation of the site through intensive field work. After that, students were divided in to 2 groups, 4 to 5 members, and decided the masterplan including the entire concept, land use plan, transportation plan, equipment layout plan, landscape design. For the rest of the half, students designed their own "Mamushi-Valley Center" according to their team's masterplan. 9 "Mamushi-Valley Center" were proposed in total. Surrounded by the steep slopes, many facilities already exist on the flat ground of the valley, so it is hard to find some space that is left opened, but I think some projects made good use out of the big slops and the topography of the valley. They were wonderful.

　2018 年スタジオ B の課題は、まむし谷全体のマスタープランと、拠点となる「まむし谷センター」の設計である。前半では、まず現地のフィールドワークを通じて現状の課題や問題点を議論した。そこから、4 から 5 名の 2 つのグループに分かれて、全体のコンセプトから、土地利用計画、交通計画、施設配置計画、景観デザインなどを含むマスタープランをまとめた。後半では、各グループのマスタープランに基づき、個人単位で、「まむし谷センター」の設計をし、計 9 つのまむし谷センターの提案がなされた。まむし谷は、急峻な斜面に挟まれた谷であり、わずかばかりの平地に、すでにさまざまな施設が整備されているため、残された土地は少なく、難しい土地である。高低差のある斜面や、谷の地形を生かした提案の中に素晴らしいものがあったと思います。

Interview ———————————————————————————————— p.26-33

Saikawa Studio

The Poetics of Water Scenery | Yumi Ishii ——————————————— p.34
水が紡ぐ風景の詩 | 石井結実

Piers as a node-revitalize the community through sports | Yusuke Ono ——— p.35
結の桟橋 - スポーツを通じた地域活性化 - | 小野裕介

WINDPATH | Takuomi Samejima —————————————————————— p.36
風の通り道 | 鮫島卓臣

Kur Mamushi Valley | Yuichi Tatsumi ——————————————————— p.37
まむし谷サナトリウム | 巽祐一

Kondo Studio

Detour × Space | Itaru Iwasaki ————————————————————————— p.38
獣道×空間 | 岩崎達

Mamushi Retaining Patchwork | Keitaro Onishi —————————————— p.39
まむし谷を守るパッチワーク | 大西慶太郎

Tangling Path | Yang Xuang ——————————————————————————— p.40
からまる小道 | 楊宣

With the forest | Kyoko Suganuma —————————————————————— p.41
森とともに | 菅沼響子

Mamushi-dani Circle | Manon Ellie ———————————————————— p.42
蝮谷サークル | マノン・エリー

Overview of the Studio B
スタジオ B の課題概要

Overview of this Studio

 The task for the Studio B, 2018 was to propose a redevelopment masterplan for Mamushi-Valley in Hiyoshi Campus and to design the "Mamushi-Center". Mamushi-Valley is a forest located behind the campus, representing abundant nature and sports facilities, designated as sacred for student athletes. Although its potential, the number of visitors and interactions are limited due to its inaccessibility and topology. Therefore, the students were asked to suggest an alternative masterplan to create an interrelationship between nature and sport facilities, as well as human interactions, while connecting it by individual defining, and designing a "Mamushi-Center". By assigning Hiyoshi-campus (expected to be the campsite for global athletes in2020 Tokyo Olympics) as our target site, the studio aims to combine research and design to achieve the ideal framework of our education in Urban and Architectural design practice.

スタジオの概要

　2018 年度建築設計スタジオ B の授業課題は、日吉キャンパスまむし谷エリアの再開発マスタープランと「まむし谷センター」の設計である。まむし谷は日吉キャンパスの裏手に位置する自然豊かな雑木林であり、学内のさまざまなスポーツ施設が点在し、学生アスリートの聖地となっている。一方で、その敷地状況やアクセスの悪さから訪れる人々は限られている。本スタジオではこのまむし谷エリアに対してその豊かな自然とスポーツ施設を相互に関係づけ、人々の交流の場として生かすことができるマスタープランの提案と、それらをつなぐ「まむし谷センター」を独自に定義し、構想することを課題とした。来たる 2020 年東京オリンピックのキャンプ地としても認定されている日吉キャンパスをケーススタディとすることで、リサーチとデザインが融合した理想の建築・都市デザイン教育を目指し、学生は上記の理念の下に設計を行った。

Mr. Saikawa insists the students to design architecture that includes social perspectives. Mr. Saikawa who proceeded his career under Kengo Kuma's office and just opened his own office, often thinks about what an architect can do. He gave advice through his esquisse not only about design but also the ideal architect vision that can help the society for the coming era.

学生のうちから社会性をもった設計を心がけるべきだと話す齋川氏。日本の建築界をリードする隈研吾氏の下で経験を積んできた齋川氏は、近年、自身の事務所を設立したのを機に、建築家の職能について考えることが増えたという。この思考の蓄積から得られた、単に建築空間へのアドバイスにとどまらない指導方針は、齋川氏が考えるこれからの社会に必要な建築家像を生徒たちに伝えていくようであった。

Takumi Saikawa / 齋川拓未

1993-1997	Shibaura Institute of Technology
1998-2001	Massimiliano Fuksas Architect
2002-2004	Keio University (Master Course)
2004	Kengo Kuma & Associate
2016	Takumi Saikawa Architects

1993-1997	芝浦工業大学　卒業
1998-2001	Massimiliano Fuksas Architect
2002-2004	慶應義塾大学大学院　修士課程修了
2004	隈研吾建築都市設計事務所
2016	齋川拓未建築設計事務所

1. About Mamushi-Valley まむし谷に対する印象

First, what did you think was the biggest characteristic of Mamushi-Valley, compared to other sites or forests?

まむし谷は他の敷地や森と比較してどのような特徴があると感じましたか？

The student athletes, normal students and the neighboring residents are just passing through the valley to make a short cut to the station…and the forest where is not completely used, but not completely abandoned… these unconnected relations will make this valley something special.
The location of the Mamushi-Valley is in between the residential areas and Hiyoshi campus. The valley has an interesting atmosphere, something apart from the environment, and remaining the old environment…

運動する学生やそれ以外の学生、スポーツとは関係なく通過する近隣住民、なんとなく管理されている森という、あまりつながっていない関係性が特徴だと思います。
まむし谷は慶應大学キャンパスと住宅地の中間に位置しています。日吉駅を出てすぐ目の前に、慶應大学キャンパスがあり、その裏側にあるまむし谷と住宅地の存在は感じられず、少し阻害されたような、不思議な古い環境の残る場所だと思います。

There is a lot of potential when connecting each other something in such circumstance and environment, etc. That made this valley something special.

そこを利用する人、森（場所）、歴史などをつなげることで新しい多様なポテンシャルを発見できると思います。

The valley was interesting especially due to it's diverse usage among students and residents. Are there any specific points that you wanted your students to deal with, or focus on?

まむし谷は慶應の体育会所属の学生を中心に使われており、地域の住民も利用できるという面白い敷地でしたが、今回の課題で学生に特に意識してもらいたかった点はありますか？

In last year's Studio, I wanted to make students think about the responsibility of their own proposal and design, and their proposals must have a sociability of architects. The theme of this year is how to renovate existing athletic buildings and facilities of Mamushi-Valley, and it is related to the Mamushi-Valley as a camp area of the 2020 Tokyo Olympic. So, this year's proposals must have the social sense more than last year. Students need to think what kind of benefits will be provided by their proposal and design to Keio University, Hiyoshi and neighbors, etc.

Of course, good and beautiful architecture must be designed, so additionally, I asked them to have a realistic image how the environment will be changed by their proposals.

去年のスタジオでは建築をデザインする時の責任を感じて欲しいと思い、提案に社会性を持つことが大事であると伝えました。今年はテーマが日吉（まむし谷）の体育施設で、オリンピックとの関連もあり、よりリアルな社会性を持つ提案が必要だと思いました。各自のプロジェクトの提案がどのようなメリットを日吉という場所に、慶應大学に、周辺に住む住民にもたらすのか考えて欲しいなと思いました。

良いデザインができることは当然として、プロジェクトを提案することで環境がどのように変わるかを考えて欲しいと伝えました。

2. Studio theme and teaching スタジオのテーマと教育

In the studio, did you have any mind on how to lead your students?

授業をやるにあたって齋川スタジオでは学生をどのようにリードしようと考えましたか？

It is contiguous to the previous talk, I put more emphasis on observing everything in a wider perspective. I wanted the students to find some problems through their field works and observations, and improve it by absorbing them. These were the things we shared in the studio discussion.

　前の話ともつながりますが、なるべく大きな視点で全体を捉えるようにということを伝えました。フィールドワークなどから問題点を見つけて、それを各自のアイデアで改善してもらうということを、エスキスの方向性として持っていました。

As myself being a member of your studio, I remember that you mentioned "I also don't know what is the correct answer for the design". In teaching about something you also "don't know", is there something you are careful about?

僕も齋川スタジオの一人として「何が正しいかは僕にもわからない」という先生の言葉が印象に残っています。その「答えがわからない」ものを指導する上で、何か心掛けていることはありますか？

I think the important thing is to initially discover something by yourself. Discovering is actually an act that cannot be taught by someone. It's more of a spontaneous act, so even I myself discover something through the conversation with the students. I consider that it's not a good influence to them if I tell them my direct impression and discovery. I try to think it with students with the same eye level. If they realize something by themselves, even it is not completed in the studio work, it will probably help their anticipating career as an experience.

　大事なのは、自分で発見することだと思います。発見するというのは「教えてもらう」ということではなく、自分で考えて思いつく、気づくということだと思います。僕の考え方を押し付けるのではなく、学生が考えようとしていることを同じ視点で一緒に考えることが大事だと思っています。
その中で学生が自分で何かに気づくことができたら、それが課題としてまとまらなかったとしても、彼らの将来に役立つのではないかと思います。

Has your design process or way of thinking changed since you were a student?

齋川さんが学生だった時に比べて設計のプロセスや考え方に何か変化はありますか？

I actually did my undergrad in Shibaura Institute of technology and then worked in Italy for a while and later did my graduate in Keio, so it is difficult to compare my experience as a master student with you.

　僕は実は2回学生をやっていて、大学は芝浦工業大学で建築を学んで、その後イタリアで働いてその後に慶應大学で修士を卒業しました。

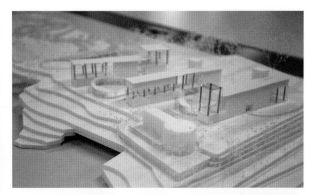

However students who can make 3D modellings and who cannot have a difference in imagination of space. If you can't use 3D, you'll have to go back and forth with plans and study models, which is old and historical style. If you can use 3D, you can study the volume and shape of the building simultaneously, allowing to create a free-form shape or making a small change immediately on screen. But it has a demerit that everything is always inside the screen. It is not a physical 3 dimensions⋯ Both technique and process is important to study the design. Sometimes people say that architecture is the cutting edge of the modern age, but it is always antique and low technology that treats real materials and gravity.

なので、自分が院生だったときと、皆さんの状況と比較することはできませんが、3D モデリングができる人とできない人で、想像力の違いがあると思います。3D モデリングができないと図面書いて模型作ってという昔から変わらないプロセスになります。3D モデリングができると形を自由に作ったり、サイズを変えたりコピーが簡単です。ただ常にモニターの中なので基本的には 2 次元で、フィジカルに 3 次元ではない欠点もあります。基本的には両方やらないといけないと思います。建築は時代を切り取る最先端のように言われることもありますが、同時にとても古くて、素材や重力を扱うローテクな分野です。

3. For the future architects　将来の建築家に向けて

Could you give an overall comment and advice to the students.
全体の総評と最後に学生たちにむけて一言お願いします。

I think each proposals were interesting and very good. They all had individual characteristics, and there were some works that made me think how I would do it, so it was enjoyable for me too. On the other hand, it was a bit disappointing to see that the works did not dramatically improve between mid-term and final-review. I think this is not only the matter of just submitting studio assignments, but also how to deal with things that you can actually devote yourself into. I hope such students increase in Keio.

　どの案も面白くてすごく良かったです。それぞれ特徴があって、僕だったらこうするなと思えることがたくさんありました。一方でちょっと残念だったのは、中間講評と最終講評であまり変化が無かったことです。たぶん、課題だけではなく、どんなことでも自分なりのこだわりをもってやりきることが大切だと思います。建築好きな学生が増えるといいなと思います。

Mr. Kondo emphasizes the importance to think and act originally. He proceeded his esquisse by questioning himself what the students truly wanted to do and gave comments. This stance of thinking connects with his design process as well. He always tries to think freely without strangling himself with conditions.

自分で考え、自身の責任で設計を進めることの大切さを語る近藤氏。実際に学生にたいしてアドバイスをする際も、この学生が本当にやりたいことはこれなのかと常に問い続けながら、スタジオでのエスキスを進めていったという。この姿勢は自身の設計活動ともつながっており、さまざまな条件に縛られることなく自分で自由に考えて設計を進めていくことを心掛けている。

Tetsuo Kondo / 近藤哲雄

1975	Born in Ehime Prefecture
1999	Graduated from Nagoya Institute of Technology
1999-2006	Worked in SANAA
2006	Established Tetsuo Kondo Architects

1975	愛媛県生まれ
1999	名古屋工業大学　卒業
1999-2006	妹島和世建築設計事務所
2006	近藤哲雄建築設計事務所設立

1. About Mamushi-Valley まむし谷に対する印象

The target site for the studio was Mamushi-Valley, usually used by student athletes from Keio univesity and simultaneously, open to the citizens. How did you feel about this site?

今回の対象敷地のまむし谷は慶應義塾大学の体育会を中心に使われ、市民にも解放されている敷地でしたが、まずその印象をお伺いしたいと思います。

First, I was surprised to see such wonderful nature still existing right next to a station that is close to the capital. This green area isn't maintained by someone, and I thought this wild and undulating nature was very characteristic. I felt how seriously Keio University is about its history, culture and nature as they try to use this rich place little by little. On the other hand, I felt that this area wsn't used well enough, even though it is open to the public. This is a familiar place for the students, so I thought it was a nice task to think about Mamushi-Valley, which has a great potential in various contexts.

　わりと都心に近い駅のすぐ近くに、こんなに豊かな自然が残されているということにまず驚きました。しかも整備された人工的な緑地ではなく、起伏の多いワイルドな自然という点も特徴的だと思いました。そんな豊かな場所を大切に少しずつ使っているところに、慶應大学の歴史の長さと文化や自然に対する真摯な姿勢を感じました。一方で、市民に開放されているとはいえ、あまりうまく使われていないようにも感じられました。学生にとっては身近な場所ですし、さまざまな文脈から大きな可能性を持ったまむし谷について考えることは良い課題だと思いました。

Please describe what makes Mamsuhi-Valley different from other forests?

他の森と違うと感じたところを詳しくお願いします。

There are many, but I though the biggest characteristic was the undulations. The terrain with the ups and downs help creating unique places such as, places with good views, places full of trees, and valleys. Each of these areas have a complicated relationship because of its height difference, so it turns out to be a very diverse area as a whole too. Some parts are already used for different purposes, and the valley is surrounded by a densely populated residential area. I thought this was a very interesting place because of all these possibilities.

　いくつかありますが、最も特徴的なのは起伏が多いところかなと思いました。アップダウンの多い地形によって、見晴らしがいいところがあったり、谷があったり、木がもじゃもじゃしているところがあったりと、あちこちにユニークな場所ができています。しかも高低差によってそれぞれが複雑な関係になっていて、全体としてとても多様な場所となっています。部分的にはすでにバラバラの用途に使われている点や、周りを割と高密度な住宅地に囲まれている点なども特徴だと思います。課題を考える上ではいろいろな可能性があって大変面白い場所だと思いました。

Are those also the elements which you wanted the students to deal with?

学生に意識してもらいたかったところもそのような点だったのでしょうか？

Yes, I agree. In cities, places like Mamushi-Valley will be developed right away, unless everybody consciously kept it under everyone's agreement. But, it didn't seem like it was preserved because it's hard to handle. I felt like there was some sort of coexistence between the city and the nature with moderate use. On the other hand, I guess it has been used in a disorderly way so far, so I thought it could become more interesting by considering the possibility of Mamushi-Valley. I am sure the students had the same problem as well.

　そうですね。都市部ではまむし谷のようなところは、みんなの合意のもと、意識して残さないとすぐに開発されてしまいます。でも、腫れ物に触るように保存しているわけでもなく、ほどほどに使いながら都市と自然がなんとなく共存しているように感じられました。それはとても良いことだと思います。一方で、今のところはわりと無秩序に使われているように見え、まむし谷の可能性を考えるともっとおもしろい場所にできるのではないかとも思いました。学生たちも同じような問題意識を共有できていたと思います。

2. Studio theme and Teaching スタジオのテーマと教育

How did you lead the student in your studio?

近藤さんのスタジオでは実際どのように学生をリードしていこうと考えていますか？

I won't say that I led them, but I hope that the possibilities have expanded through my esquisse. There are many international students in this studio, and there were people with various backgrounds, so their interests and preferences should be different too. I did the esquisse thinking, if the students ended up proposing something similar in such a highly flexible task, my teaching is wrong. But fortunately, I guess the students ended up observing Mamushi Valley from their own perspectives and showed many possibilities.

　特にリードというのはないのですが、エスキスを通して可能性が広がるといいなと思っています。このスタジオは留学生も多いですし、いろいろなバックグラウンドを持っている人がいて、興味や好みも一人ひとり違うはずです。今回のような自由度の高い課題で、もし学生たちの提案が似たようなものになってしまったらそれはぼくの教え方が悪いと思ってエスキスをしていました。幸い、学生たちはそれぞれ独自の視点でまむし谷を観察し、多くの可能性を見せてくれたと思います。

You also hold studio classes in other universities.
Are there any studio classes that also requires to build something in the forest?

近藤さんは他の大学でもスタジオを持っていらっしゃいますよね。そこでも敷地が森だったりするのでしょうか？

Not actually. Usually in graduate school studios, most of the tasks require you to choose the site by yourself, and it is quite interesting to do so, because this selection is also where you can feel the student's individuality. When I took part in a studio in a foreign university, I remember some students choosing the amazon, a desert, or an island where penguins lived. For some countries, such places may be familiar, so it's interesting.

　そんなことはないですね（笑）。大学院のスタジオだと、自分で敷地を選んでくださいという課題を出すことが多いのですが、敷地選びにも個性が出るのでなかなか興味深いです。海外の大学でスタジオをやった時には、アマゾンや砂漠やペンギンの住んでいる島などを敷地に選んでくる学生もいました（笑）。たしかに、国によってはそういった場所がそれなりに身近なのかもしれません。おもしろいですよね。

Were there any works that were impressive?

今回のスタジオで印象に残っている作品はありますか？

There are some people who I remember. For example, one student was struggling how to get things right, even though he had a unique point of view. The student had an option to shift to the easy way, but he repeated his study with his strong will, "I want to do this". And I think he managed to organize it well in the end. Maybe he himself wasn't satisfied with it, but I am sure this experience will be useful in the future.

　印象に残っている人は何人かいます。例えば、着眼点はユニークだけどなかなかうまく案に結び付けられなくて苦労していた学生がいました。まとめやすい方向にシフトする選択肢もあったかもしれないけど、その学生は「自分はこれをやりたいんだ」という強い意志でスタディを重ねて、最後にはまあまあ上手にまとめていました。もしかしたら満足のいくレベルには達していなかったかもしれないけれど、苦しい状況でも自分に正直にやりたいことをつきつめていったという経験は、きっと今後役に立つと思います。

3. For the future architects 　将来の建築家に向けて

Can you tell us what we should think or to do as students?

学生のうちに考えておくべきこと、やっておいたほうがいいと思うことがあれば教えてください。

After graduation, I think some people will go on to design, and some others will choose a different way. However, no matter what field you choose, I would like the students to have literacy and trust in space. For that, it is important to look at various things and to think carefully. This sounds natural, but it's not easy to digest and understand things properly. And then, I hope the students work on something with the spirit of inquiry, honest, and greed. Well, of course not just while you're a student, but after you graduate too.

　卒業後は設計に進む人もいれば違う道に進む人もいると思います。ただ、どんな分野に進むことになっても、建築を勉強した人たちなので空間に対するリテラシーや信頼を持っていてほしいなと思います。そのためにはいろいろなものを見て、よく考えるということが大事です。そんなことわかっているよと言われそうですが、表面的ではなく、きちんと自分の中で消化して理解するというのはそんなに簡単なことではありません。それから、探究心を持って、正直に、貪欲に、何かに取り組んでほしいと思います。まあ、それは学生の間だけでなくてずっとですが（笑）。

Yumi Ishii
石井結実
Saikawa Studio

Mamushi-Valley which is a "Satoyama" is opened to the city. However, students, residents, and the relation between the nature is somehow isolated. This project aims to propose a Hydrophilic space using bamboos and water of the valley. By rethinking the relationship of people and nature, this proposal weaves a new landscape through the "Satoyama".

「里山」であるまむし谷は街に開いている。しかし、学生と地域住民、そして自然との関わりが閉じている。そこでまむし谷の水と竹を用いて、人が集い、自然が育まれる親水空間を提案する。人と人、人と自然の関係性を問い直すことで、「里山」に新たな風景を紡いでいく。

Sketch

まむしの水のシステムの再編
Restructuring of water system in Mamushi-dani

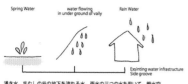

Spring Water　　water flowing in under ground of vally　　Rain Water

Exsinting water infrastructure
Side groove

湧き水、まむしの谷の地下を流れる水、雨水の三つの水を用いて、親水空間をつくる。これらを既存のインフラストラクチャ〜である側溝によってつなぐ。

広島県土砂災害事例
Case of Hiroshima prefecture landslide

Before　　After

かつて広島県で起きた土砂災害の対策として、一階部分にコンクリートによる補強壁を立てた事例がある。そこで土砂災害危険区域にコンクリート壁を建てる

竹を型枠としたコンクリート壁
Concrate casting with Bamboo form

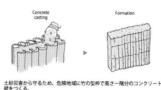

Concrete casting　　Formation

土砂災害から守るため、危険地域に竹の型枠で高さ一階分のコンクリート壁をつくる。

法面の水抜きパイプ
Pipe in Retaining wall

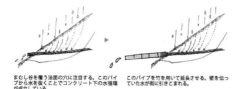

まむし谷を覆う法面の穴に注目する。このパイプから水を抜くことでコンクリート下の水循環が成立している。

このパイプを用いて延長させる。壁を伝っていた水が街に引きこまれる。

竹のジョイント
Bamboo joint

仮設的にも建てられるように紐で結ぶことで竹をジョイントさせる。

水と竹
Water & Bamboo

竹の中心に穴を開けて水を通す。

竹を半分に割り交互に重ねることで、雨よけになる。

竹をしならせ、雨が竹を伝う。

水の中の竹は生き物の居場所となる。

Details

34

02 Piers as a node-revitalize the community through sports
結の桟橋 - スポーツを通じた地域活性化 -

Yusuke Ono
小野裕介
Saikawa Studio

Mamushi-Valley locates between two mountains, and with its geographical characteristic, the sports facilities and the residents are disconnected. This project proposes a new sports clubhouse for both students and residents which behaves as a node connecting the facilities and residents, and as a result, revitalizing the community.

まむし谷の二つの山に挟まれるという地形的特徴から各施設と近隣住民は分断されている。このプロジェクトでは学生と住民のためのクラブハウスを新たに設計することでスポーツ施設と利用者を繋ぐノードを作り出し、コミュニティを活性化することを目的とした。

Perspective

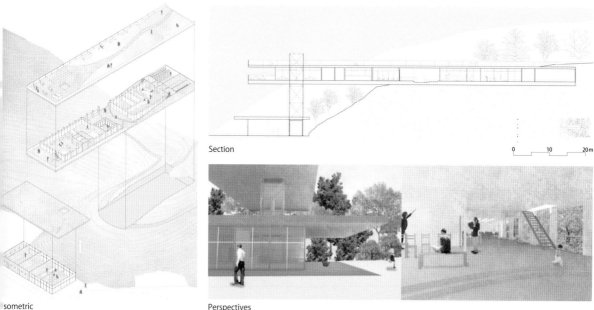

Section

0   10   20m

sometric

Perspectives

WINDPATH
風の通り道

Takuomi Samejima
鮫島卓臣
Saikawa Studio

This proposal was inspired from the Microclimate of Mamushi-Valley. By considering those features into the design, multidisciplinary activities occur inside the building. Students, athletes, and the local residents will realize the true nature and value of the valley through them.

　この提案はまむし谷の微気候に着目した。それらを取り込むことによって建物内で横断的なアクティビティが生まれ、学生やアスリート、地域住民はまむし谷の自然に触れ合いその価値を認識する。

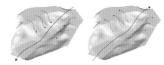

Yama-kaze and Tani-kaze
山風と谷風の概要

Perspective

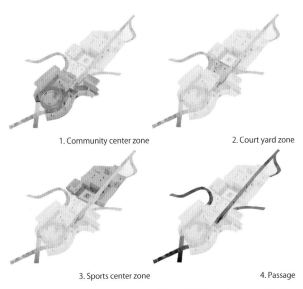

1. Community center zone   2. Court yard zone

3. Sports center zone   4. Passage

Relationship between the users of Mamushi-Valley and program definition
蝮谷の利用者の相互の関係性とそこから想起されるプログラムの概要
Diagram

Natural sunlight streams into the dark pilot
暗いピロティにスポットライトのように光が差す

Kur Mamushi Valley
まむし谷サナトリウム

Yuichi Tatsumi
巽祐一
Saikawa Studio

This project focused on designing a "Kur House" and a promenade, where students and residents can interact, devoting themselves into the vast nature of Mamushi. The design was driven by tracing the landscape, providing a continuous experience of sightseeing and walking inside the warm stream.

まむし谷の広大な自然を全身で体験しながら、生徒と住民が交流を図れるコミュニティの場として「クアハウス＝温泉施設」及び遊歩道を設計した。地形をトレースしながら円環を描き、内部を歩行湯でつなぐことで景色と湯に浸かる体験が連続することを目指した。

Perspectives

Exsiting pass

proposal

Site analysis

Diagram

Perspectives

Section S=1/1000

0   10   20m

05 Detour × Space
獣道 × 空間

Itaru Iwasaki
岩崎達
Kondo Studio

The aim of this project is to centralize the Mamushi-Valley, which is actually dividing Hiyoshi station and the residents, by inserting new functions like Cafes and Event halls. Each facilities are intentionally connected with a "Detour Trail". The steps of the users will turn into an "Animal Trail", offering opportunities to create a new space.

このプロジェクトでは日吉駅と住宅街を分断している既存のまむし谷にカフェやホールといった新たな機能を挿入することで、まむし谷が日吉地区の中心となることを目指した。各プログラムは「迂回道」で繋がり、人々の歩みはやがて「獣道」になり、新たな空間を創出していく。

HIYOSHI - CAMPUS
MAMUSHI - VALLEY
YAGAMI - CAMPUS
MAMUSHI - VALLEY

Perspective

Site analysis

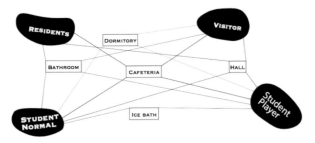

Relationship between the users of Mamushi-Valley and program definition
蝮谷の利用者の相互の関係性とそこから想起されるプログラムの概要

View from the Dormitory
宿泊施設からの眺め

06 Mamushi Retaining Patchwork
まむし谷を守るパッチワーク

Keitaro Onishi
大西慶太郎
Kondo Studio

This proposal criticizes the current disconnection of the sports facilities, the campus, and the locals yielded by the steep landscape. By proposing a new retaining walls as an infrastructure, which people can use and interact on a daily basis. The retaining walls will create a bright vision towards the future of the valley.

この提案ではスポーツ施設やキャンパス、周辺地域が地形によって分断されている現状を意識した。人々が日常的に関わりを持ち、使うことができるような新たな土留めをインフラとして斜面地に設計することで、まむし谷の未来の明るい風景を紡ぎ出すことを目指した。

Perspective

woden stair garden   community stone stair   observation bamboo rest hut   drain pipe architecture   wooden land slide protection

Diagram

Perspective

Tangling Path
からまる道

Xuang   Yang
楊宣
Kondo Studio

The concept of the building is to connect two hills, by using the factors extracted from the research of Mamushi-Valley. The vertical columns support and hide the narrow paths which crosses the whole building from top to bottom, connecting the various function inside.

この設計ではまむし谷を調査する中で見つけたさまざまな要素を用いて二つの丘を建物でつなぐことをコンセプトとした。垂直に並べられた柱は、建物内を上から下まで巡る細い小道を支え、隠しながら内部の多様な機能や空間をつないでいく。

Perspective

Various activities gets into the building from outside through the narrow path
建物内には外部から多様なアクティビティが小道を介して貫入する

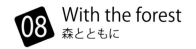

08 With the forest
森とともに

Kyoko Suganuma
菅沼響子
Kondo Studio

Since the old days, human used to live with the forest. Nowadays, the forest disappeared from people's daily life due to urbanization. This proposal aims to offer a space which triggers people to interact with the forest by designing a big roof in Mamushi-Valley.

昔から人びとは、森とともに住んでいた。しかし、人口増加によって土地が開発されると、人びとの生活から森が消えた。このプロジェクトでは人々が再び森と関わり合いを持つきっかけとなる空間を、まむし谷の森に大きな屋根をかけることで実現することを目的とした。

森の停留点　　人の交流点

Perspective

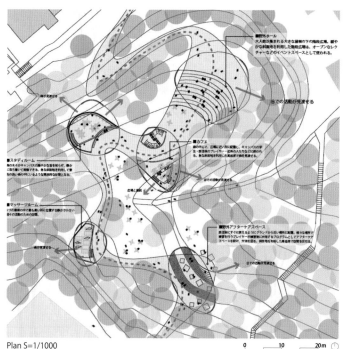

Plan S=1/1000

0　　　10　　　20m

View of the interior staircase
階段状の屋内空間

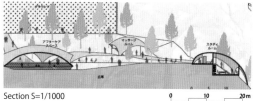

Section S=1/1000

0　　　10　　　20m

41

09 Mamushi-dani Circle
蝮谷サークル

Manon Ellie
マノン・エリー
Kondo Studio

"Mamushi-Dani Circle" allows people to gather and creates a new "Common Space" for sports players, students, and the residents of the surrounding area. The new center and the boardwalk gives new experience at the valley, creates a new way to circulate, and provides a space to enjoy sports and nature.

この提案ではスポーツアスリートや学生、住民が集えるような新しい「コモンスペース」として円環状の「まむし谷サークル」を設計した。新しい建物と遊歩道はまむし谷における新たな体験と人々の流れを生み出し、スポーツを楽しみながら自然を感じる空間を提供する。

Idea of place making
空間の作り方

Perspective

1.Open Public space
開けた公共空間

2.Circle walkway
円状の遊歩道

3.Integration
地形との統合

4.Volume placement
ボリューム配置

Diagram

Section S=1/1000

0   10   20 m

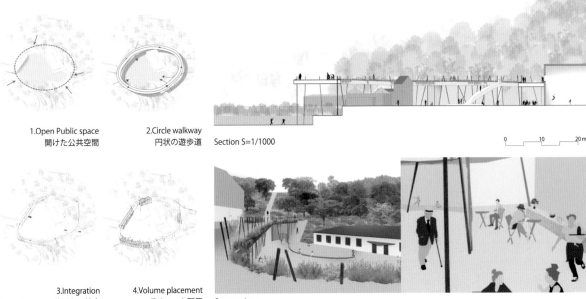

Perspectives

42

Column 2

The snapshots from production of
Keio Architecture

POSTER1

Exhibition & Lexture's Poster 2018
展示会とレクチャーポスター 2018

Guest lecture was held as part of CDW. A lecture was given that will be a hint
of investigation and design of the target area from a wide viewpoint, such as
domestic architects and overseas researchers, and the poster was also made the
student main subject.
CDWの一環として、ゲストレクチャーが行われた。国内の建築家や海外の研究者など、幅広い視点
から対象地域の調査、設計のヒントとなるような講演が行われ、そのポスターも生徒主体となっ
て製作された。

KEIO ARCHITECTURE EXHIBITION

CDW A Comprehensive Design Workshop for the Athletic and Recreational Facilities of the Hiyoshi, Shimoda, and Yagami Campuses

2018/07/21 - 07/24 7/21 13:00 - 19:00   7/23 09:00 - 19:00   **Raiosha 1F**
                  7/22 closed   7/24 09:00 - 15:00

43

M

The snapshots from production of
Keio Architecture
MODEL1
Site model of Mamushi Valley area
まむし谷エリアの敷地模型

It was the site model of the Mamushi Valley area which was produced regarding the opening of CDW. We made a model with a scale of 1/500 on a 1.25-square area over a month.

CDWの開催に合わせて製作されたのが、敷地となるまむし谷エリアの敷地模型である。1.25km四方のエリアを1/500スケールにした模型を1か月以上かけて製作した。

Chapter 3
Seizu 3 2018
Designing of Mamushi Center

第 3 章　2018 年度　製図 3　慶應義塾大学まむし谷センターの設計

"Space Design III" was coordinated by Prof. Darko Radovic in Spring of year 2018. A total of 10 students participated, divided into three groups, each one lead by one instructor. Jorge Almazán's group assignment focused on Urban Acupuncture in Mamushi Valley. Professor Tatsuya Kishimoto's group assignment was entitle, "The Proposal of the Masterplan and Architecture program that improves Mamushi-Valley Space". Professor Darko Radović Studio assignment was centered on the concepts of "Smart + Sensual – The Spaces for Ideas and Bodies on the Move –"

「空間設計製図Ⅲ」は 2018 年春学期に実施、ダルコ・ラドヴィッチ教授が主担当となった。参加した 10 名の生徒は 3 つのグループに分かれ、各グループは担当教授によって指導された。アルマザン・ホルヘ班ではまむし谷における都市の鍼治療について考えた。岸本達也班の課題は、まむし谷の空間システムとそれを改善するマスタープラン及び建築プログラムの提案であった。ダルコ・ラドヴィッチ班の課題は「スマート＋センシュアル　進行し続けるアイデアと体のための空間」。

Studio Works
作品一覧

Interview ——————————————————————————————— p.50-53

Radović Studio

Architecture Trail │ Hiroki Shigemura ——————————————————— p.56
アーキテクチャトレイル │ 重村浩規

Re: │ Motomi Matsubara ——————————————————————————— p.58
Re: │ 松原元実

In Search of Lost Space │ Junpei Kawamoto ————————————— p.58
失われた空間を求めて │ 川本純平

"my" forest │ Amami Iwata ——————————————————————— p.58
「私」の森 │ 岩田あま美

Mamu-Heal │ Shinichi Nishibori ——————————————————— p.58
まむ治癒 │ 西堀槙一

Almazán Studio

The Entrance to the Forest │ Kyoko Ito ——————————————— p.54-55
森への入り口 │ 伊藤京子

Back Bone of Mamushi │ Yoshihisa Moriya ——————————————— p.57
まむし谷の背骨 │ 守屋嘉久

G-GYM -crossing flows- │ Kousuke Miyano ————————————— p.59
慶應スポーツギャラリーとジム │ 宮野公輔

En behind Mamushi memorial │ Akari Hara ——————————————— p.59
まむし谷広縁墳 │ 原明里

valley gathering place │ Yuki Wada ——————————————————— p.59
谷底の集い場 │ 和田雄樹

Overview of the Seizu 3
製図 3 の課題概要

Overview of this competition

 This competition was organized for senior students from the department of System Design Engineering. As the culmination of undergraduate architecture studies, 10 students from architecture design laboratories participated in the competition. The final presentation took place in Raiosha, Hiyoshi Campus.

Final presentation

		最終プレゼンテーション
Jury	Darko Radović	審査員 ダルコ・ラドヴィッチ
	Jorge Almazán	アルマザン・ホルヘ
	Tatsuya Kishimoto	岸本達也
	Hiroyuki Ito	伊藤博之
	Motoo Chiba	千葉元生

コンペの概要

　この設計競技会は、理工学部システムデザイン工学科の建築を学んでいる四年生を対象としたものである。学部の集大成として、意匠系の 2 つの研究室から計 10 人が参加した。最終プレゼンテーションは慶應義塾大学日吉キャンパスの来往舎にて行われた。

Q&A

Hiroyuki Ito / 伊藤博之

1993	Graduated from Architecture Engingeering Department at Tokyo University	1993	東京大学工学部建築学科卒業
1995	Completed Master Degree of Architecture Engingeering at Tokyo University	1995	東京大学大学院修士課程修了
1995	Joined Nikken Sekkei	1995	日建設計入社
1998	Established O.F.D.A	1998	O.F.D.A 設立
1999	Established Hiroyuki Ito Architecture Design Office	1999	伊藤博之建築設計事務所設立

1. Please tell us about the characteristcs of the site Mamushi-Valley.
  And were the students dealing well with those points?

まむし谷という敷地に対し、先生自身が受けた印象・注目すべき特徴について教えてく
ださい。また、学生はそれらのポイントに対し、うまく対応できていましたか？

 Mamushi-Valley was an area that I had hardly stepped in, even though I often come to Yagami Campus as a part-time instructor. As I visited this site for this review, I was surprised to see how the precious greenery remained with this complex city landscape. On the other hand, the facilities for each sport club seemed to be jammed into the flat spaces by force. Each of them are connected with the shortest route allowed by the landscape too, so it was hard to find any kind of relationship between each facilities or with the nature around them. With this poor environment, I believe students will never show interest to their surroundings. If needed, I suppose they will cut down some trees to expand their own territory, changing the space into something completely different. How do we open this closed area to athletes, other students who do not take part in sports, and to the neighbors, keeping the trees at they are, or maybe even growing them more. This problem is about how to introduce ideas or logics to the area except the spaces that are functionally required for each sport facility, for instance, the flow lines between changing rooms and the practice field. Several elements have the power to make Mamushi-Valley attractive, for instance, facilities for common use, the group of Hiyoshi and Yagami Campus buildings, neighborhood residences, the long history, and the landscape full of nature. I thought this was a wonderful assignment, because the students were required to come up with new ideas, without just applying theories of the old days.

　まむし谷は、僕自身、非常勤として矢上キャンパスに通っていながら、ほとんど足を踏み入れたことのない場所でした。この課題の講評に際して訪れ、都市部では貴重な自然が、複雑な地形と共に残っていることに驚きました。一方で、各部活動に必要な施設が、平場に埋め込まれるように配置され、地形が許す最短のルートで結ばれているのが現状で、施設同士、あるいは施設と周囲との積極的な関係が作られているとは言えません。学生が、所属する部の施設以外の環境を意識することはあまりなさそうですし、ともすると個々の必要に従って、次第に木が伐採され、変わっていってしまうかもしれないとも感じました。環境を保全しつつ、できればより豊かに育てながら、運動部員だけでなくそれ以外の学生、そして周辺住民に対して、この場所をどのように開くことができるのか。練習場と部室、およびそれらへの動線など、個別の部活動の機能的な要請の間に残された空白に、どのような視点や論理を導入し、全体を再構成できるかが問題です。各部共通で使えるスポーツ関連の機能も手掛かりになるでしょうし、日吉の校舎群、矢上キャンパス、周辺住宅街、古代や近代の場所の歴史など、地形と自然に加えて、まむし谷の場所の個性と魅力を引き出す手掛かりはたくさんありそうです。古典的なマスタープランを当てはめることが困難だからこそ、より今日的なアイデアや方法が求められる、良い課題だと思いました。

2. Which points were good about the students proposal as a whole, and also points that could be improved.

生徒全体の提案について良かった点、改善できた点等を教えてください。

First of all, I was surprised with the level of the presentations. Each student had their own original view for site selection and planning. Ms. Ito's proposed interspersing buildings where you can fully enjoy the woods, and I thought this idea came from her careful observation skills of the site. Using wood makes sense being friendly to the environment, and also because of its own ability. Her wonderful drawing and the interesting way how she framed them really well brought out the charm. I though this idea had the power to grow a new vision to Mamushi-Valley woods, effecting other plans in the future. It would have been better if she worked on a bigger scale, thinking of how other existing buildings could take part in this proposal, for example by renovating the buildings with the same wooden frames. The proposal of Mr. Shigemura "the pathway of the woods" created a nice relationship between the woods and the surrounding city blocks. The gentle curves following the contour, showed a clear vision of how the future architecture in Mamushi-Valley should look like. If he could have proposed more about the details and materials in a scale we can simply imagine, the proposal would have been more attractive. A work becomes highly convincing when both the clearness of the vision/method and the attractiveness of the architecture as an entity are proposed in highly standard. The same applies to the other students too. Re-considering their own works from these two points will help them jump a higher level.

　プレゼンテーションのレベルが全体的に高かった点と、敷地選定と計画において、どの提案もそれぞれオリジナルな方向性を持っていた点が良かったと思います。森の経験を享受できる建物を散在させる伊藤さんの提案は、まむし谷をとても丁寧に評価する姿勢から生まれたものだと思います。木造の選択は、環境へのインパクトの少なさや性能面から十分納得できるし、その架構の独特な利用の仕方と繊細なドローイングは、それぞれの場所の魅力を引き出し、伝えています。今までのまむし谷になかった森への視点が、今後の他の計画をも変えてゆく力を持つと思わせるに十分でしたが、他の既存建物が、どのように変わってゆくかを含む全体のビジョンを、例えば同様の木を用いた増改築などとして示すこともできたかもしれません。

3. What do you expect for the students in their future design assignments or other classes.

設計課題や、今後の学習にあたって、学生だからこそ大切にしてほしいことを教えてください。

If you put the vision and the entity of architecture in other words, it will be a proposal in a bigger and wider scale, and a proposal in a small scale in the real size. In the real world, these two are related to each other, and architects are expected to commit to all of these steps. An abstract concept, and the details are never two different things. Architects must try to make an overall experience where you can perceive these two at the same time. The richness of this experience must be decided by your own. And in order to figure out your own level of richness, it goes without saying that you should experience something that attracts you. In this sense, I think it is important for students to travel a lot while they are young and pure. When I was a student, I visited many villages all around the world, and these experiences really help me a lot even now. Traveling makes you learn a lot, but books help you too. It is easy to collect information from the internet, but it is a bit different from what I am trying to say here. Reading, which is an action that comes from you own spirit of inquiry, makes you remember something very well. This is why I think reading helps students to establish their basic attitude toward architecture. Actually, student life itself could be a journey already. I hope every student goes on somewhere, to figure out how far they can go, and to know what they can encounter.

　建築のビジョンと実体とは、より広範囲の大きなスケールにおける提案と、実物大の小さなスケールにおける提案とも言えます。実はそれらは連続していて、建築家はその全体にコミットすることが求められます。抽象的なコンセプトと、もののディテールは、別々のものではなく、それらが同時に知覚されるような総合的な体験の豊かさを作り出すことが目標であるべきです。そしてその豊かさの基準は、みなさん自身がそれぞれに持つべきものであって、それを得るためには、少なくとも本人が魅力的と思う、一つでも多くの体験をすべきであることは、言うまでもないでしょう。その意味で、新鮮な感覚を持った若いうちに、旅をすることは大切だと思います。僕自身、学生の時に国内外のたくさんの集落を訪れたことは大きな糧になっています。実際の旅は建築家に多くの刺激を与えてくれますが、一方で、よく例えられるように、本を読むことも旅の一つだと思います。ネット検索は情報収集には便利ですが、ここでいう体験とは少し異なります。自分の意志による探求である読書が、より深く心に刻まれるのは自然なことで、だからこそ建築に向かう基本的な姿勢の形成に役立つように思います。考えてみれば、学生生活自体、旅のようなものかもしれません。どこまで行けるのか、何と出会えるのか、より多くの冒険に出かけてもらえたらと思います。

Chiba Jury Interview
千葉審査員インタビュー

Motoo Chiba / 千葉元生
2009 Tokyo Institute of Technology
2010 Eidgenössische Technische Hochoschule Zürich
2011 Jonathan Woolf Architects London
2012 Tokyo Institute of Technology (Master Course)
2013 Established Tsubame Architects
2015 Keio University part-time lecture

2009 東京工業大学　卒業
2010 スイス連邦工科大学　卒業
2011 Jonathan Woolf Architects London
2012 東京工業大学大学院　修士課程修了
2013 ツバメアーキテクツ設立
2019 慶應義塾大学理工学部 非常勤講師

1. Please tell us about the characteristcs of the site Mamushi-Valley.
   And were the students dealing well with those points?

まむし谷という敷地に対し、先生自身が受けた印象・注目すべき特徴について教えてください。
また、学生はそれらのポイントに対し、うまく対応できていましたか？

At first, it is important to think about the boundary of the university campus and the city for future education and cities itself, not limited to this site. It is easy to imagine the potential of having a universities in cities. For instance, you can provide an open space in the city. You can create a space where young people can gather easily in a highly aging society. There might be a chance to create a core community space. You can contribute to social development by providing collaborative practical education. When considering all these possibilities, it is necessary to think about how the boundaries between the university and the city should be defined. Speaking about Mamushi-Valley in particular, there is also a geographic boundary, so I thought this assignment and site was quite complex, containing several issues at the same time. But complexity brings many ideas. From this point of view, I thought many of the students did a great job, finding their own tasks and proposing something from it in the right way. However, I expected to see more provocative and ambitious ideas, proposing the way how Hiyoshi or Keio University should be like from now on.

　まず、この敷地に限らず大学のキャンパスと街との境界を考えることは、これからの教育や都市のあり方を考える上で非常に重要です。都市における大学のキャンパスの可能性は、少し考えただけでもさまざま浮かんできます。例えば、都心においてオープンスペースを提供できること、高齢化社会の中で若者が多く集う場所となること、地域的なコミュニティの核となれる可能性があること、産学協同など実践的な教育を提供できるとともに社会の発展に貢献できることなど。これらの可能性を考えたときに、大学と街とのつながりがどうあるべきなのか、その境界のあり方が問われます。まむし谷に関して言えば、こうした大学と街との境界であると同時に、地形的な境界にもなっているため、その強い境界をどう調整していくのか、課題の多い敷地だと思いました。課題が多いということはさまざまな提案の可能性があるということです。そういった意味ではそれぞれに課題を見つけ、そこに対する提案ができている学生が多かったように思います。ただ、日吉という街のあり方そのものや、慶應義塾大学のあり方そのものの、今後について提案していくような野心的な提案がもっとあると良かったと思います。

2. Which points were good about the students proposal as a whole, and also points that could be improved.

生徒全体の提案について良かった点、改善できた点等を教えてください。

I thought it was good where each student followed the assignment rules carefully. Every proposal came from close research, and I think that is why this class ended up in a great success. The most difficult and exciting part of proposing an idea is when your proposal jumps to the next step form what you found from a good investigation. So, the students could have spent more time with their research outcomes. I expected to see the works designed in a way that couldn't have come without the exact research.

　リサーチから提案までという課題設定に忠実に思考を詰めていった人が多かった点は良かったと思います。ただ、最も難しく、エキサイティングなのはリサーチの中で何かを発見し、その発見が提案のジャンプに生かされるというプロセスです。その発見がなければ想像できなかったような建築の提案につながっている人は少なかったように思います。なので、改善できる点としては、リサーチの結果ともっと向き合って、そのリサーチがなければ浮かばなかったような建築の形にたどりつくことを、より意識すると良いのではないかと思いました。

3. What do you expect for the students in their future design assignments or other classes.

設計課題や、今後の学習にあたって、学生だからこそ大切にしてほしいことを教えてください。

It is important to consider things from both perspectives, diachronic and synchronic. By having a diachronic point of view, you will learn about the transition of the history or the culture, or things that have been taken care of universally. Whenever you think of architecture in the future, you must position your own design by thinking where you are standing and what you should do in this continuous history. By having the synchronic point of view, you will learn what is happening these days, and foresee what is being required from the world. A new space comes to life when the society and the way of living changes. To cut the long story short, learn from the past and from the latest social conditions at the same time. Whenever you look at architecture or read a book, I think it is important to think about it from these two standing points. And my last advice is to be active. Go and see a lot of architecture and meet many people when you still have time. When you start working, it becomes really hard to make time.

　通時的な視点と、共時的な視点を両方もって物事を考えることが大切です。通時的な視点をもつことで、歴史や文化の変遷や普遍的に大切にされてきたことを学べます。これからの建築を考えるときに、今自分たちがどこにいて、なにをすべきなのか、歴史的な連続のなかで考えて、自分が設計するものを位置付けていくことが大切です。共時的な視点を持つことで、現代の社会の状況を学び、いま何が求められているのか考えることが出来ます。社会が変化して、人の暮らし方の枠組みが変化するときにこそ、新しい空間が生まれます。簡単に言えば、過去からよく学ぶと同時に、最新の社会の状況にも目を向けることです。建築をみるときにでも、本を読むときにでも、こうした二つの視点でその意味を捉えて考えることを大切にすると良いと思います。あとは時間のある学生のうちに、フットワークを軽くしてたくさん建築を見たり、人と会ったりすると良いと思います。働き始めるとなかなかそういう時間がつくりづらくなります。

The Entrance to the Forest
森への入り口

Kyoko Ito
伊藤京子
Almazán Studio

Concept

 The forest that spreads all over Mamushi-Valley has always been a part of the people's lives. In between the living area and the forest, I have designed an unusual space where people can take a break.

 It is difficult to feel the charm of the vague space created by the forest just by passing through Mamushi-Valley, so I have designed an architecture in order to bring out the charm of the valley. Visitors will stop by and look carefully to the surrounding, experiencing activities particular to that space.

 This architecture will help the locals rediscover the beauty of the forest, and the forest will be the part of their daily life.

設計趣旨文

　まむし谷に広がる森は、昔から人々の活動のそばにある。暮らしと森の境目に、少しだけ日常から離れ、ひと息つくことのできるような居場所を設計した。

　森によって形づくられる、ぼんやりとした空間の魅力はまむし谷を通り抜けるだけでは気付かない。足を止めて丁寧に観察し、その場所の魅力を引き出す建築をつくることによって、その場でしか味わうことのできない体験が生まれる。

　この建築をきっかけとして、人々が森の魅力を再確認し、森と暮らしが寄り添いあっていく。

Concept Diagram

There is no relationship between people's activities and forest in Mamushi Valley.

まむし谷の森と人々の活動の
関係性は希薄である

The architecture is designed in gap space between the daily life and forest.

活動の場と森との境目に
居場所となる建築を設計する

The architecture connect forest and people's life in Mamushi Valley.

居場所ができることで人々の
生活に森との関わりが生まれる

Site Plan S=1/2500

0　10　20 m

research in Mamushi

森に形づくられる
空間を探す

↓

simple volume

シンプルなボリューム
を配置する

↓

fit to site

敷地に合わせて
変形させる

Research Sketches

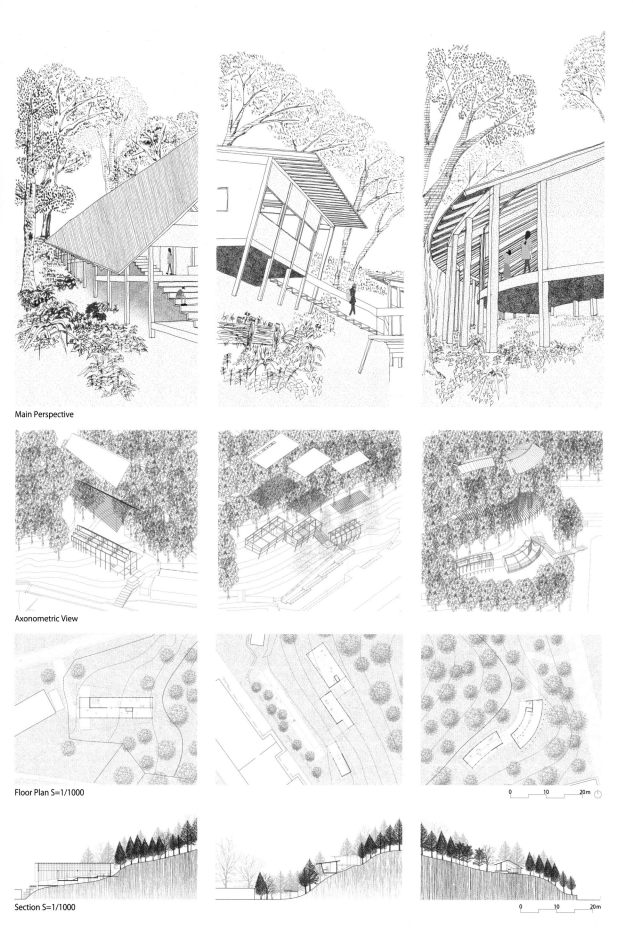

Main Perspective

Axonometric View

Floor Plan S=1/1000

0　　10　　20m

Section S=1/1000

0　　10　　20m

Concept

Mamushi-Valley is consisted of several facilities such as sports facilities, residential areas which are divided by the slope located in the center. At the moment, the slop is only used as a staircase, so I designed a new facility where people can gather around. The simple path will turn into a hub bringing opportunities for the University students and the locals to interact. As people walk along the "Architecture Trail" they will encounter several activities, feeling the rich greenery. I hope my design creates a stronger bond between the locals and the students of Keio University, bringing a harmony to Hiyoshi.

設計趣旨文

さまざまなアクティビティが起こるまむし谷は、中央に位置する斜面によって慶應義塾大学、スポーツ施設、住宅街に分断されている。その斜面では、ただただ人が上り下りしているだけで、交流が生まれる気配はない。その斜面が位置する森の中に、人々が集う新しい施設を設計する。今まで単に通り過ぎるだけであった場所を新たな居場所へと変化。森や周囲との関係性を持ちながら、離れた場所同士をつなぐ"アーキテクチャトレイル"。この通りは、まむし谷に新たなアクティビティ空間を創り出し、慶應義塾大学の学生と地域住民の交流を促進する。

Main Perspective

Diagram

Plan S=3500   0 10 20 m

Interior Perspective

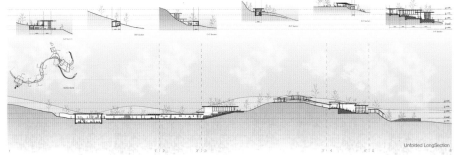

Section S=3000   0 10 20 m

Back Bone of Mamushi
まむし谷の背骨

Yoshihisa Moriya
守屋嘉久
Almazán Studio

Concept

Even though Mamushi is surrounded by hills, there are residences. In order to make a space for people to gather, I will propose a "Street Corner Community Center" that is equipped with several urban functions. This architecture is consisted of roofs and pillars based on a simple grid pattern. By keeping the boundary of the entrance to the university and the private space of the residents unclear, so as the overflowing appear nice. This flexible space attracts both the university students and the residents and connect them.

Main Perspective

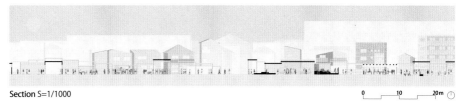

Section S=1/1000

0   10   20m

設計趣旨文

　まむし谷は湾曲型傾斜地に囲まれているにもかかわらず、住宅という機能しか持ちあわせてない。そこで私は、都市機能を備えた「まちかど交流センター」を提案する。シンプルなグリッドを基に、屋根と柱を配置してできるこの建築は、周辺の住人が彩る境界によって経年変化されていく。そのために大学へのアプローチ空間と周辺住人のプライベート空間の境界を曖昧にし、溢れ出しが魅力的な場所となるよう設計した。人を集めるようなコアスペースと、それによって生かされるフレキシブルスペースは住人や学生をケアすることによって結ぶ。

Main Concept

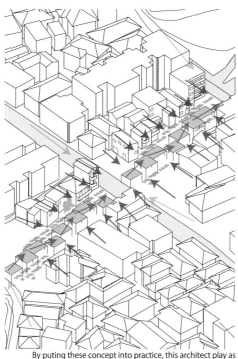

By puting these concept into practice, this architect play as "Communitiy center on the road."
右記のコンセプトを実現することで、「まちかど交流センター」ができる。

Diagram

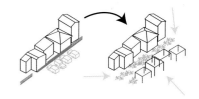

Core space that has social function gather neighbor
生活に必要なコアで住人を集める

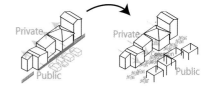

Share the thoughts of residents and create a common space
住人たちの思いを共有してコモンスペースとする

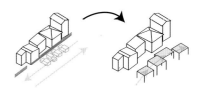

People do not just pass through, but will take a break
通り過ぎるだけでなく、一息つける場所がある

Re:
Re:

Motomi Matsubara
松原元実
Radović Studio

ReUse,Reserve,Recreate

リユース、リザーブ、リクリエイト

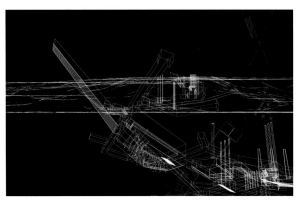

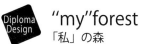

"my"forest
「私」の森

Amami Iwata
岩田あま美
Radović Studio

"Hiyoshi Forest" is located between the Campus and the town. This forest which used to be a "Satoyama", has lost its presence as the time goes by. Through my design, people will feel the growth of the trees season by season, and rediscover the value of "Satoyama". I hope each visitors find their own "my" forest.

日吉キャンパスと町の間を日吉の森が隔てている。かつて里山だったこの森は時代によって存在が希薄になりつつある。四季の変化、木々の成長。森を感じながら活動をすることで新たな里山の価値を発見したい。利用者一人一人、「私」の森を発見できる建築を提案する。

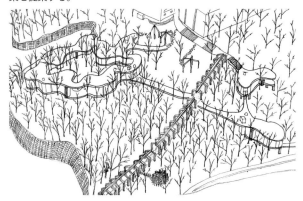

In Search of Lost Space
失われた空間を求めて

Junpei Kawamoto
川本純平
Radović Studio

Aging society has increased the number of multi-family housings in cities. The memory and the lifestyle of the countryside is being forgotten. This is a case study redesigning my family's house in Miyazaki to Hiyoshi. I intend to show the method of designing a multi-family house in future cities.

高齢化社会では多世代同居が都市化する傾向が見られ、地方暮らしの人たちの記憶が軽視される傾向にある。本提案ではケーススタディとして、宮崎市にある私の家族の家を生活の歴史として孫世代である私が住む横浜市・日吉に再設計し直した。将来の多世代住宅の設計手法を示す。

Mamu-Heal
まむ治癒

Shinichi Nishibori
西堀槙一
Radović Studio

Though Mamushi-Valley is full of nature and has many sports facilities, the relationship between the University and the locals are scarce. Now, existing sports facilities are used only for club activities and classes. By creating a "Healing Facility" with a core spa, I intend to create a stronger bond between the two.

自然が豊富でスポーツ施設の多いまむし谷。学生と地域双方から親しまれているものの、そこに交流はない。既存スポーツ施設は主に部活動と授業のために使われ、いわゆる "Healing Sports" としての利用は乏しい。コミュニティの形成を主眼に、銭湯を中心とした Healing 施設を設計する。

58

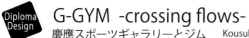

G-GYM -crossing flows-
慶應スポーツギャラリーとジム

Kousuke Miyano
宮野公輔

Almazán Studio

En behind Mamushi memorial
まむし谷広縁墳

Akari Hara
原明里

Almazán Studio

The virtue of sports lies in the involvement with other people. In Hiyoshi, due to the trend to revitalize university sports, it is expected to establish a stronger relationship between the university and the neighbors. As a pioneer, I designed a facility that positively creates a link between them.

スポーツの良さは個人が楽しむ以上に、人々の交流から新たなコミュニティが生まれることにある。大学スポーツ活性化の流れを受け、ここ日吉では、大学と地域の繋がりが求められている。その関係性構築の先駆けとなる施設として、「慶應スポーツギャラリーと地域に開かれたスポーツジム」を提案する。

By constructing a formal facility on a sloping ground, informal activities occur in between the gap space created by the topography and the structure. Different types of activities are connected at the edge of the space (縁 -edge), and people's relation (縁 -En) emerges on a connecting line.

まむし谷において、広く平面的な空間をもつフォーマルな施設をあえて連続的に傾斜地に建てる。すると、建物同士や地形とのギャップで生じる隙間空間にインフォーマルで小さいアクティビティが入り込む。活動同士が空間の縁（ふち）で連続し、人々の縁（えん）が両エリアをつなぐ動線上に生まれる。

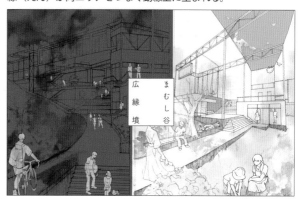

valley gathering place
谷底の集い場

Yuki Wada
和田雄樹

Almazán Studio

By keeping the old frames, I will renovate Mamushi-Valley Gymnasium into a recreation facility that is fully opened to the locals. The building was designed so to feel the rich greenery through the frames, hoping to create and enhance the relationship between the University and the residents.

現まむし谷体育館の躯体だけを残し、地域に開かれたレクリエーション施設へと改修する。学生だけでなく地域住民にも利用されるまむし谷。既存スポーツ施設を開放することで、学生と地域の間に新たな関係を生む。躯体を介して斜面の自然を感じられるよう、建物全体が緑に埋もれるように設計した。

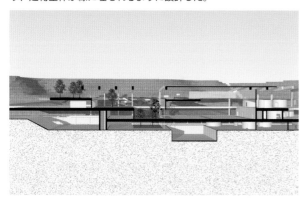

P

The snapshots from production of
Keio Architecture
PAVILION1
colabo Research Pavilion 2018
colabo リサーチパビリオン 2018

Objective and sandrequitements.
Fot the education of architecture in Keio, pavilion focusing on portability and interactivity.
with the local community had important role. Having this in mind, we explore a new urban
research pavilion for coming research activities. This pavilion making process is to discuss
its conceptual design and to step forward to its design development and construction in
the monetary limitation of 500,000 JPY.

目的と要件.
慶應義塾大学の建築教育において、簡単に持ち運ぶことができて、地域の人々と関わる
ことができるパビリオンはとても重要な意味を持っていた。その背景から、私たちはこ
れからの都市調査のため、新しいリサーチパビリオンの提案を500,000円という予算の
範囲内で行った。

Create a new pavilion as a method of investigating the target site. We
divided the group from three themes and exhibited each of them.

対象敷地の調査手法として新たなパビリオンを製作する。3つのテーマからグル
ープを分け、テーマごとの提案を展示した。

Brainstoming

TENTION

ASSEMBLE

INTERACTIVE

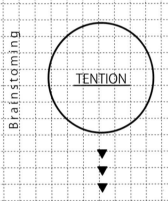
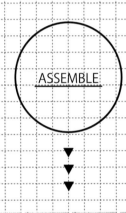
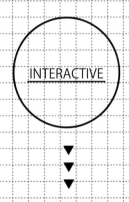

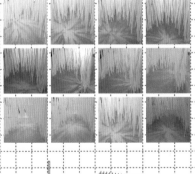

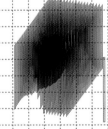

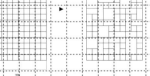

Chapter 4
Keio Architecture
Exhibition 2018

第 4 章　2018 年度　慶應アーキテクチャ展示会

First CDW Exhibition was held at Keio Hiyoshi Campus in July 2018. In the spirit of Keio Architecture, not only the exhibits but total design and production of all fittings and the grand 2.5x2.5 meters physical model were done by our students. The quality of their work best communicated the achievements of the work in participating laboratories and set high expectations from every subsequent presentation. This event also celebrated the strategic partnership, well established and fruitful collaboration between one of the best European schools of architecture and urbanism, Politecnico di Milano and our nascent Keio Architecture.

　初の CDW 展示会は 2018 年 6 月に慶應日吉キャンパスで開かれました。慶應アーキテクチャの精神に基づいて、展示物だけでなく、全ての会場デザイン・設置物、そして 2.5m × 2.5m の特大模型は、学生の手によって造られました。生徒によって造られた会場デザインなどは、各研究室の展示作品とうまく調和し、その後の講評会やプレゼンテーションに高い期待が寄せられました。またこの展示会では、建築・都市の分野でヨーロッパの頂点を走るミラノ工科大学と初期段階の慶應アーキテクチャとが、実に有益なコラボレーションをして成功しました。

Exhibition Appearance 2018
展示会風景

As the Keio Architecture Kick-Off Event, CDW Keio Exhibition 2018 was held at Hiyoshi Campus in July. Many visitors came to see works of the graduate and undergraduate students of the Faculty of Science and Technology and SFC. Some pavilions and the whole model of the Mamushi-Valley were exhibited as well.

慶應アーキテクチャキックオフイベントとして、7月、日吉キャンパス来往舎にて CDW 慶應展示会 2018 が実施された。理工学部と SFC による院生と学部生の設計作品およびパビリオンやまむし谷全体模型などが展示され、多くの来場者が訪れた。

Exhibition Scedule 2018
展示会スケジュール

Before the exhibition, a Keio Architecture Kick-Off Event was held with lectures by Shigeru Ban and Kengo Kuma. During the exhibition period, there was a lecture by Fumihiko Maki and students' works from graduate program "Studio B" and undergraduate program "Architectural space planning and design 3" were exhibited.

　展示会に先駆け、慶應アーキテクチャのキックオフイベントが開催され、坂茂氏・隈研吾氏による講演も行われた。展示会期間中には槇文彦氏による講演があり、修士課程「スタジオ B」と学部生による「空間設計製図 3」の設計課題の作品が展示された。

Before Exhibition

坂茂氏による講演
Lecture by Shugeru Ban

隈研吾氏による講演
Lecture by Kuma Kengo

キックオフイベント
Kick off event

Day 1

CDW展示会開会
CDW Exhibition Door Open

デザインコンペティション
CDW Design Competitoin

槇文彦氏による講演
Lecture by Humihiko Maki

Day 2 / 3

展示会
Exhibition

訪問者賞発表
Students and Visitors Awards

展示会閉会
Closing Down

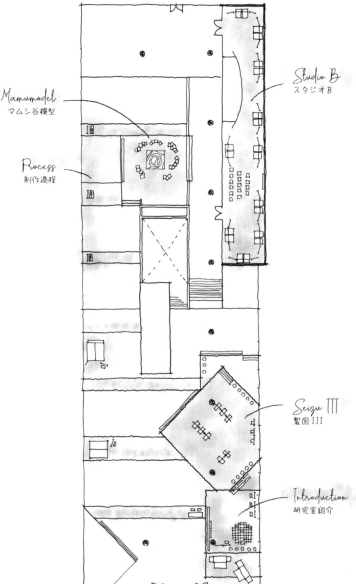

Studio B
スタジオB

Mamumodel
マムシ谷模型

Process
制作過程

Seizu Ⅲ
製図Ⅲ

Introduction
研究室紹介

1.Exhibition space

The works from the design studio of the undergraduate class "Architectural space planning and design3" and the master course "Studio B" were exhibited. A variety of unique works were arranged in panels and models, and visitors were paying close attention to the details.

1.展示会場

学部授業「空間設計製図3」の設計課題と修士課程「スタジオB」の設計課題の作品が展示された。ボードと模型にまとめられた個性豊かな作品が並び、来場者はディティールに目を凝らしていた。

2.Mamushi-Valley Model

The Model of Hiyoshi-Yagami was exhibited, which was made by the students. A 2.5m × 2.5m diorama model, composed of 25 pieces of 50cm × 50cm square models. Many visitors were looking at the terrain and buildings with fascination.

2.まむし谷模型

学生で作成した日吉・矢上キャンパス周辺模型が展示されていた。50cm四方の模型25ピースからなる、全体で2.5m四方のジオラマ模型の地形と建物に、来場者の多くが興味深く眺めていた。

3. Lab Introduction

Near the reception, each laboratory exhibited their activities boards and pavilions. We never had an opportunity to share activities together, and this created a connection that goes beyond the boundaries of each laboratories.

3.研究室紹介

受付近くのエリアには、それぞれの研究室の活動などが紹介されているボードやこれまでに製作してきたパビリオンなどが展示された。こうした研究活動を一緒に展示し、一覧できるようにする機会はこれまでなく、研究室の垣根を超えた繋がりを生むことができた。

4. SFC Pavilion

A wooden pavilion made by SFC students was exhibited. By assembling parts cut out of veneer boards, the structure of this pavilion becomes very strong. Previous research activities and ongoing ones were also displayed inside.

4.SFC パビリオン

SFC の学生が製作した木製のパビリオンが展示された。ベニヤボードから切り出したパーツを組み立てることで構造強度が高くなる。パビリオン内にはこれまでの研究活動や現在進行形の研究活動も展示された。

5. Urban Cupboard

As a part of a research, large furniture made in Radović laboratory was installed at the exhibition space. Materials related to past publications and research activities were displayed too.

5.アーバンカップボード

研究活動の一環としてラドヴィッチ研究室で製作した大型の家具が展示会場に設置された。過去の出版物やこれまでの研究活動などに関わる資料も展示された。

6. Original CDW Bag

Visitors were presented with handbags made for this exhibition. Students designed the bags and the visitors seemed happy to take them home.

6.CDW手さげバッグ

来場者には、展示会のために製作された手提げバッグがプレゼントされた。これらは学生がデザインを手がけたもので、受け取った来場者の方は喜んで持って帰っていた。

Architecture and City after Olympics

Kengo Kuma

隈研吾
オリンピック後の建築と都市

I would like to speak about architecture as a relationship today. In the 20th century, architecture was considered as a beautiful sculpture isolated from the environment. But, I wanted to change the definition of architecture to a representation of a relationship.

I will tell you a story about Satoyama, a village in the mountain. Hiyoshi Campus and the surrounding area used to be Satoyama. Satoyama had a very close relationship with the village and the people who lived there. While Yokohama is a big city with a large population, there are still many Satoyama remaining in the area. I was born in Okurayama, where my mother still lives. My childhood home was very close to Satoyama. The topography and vegetation of Hiyoshi and Okurayama are quite similar. Satoyama was my playground in the 1960s and I spent a lot of time there. I still hold memories of a quiet life in Satoyama dear to my heart.

『Nakagawa-machi, Bato Hiroshige Museum of Art』

The Hiroshige Museum [of Art] is very much related to the concept of Satoyama. The building materials for this project came from Satoyama and the forest near the site. This doesn't happen often these days because most of the construction materials are produced at big factories in cities. Since the relationship between the land and the people's life was weak, I wanted to use local materials, local workers and craftsmanship as much as possible.

A shape of the museum is associated with Satoyama. The main street of the village and Satoyama form an unlikely pair. People like to live at the foot of Satoyama [mountain]. It is because they were dependent on natural resources of Satoyama since they first arrived and settled in the area. Then they built a shrine on the edge of Satoyama. Religious buildings are placed in a town center in the West.

In Japan, however, they are located on the border of a village and Satoyama. This is because shrines symbolically represent a meeting point between nature and the community to convey a significant message, "Do not destroy Satoyama. If you destroy it, you will not survive". In the 20th century, unfortunately, people started to forget the importance of Satoyama and consequently, many shrines [throughout Japan] have fallen into ruins and so was the one in Bato. I disagreed with a standpoint that the entrance should face the parking lot because it would mean we literally turn our backs to Satoyama. People would forget the shrine yet again. I proposed to "cut" the building to make an entrance facing Satoyama and the shrine. We should strive to connect Satoyama and the community, and this connection is very important for us and nature. A passageway inside the museum highlights the connection to the shrine; people can enjoy the beauty of nature. Another proposal [for the client] was to make two museum shops. The second one can be a place to sell locally-grown vegetables and other produce. Many museums offer a sophisticated view from the inside, but I felt that was not enough, so I proposed a second museum shop. This greatly contributed to the atmosphere of this place. The entrance also became a tunnel that allowed direct access from the center of the village to the shrine. Local materials were, as I said earlier, used for the exterior and interior including rice paper produced by craftsmen in the village and stone from a quarry in the mountain. Talking about sustainability, using local timber can greatly decrease CO_2 emission during the construction process and transportation.

『CHIDORI』& 『GC Museum』

Wood is very important for our daily life. It is particularly an essential material in Satoyama.

Nakagawa-machi Bato Hiroshige Museum of Art
那珂川町馬頭広重美術館

KENGO KUMA AND ASSOCIATES
隈研吾建築都市設計事務所

今日はつながりとしての建築についてお話します。

20世紀中ごろ、建築はそれ単独で存在する美しい造形物として多くの人に捉えられていました。しかし、私は建築物の意味合いを、孤立した造形物からつながりを表すものへと変えたいと考えています。

はじめに里山についてお話ししましょう。日吉キャンパス周辺もかつては里山の一つでした。里山はその地域の村と密接な関係にあり、村人に大変親しまれていました。横浜は人口も多く、大都市ですが、多くの里山が現存します。実は、私は大倉山の生まれで、現在も母が暮らしている実家は里山から非常に近い場所にあります。日吉と大倉山の地形と植生はとても似ています。里山は私の遊び場であり、よく遊びに行っていたので、今でも60年代のあの里山の雰囲気を時折思い出します。

『馬頭広重美術館』

この広重美術館のプロジェクトは里山から構想を得ています。この建築物の材料は里山由来のもので、建物の奥にある森から調達しました。大都市の大きな工場から建材が出荷されることが多い近年において、このようなことは珍しいです。この村では地域と住民の関係性が薄れていたので、この美術館ではなるべく地域の資材を利用し、地元の職人と工芸技術を使うことを心掛けました。

美術館の形は里山に由来しています。村人たちは里山のふもとに住むような形で里山と目抜き通りの間に住むことを好みます。なぜなら彼らの生活は里山に大きく依存しており、建築材料から薪まで、すべて里山から調達していたからです。やがて、里山のふもとに神社がつくられました。ここで注目すべきはその立地です。宗教建築の多くは、まちの中心部に位置するように作られますが、西洋と異なり、日本ではコミュニティや自然の境界に作られます。なぜなら、日本における宗教建築は人々に対して自然や里山の領域を明確に

し、「里山を破壊するな、里山を破壊したら生活ができなくなってしまうぞ」と警告を発する役割を担っていたからです。しかし、20世紀になり残念なことに人々は里山の重要性を忘れ始めてしまいました。馬頭町も例にもれず、神社は廃墟へと化してきていました。私がこの馬頭広重美術館を設計する前、この敷地にはすでに大きな駐車場がつくられていました。村長は私の設計案を見たとき、エントランスは駐車場に面するべきだといいましたが、それだと里山が裏側扱いをされてしまうので私は彼の意見に反対しました。そんなことをしたらまた里山と神社が人々に忘れ去られてしまいます。そこで私は建物を切断し、里山と神社に面するエントランスを作ることを提案しました。日本において里山は私たちの生活と環境において重要であり、本来、村とつながっているべきものなのです。美術館を横切る通路からは神社が見え、来場者は自然の美しさを感じることができます。また、私はミュージアムショップを二つ設けることも提案しました。ミュージアムショップの多くはポスターやカタログといったものの販売が多いですが、ここでは二つ目のミュージアムショップで、地元で採れた野菜を販売することを考えました。多くの美術館では内部から洗練された景色を見ることができますが、それだけでは不十分だと感じたため、二つ目のミュージアムショップを提案したのです。これはこの場所の雰囲気づくりに大きく貢献しました。また、素材に関しては先程お話した通り、内外共に地元の素材を用いました。地元の職人が製造したわら紙や山で採れた石を使っています。そして、環境対策としても地元の木材を用いることで、CO_2の吸収を促進したり、輸送におけるエネルギーを節約したりしています。

『千鳥』と『GC museum』

木は私たちの暮らしにおいて非常に重要です。特に里山の暮らしにおいて、木は必要不可欠なものです。

Nakagawa-machi Bato Hiroshige Museum of Art
那珂川町馬頭広重美術館　　　KENGO KUMA AND ASSOCIATES
　　　　　　　　　　　　　隈研吾建築都市設計事務所

GC museum
GC ミュージアム　　　KENGO KUMA AND ASSOCIATES
　　　　　　　　　隈研吾建築都市設計事務所

One of the unique traditional technologies in Japan is Chidori, which can join wood without metal fittings. Hida Takayama, a city near the northern Japan Alps of Gifu prefecture, has a tradition of this technique for a long time and it still lives with local wood-workers. I found it fascinating and designed a toy inspired by the concept of Chidori. As a next step, we decided to build a pavilion with the toys. Chidori has three types of joints, which enable construction of complex shapes. It was the collaborative project with students of Keio University for the Milan Salone. The students built the pavilion without professional carpenters, except for the joint cutting which required experiences and expertise.

After coming back to Japan [from Milan], I applied this technique to an actual building. Since the pavilion was a temporary structure, components were as small as 3x3cm. Wood parts for the actual building, however, measured about 6x6cm. They are still very small compared to ones for usual wooden structures. After a tensile strength test, the 6x6cm wooden part proved strong enough to build a three-story building, which is approximately 10 meters in height. The museum was built in Aichi prefecture. In the 20th century, a building frame only worked to hold the structure and was separated from other systems such as air-conditioning, pipes, and ducts, etc. My idea is that a single unit can accomodate everything like works of traditional carpenters, who used to build everything in the architecture by themselves. For example, a single wall can also serve as shelves, boxes, etc. This system, -let's call it "a cell system"-, is very similar to a human body. Although organs such as the stomach and the lung seem to work separately, they are aggregate of cells, a basic unit of the human body.

『Nagaoka city hall Aore』

We designed the city hall in the center of the city. First, let me introduce the background of this project. Ohtemachi.Dori street in front of Nagaoka Station and near the city hall used to bustle with people. As a large shopping mall opened in the suburb, almost all of the important facilities including a concert hall moved out of the city center and relocated. Then, the shops have been slowly closing down on the main street. This is a very serious problem happening everywhere in Japan. Mayor of Nagaoka city, Mr. Mori wanted to activate the street again by moving the city hall from the suburb to the city center. The city held an architectural competition with Mr. Fumihiko Maki as the head of the jury and they chose our plan to build the Doma space in the center of the hall. Doma space is typical in traditional Japanese farmer's house. Doma is a semi-outdoor place where most of the daily activities take place, while the tatami space is rather considered formal and ceremonial. "Do" means the earth or "the ground", and "Ma" means space". I wanted to introduce this idea into a public building. The atmosphere of Doma covered by soil is humid, and therefore very comfortable for people to spend time in. At the city hall, the ground is made of multiple compressed layers of soil, and the walls are of wood. The wood used in the project was locally supplied from forests in a 50km range based on my idea toward Satoyama village. To add warmth to the space, the texture of the wood was considered more important than the beauty of the surface.

People of Nagaoka enjoy the architecture very much, and children use the space after school. Elderly people also spend some time there to have a chat with their friends. Many places were broadly designated as a "community center" before the 19th century. After the 20th century and the arrival of a concrete building, such spaces have gradually disappeared. That's why I wanted to provide a new space for the community. 5 million people have visited there since the opening four years ago, which was unusual, to say the least, considering the population of Nagaoka [estimated population of 273,746 as of June 1, 2016]. The sports arena is open to the public where basketball games are held, and children play table tennis. The assembly hall can be seen from the surrounding Doma area. It is open to the public as well and is sometimes used as a concert hall.

Using local materials is an important element of my designs. For instance, the special rice paper made with snow is called white rice paper. This locally produced paper is used for the interior, including the walls and finishing texture of furniture. It is dyed by Kaki-Shibu, Japanese traditional persimmon tannin.

GC museum
GC ミュージアム

KENGO KUMA AND ASSOCIATES
隈研吾建築都市設計事務所

さて、日本には数々の伝統的で特別な技法が存在します。その一つとして、金具を用いることなく木材を接合する千鳥という技法があります。岐阜県の飛騨高山では昔から千鳥の技法が伝わっており、今でも多くの木工職人の方々がいらっしゃいます。私は非常に興味を惹かれ、飛騨高山の技法からこの千鳥のおもちゃの構想を得ました。次に、これらの千鳥のおもちゃを用いてパビリオンを制作することを考えました。千鳥のおもちゃには三種類の接合が用いられているため、複雑な形状のものを建設することが可能です。この技術を用いて、慶應大学の学生と合同で、大工なしでミラノにパビリオンを作るというプロジェクトです。接合部の木材の加工は専門的な技術と経験を要するため、この部分は学生に代わり職人の方々が作業を行いましたが、最終的な建設作業は学生がミラノで行いました。

日本に帰国後、私はこの技術を用いて実際に建物をつくることにしました。ミラノのパビリオンは一時的なものだったので各部材は非常に小さく、3cm角の部材が用いられていましたが、実際の建物になると部材の大きさは6cm角くらいになります。パビリオンの部材より大きいとはいえ、一般的な建材と比べるとこれは非常に小さいです。また、人工的な建材とは違い、自然に由来しているものであるため各々性質が違います。そのため、強度を検証しなくてはなりませんでした。結果的に、構造家の方に6cm角の木材であれば、高さ10m程度の三階建ての建築物をつくることが可能だと言われました。このミュージアムは愛知県に建てられました。一つの部材からすべてを作ることができる建物といったアイデアのもと設計を行いました。20世紀において、構造は空調やパイプなどといったものから切り離されて単独で存在していますが、かつては全て統合されており、大工が建設することができました。私はそのアイデアに立ち返り、一つの部材が壁のみならず建物内部の棚や箱などの全てに対して機能するようにしたかったのです。細胞の集合が人体を形成するように、私たちはこのシステムのことをセルシステムと呼んでいます。胃や肺といった内蔵は一見独立したシステムであるように思えて、すべて細胞という基本単位から成り立っています。

『シティホールプラザアオーレ長岡』
私たちはこのシティホールを街の中心部に設計しました。まず、このプロジェクトの背景をお話しましょう。長岡駅の前には大手町通りという大通りがあります。市役所の近くに位置したこの大通りはかつて市の中心となる役割を担っていました。しかし、大規模な商業施設が郊外に作られたことで、この地域は以前より人口が減少していました。商業施設のみならず、コンサートホールや他の重要な施設までも市の郊外に作られています。その為、大通り沿いでは閉店したお店が目立ちます。日本ではこのような場所をシャッター街と呼び、近年各地で見られ、非常に重大な問題になっています。長岡市の森市長は大手町通りをもう一度活性化し、市役所を郊外から市の中心へと移動させることを考えました。そこで長岡市は槇文彦を審査員として招いてコンペを開催し、市の中心に土間を設けるという私たちの提案が選ばれました。土間づくりは日本の農家によく見られます。半屋外空間である土間では日常生活の多くが営まれ、家の中で最も活動的な場所です。よりフォーマルで、どちらかというと儀式的な活動が行われる畳空間と違い、土間空間はインフォーマルで農家の日常生活に使われます。私はこの仕組みを公共施設に用いたいと考えました。西洋では建物内部の公共空間は石などの堅い素材で作られていることが多いですが、土間は土で作られ、うるおいがあるため人々にとって居心地のいい空間になります。アオーレ長岡の地面は土を用い、壁は木で作られています。用

いられている木材は私の里山の考えに基づき、50km圏内の森から採られたものです。より空間に温かみを与えるため、このプロジェクトでは木材の綺麗さではなく、質感を重視しました。

長岡市民の方々はこの空間を非常に楽しんでくれていて、放課後には子供たちも使ってくれています。高齢者の方々もコミュニケーションの場として使ってくれています。19世紀以前はコミュニティーセンターの役目をもつ場所がありましたが、20世紀になりコンクリートの建物が増えるにつれ、そのような場所は減少してしまいました。そのため、私はコミュニティにそのような場所を復活させたかったのです。建設後は4年間で50万人もの人々が来てくれました。これは長岡市の大きさを考えると珍しいことです。長岡市は現在住民と来訪者に対して新たなサービスを提供しようと試みています。アオーレ長岡は市全体を変化させました。スポーツアリーナは一般開放されており子どもたちが卓球台で遊ぶ様子が見られ、時にはバスケットボールの試合が開催されます。集会所は土間空間を臨むように作られており、コンサートホールとしても使われます。

私の設計において地元の素材を用いることは大変重要な要素の一つです。この特別なわら半紙は白わら半紙と呼ばれ、雪から作られています。地元でつくられたわら半紙は壁や家具の質感などの内装に用いられます。色は柿渋によって付けられています。私たちは柿渋を用いて絹を染めている農家にも出会いました。この絹はカウンターのデザインに用いられています。この空間は絹、木材、半紙といった地元の素材を用いることで地元のつながりを創出しています。

Nagaoka city hall Aore
シティホールプラザアオーレ長岡

KENGO KUMA AND ASSOCIATES
隈研吾建築都市設計事務所

Kengo Kuma

Kengo Kuma was born in 1954. Before establishing Kengo Kuma & Associates in 1990, he received his Master's Degree in Architecture from the University of Tokyo, where he currently holds position of Professor of Architecture. After his time as a Visiting Scholar at Columbia University, he established his office in Tokyo. Since then, Kengo Kuma & Associates have designed architectural works in over twenty countries and was awarded numerous prestigious awards.

隈研吾

1954年生。東京大学大学院修了。1990年隈研吾建築都市設計事務所設立。現在、東京大学教授。コロンビア大学客員研究員を経て、1990年、隈研吾建築都市設計事務所を設立。これまで20か国を超す国々で建築を設計し、(日本建築学会賞、フィンランドより国際木の建築賞、イタリアより国際石の建築賞、他)、国内外でさまざまな賞を受けている。

"Delight" in architectural space

According to the famous ancient Roman scholar Vitruvius, the most important elements in architecture are summarized in firmitas (strength), utilitas (function), and "venustas". When I was a student, "venustas" was translated as "beauty" and its interpretation has been accepted for centuries. However, a scholar has recently taken this interpretation a step further and suggested that Vitruvius's intended meaning was "delight". This idea was supported by various scholars because the concept of "beauty" changes over time and includes personal preferences.

I think "venustas" has meanings of both "beauty" and "delight". As you can see from the past architectures, good architecture has both qualities. Beauty is expressed in the exterior of architecture, and the space inside creates delight. I would like to talk in this lecture with an emphasis on how places and spaces bring delight to people.

Inheriting the university library which became an important cultural property

Keio University Library, Mita Campus, Tokyo (1981)

I would like to start with an explanation of the Keio University Mita Campus Library in Tokyo. The old library was built in the early 20th century. The library on the hill could be seen from Ginza back then. 75 years later, I was assigned to design a new library. The old library was designed by Mr. Tatsuzo Sone, one of the first graduates of the Department of Architecture, the University of Tokyo, which I also graduated from.

Since the area required for the new library was much larger than that of the old library, I tried to match the scale of the two libraries by placing all the bookshelves underground. When I was a student at Keio primary school, I often climbed the hill seeing this library on my way to Tamachi station to take a bus to my home. I was able to see the beautiful Tokyo Bay right below at the time.

Many western architectural techniques were used in the old library, most of which could be reproduced in Japan. Only iron sashes were imported from the UK because they could not be manufactured domestically.

I was also responsible for the design of the remodeling of the old library to meeting rooms. The old library is designated as an important cultural property and we are not allowed to change some parts of it, while restoration is permitted. It was extremely difficult to restore the original colors because there were only black and white photos left as you know. But the development of technologies has made it possible to identify colors from black and white photos. We built a small exhibition room in the underground space where changes were allowed.

Public Policy Center connecting Modern and Classic

University of Pennsylvania, Annenberg Public Policy Center,

Despite the short history of only a few centuries, the United States is dotted with numerous buildings that match the styles of different eras, from ancient Greece, Renaissance, Neoclassic to modernism.

When I visited the site, I saw modernist architecture on one side of the road and classical architecture on the other side. I wanted to create harmony by following both styles. I designed the façade of glass and aluminum representing modernist architecture, and movable wooden panels to portray the warmth of classical architecture.

When I was standing in front of the building on the day after completion, a man walked up to me and said that it was a very good building. Of course, he didn't know I was the designer of the architect. He turned out to be a researcher at the University of Pennsylvania. I think that interactions with strangers like him are very important, and I am especially grateful that he, who was not an architect, gave me his view frankly.. This architecture seems to have a good reputation on the university campus. If you have a chance to visit, please go see it.

Keio Library, Mita Campus, Tokyo(1981)
慶應義塾大学図書館、三田キャンパス、東京都(1981)

建築空間の「喜び」

かの有名な古代ローマの学者ウィトルウィウスによれば、建築における最も重要な要素はfirmitas（強さ）、utilitas（機能）、そして"venustas"に集約されます。私が学生のとき、"venustas"は「美」として訳されており、その解釈は何世紀もの間受け入れられてきました。しかし、最近になってある学者がこの解釈を一歩推し進め、ウィトルウィウスの意図した意味は「喜び」だったのではないかと提唱しました。「美」の概念は時間と共に変化し、また個人的な好みも含むものであるため、この意見はさまざまな学者に支持されました。

しかし私は"venustas"が「美」と「喜び」の両方の意味を持っていると考えています。歴代の建築を見てもわかるように、優れた建築はその両者を兼ね備えています。美は建築の外観に表現され、空間は喜びを生み出す。私はこの講義で場所や空間がどのように人々に喜びをもたらすかに重点を置いて話したいと思います。

重要文化財となった大学図書館を受け継いで
慶應義塾大学図書館, 三田キャンパス, 東京都（1981）

東京都にある慶應義塾大学三田キャンパス図書館の説明から始めたいと思います。旧図書館が建てられたのは20世紀初頭。その頃は銀座からもこの丘の上の図書館が見えたといいます。それから75年経て、私は新しい図書館の設計を任されることになりました。旧図書館は私も在籍していた東京大学の（工学部建築学科）第一期卒業生の曽禰達蔵さんによって設計されました。

新図書館に求められた面積は旧図書館と比べ、極めて大きかったため、私は新図書館の書架を全て地下に配置することで新旧図書館のスケール感を合わせる試みをしました。私が慶應義塾幼稚舎に通っていた頃、家に向かうバスに乗るために田町駅に向かう途中で、よくこの図書館のある丘を登っていました。当時はそこから真下に美しい東京湾が見えていました。

旧図書館は多くの西洋建築技術を用いており、そのほとんどは国内で再現することができましたが、鉄サッシだけは日本で製造することができなかったためイギリスからの輸入品を使っています。

またそれに加えて旧図書館を会議室群として使うための設計も任されましたが、旧図書館は国の重要文化財として指定されており、場所によっては変更ができず、復元のみが許されていました。皆もご存じの通り、当時は白黒写真しかなかったため色の復元が最も難しいところでしたが、今日では技術の発展により白黒写真からでも色の判別が可能になりました。変更の許された地下スペースには、小さな展示室を作りました。

モダンとクラシックを繋ぐ公共政策センター
ペンシルベニア大学, アネンベルグ公共政策センター, 米国ペンシルベニア州（2009）

アメリカ合衆国には数世紀のみの短い歴史にも関わらずギリシャ、ルネッサンス、ネオクラシックからモダンにわたってさまざまな時代の様式に合わせた建築が多数点在しています。

敷地を見に行くと片側の道にはモダニズム建築が立ち並び、その反対側にはクラシックな建築が立ち並んでいました。私はファサードに両方の様式を踏襲することによって調和を生むことを目指しました。外側の層にはモダニズム建築を意識したガラスとアルミのファサードがあり、その内側ではクラシックな建築を意識した可動性の木パネルで温かみを表現しました。

Photo credit: Jeff Totaro

Pennsylvania University, Annenberg Public Policy Center, America Pennsylvania
ペンシルベニア大学, アネンベルグ公共政策センター, 米国ペンシルベニア州

竣工の翌日、私が建物の前に立っていると見知らぬ方が私のほうに歩み寄り、とても良い建築だねと話しかけてきました。もちろん彼はその建築が私の設計であるとは知りませんでした。話しているうちに、どうやら彼は建築家ではなくペンシルベニア大学の研究者であることがわかりました。しかし私はこういった見知らぬ人との話し合いはとても大事だと考えており、特に建築家でもない彼が見知らぬ私にこのように思いを打ち明けてくれたことに感謝しています。この建築は大学キャンパス内でも評判が良いようですので、もし訪れる機会があれば是非見に行ってください。

Republic Politecnic, Shingapore(2007)
パブリックポリテクニック、シンガポール(2007)

University campus providing a place for each

Republic Polytechnic, Singapore (2007)

This is the campus of the Singapore Institute of Technology, located in the northwestern part of the country near the border with Malaysia. It took approximately five years to design and complete the site. Here again, there are dormitories, offices, and cultural centers around a loop road.

The university adopts a learning theory called problem-solving learning that originated in the UK and does not value traditional classrooms where teachers and students gather. Students are divided into different spaces like the atelier system of the Department of Architecture. A teacher gives a day's assignments in the morning, and the students meet again to report the results of the day in the evening. The central area, called Agora, is open to students throughout the day. The library corner is also a very important place where students can gather and discuss their assignments without hesitation.

The hallways and open spaces are transparent so that people can see through, and Agora has a learning area abundant with indirect natural light, controlling severe solar radiation in the subtropical climate. Also, outdoor plazas are systematically placed on the site, creating a sense of the overall scale and a closer relationship between the inside and outside. We also designed a rest area for students and installed a pool table which worked out quite well.

Since these spaces are connected with a gentle slope, a small hangout is formed at the joint. Students enjoy staying in such places. It is very interesting to know what kind of space people like psychologically and behaviorally. The need for a place suitable for one person or for a group has a common ground in both architecture and urban space. At the root of this, architects consider it important to provide diverse spaces to individuals and groups after carefully considering the behavior of people.

Evolving campus

Keio University Shonan Fujisawa Campus, Kanagawa Prefecture (1992)

After the planning of the Mita Campus Library was over, I was pleased to accept an offer to design Shonan Fujisawa Campus by Mr. Tadao Ishikawa, the head of the school at that time.

The concept of the plan was not to use architecture with strong axes. A plan with a large building in the center was the mainstream of the campus design at the time. Such a plan was not required but a campus where small buildings gathered like villages. A graduate school, a gymnasium, a tennis court, and guest houses are located outside the loop road, and a research building, classrooms, a student hall, and an auditorium are planned inside. The most important part of the campus was the library. I think it is a place where the latest information and knowledge gathers, and should be central to any campus. In recent years, the way that a college library should be is changing, and it seems that importance as a place of education is increasing. The entrance to this campus is a symbolic space in a sense, and you can see the library and information center with a translucent facade. There is a space around the student hall where students can spend their time freely, such as a pond, where many students gather in the lunch break.

Various buildings have been added to the basic plan since then. Currently, we are planning to expand the eastern part of the campus, especially the graduate school annex where teachers and students can stay on campus for 24 hours. Unlike in the past, international universities often operate all day to accommodate time differences. Such facilities need to be provided as places to take a nap and to make simple dishes. Soon, you will be able to stay in a hotel-like facility where you can have a good meal.

Like urban design, university campus design and design elements tend to be a collection of different things. My proposition here was how to maintain unity among various factors. For that purpose, it is important to design the external space at an appropriate scale and to give users a place to relax.

それぞれのための場所を提供する大学キャンパス
リパブリック・ポリテクニック, シンガポール (2007)
　次に紹介するのはマレーシア国境付近のシンガポール北西部に位置するシンガポール工科大学のキャンパスです。私達はおよそ5年かけてこの敷地をデザインし、竣工しました。ここでも先程と同様にループ道路の周りに寮や事務室、文化センター、駐車場、運動施設などを配置しました。

　この大学ではイギリス発祥の問題解決学習と呼ばれる学習理論を採用しており、従来の教師と生徒が集まる形式の教室は重視していません。生徒は建築学科のアトリエ制のようにそれぞれのスペースに分けられます。朝、教師は一日の課題を与え、そして夕方に再び集まり生徒たちは一日の成果を発表します。このAgoraと呼ばれる中心部は学生が一日中使えるよう解放されています。図書コーナーも学生が集まって与えられた課題について遠慮せず議論できる、非常に重要な場所です。

　廊下やオープンスペースでは視線が抜けるよう、すべての空間に透過性を持たせており、Agora内には自然光が間接的に差し込む学習エリアがあり、亜熱帯気候地域の厳しい日射を制御しています。また屋外広場は敷地上に計画的に配置されており、全体のスケール感を整え、内外の関係をより密なものにしています。そして学生たちの休息所も設計し、ビリヤード台などを設置しました。そして嬉しいことにそのビリヤード台はいつも賑わっています。

　これらの空間は緩やかな傾斜で繋がっているため、そのつなぎ目に小さなたまり場が形成されます。学生はこのような場所に滞在することを好みます。このように人々が心理学的に、あるいは行動学的にどういった空間を好むかを知ることは、非常に興味深いものです。一人に適した場所や、集団に適した場所の必要性は建築も都市空間も共通しているのでしょう。その根底に、建築は人々のふるまいを丁寧に考えたうえで、個人や集団に対して多様な空間を提供することが大事だと考えています。

進化し続けるキャンパス
慶應義塾大学湘南藤沢キャンパス, 神奈川県 (1990)
　三田キャンパス図書館の計画が終了した後、当時の塾長であった石川忠雄さんに湘南藤沢キャンパス設計のお話をいただき、私は喜んでこれを引き受けました。

　この計画のコンセプトは、強い軸線のある建築を用いないことでした。当時のキャンパス設計の主流はその逆で、中心に大きな建築を設けることが望まれていました。今回求められたのはそのようなプランではなく、小さな建物が村のように集まって出来上がるキャンパスでした。ループ道路の外側には大学院、体育館、テニスコート、ゲストハウスを配置しており、内側には研究棟、教室、学生会館やオーディトリアムを計画しました。その中でも最も重要なのが図書館です。図書館は最新の情報や知識の集まる場所であり、どのようなキャンパスでも中心に据えられるべきだと私は考えています。近年では図書館の在り方も変わってきており、教えの場としての重要性もさらに増しているように思います。この集合体へのエントランスはある意味で象徴的な空間になっており、半透明のファサードをもつ図書館と案内所が見えます。学生会館の周りには池など学生が自由に過ごせる空間があり、お昼時には多くの生徒たちが集まっているようです。

　その後にも、さまざまな建物が基本計画に付け加えられています。

Keio University Syonan Fujisawa Campus, Kanagawa(1990)
慶應義塾大学湘南藤沢キャンパス、神奈川県 (1990)

　現在はキャンパス東部分の増築を計画しており、特に先生や学生が24時間キャンパスに残れるための大学院別館が計画されています。昔とは違い、時差に対応するため国際的な大学においては24時間稼働していることが多くなっています。そうした施設においては、仮眠をとれる場所や、簡単な料理を作るスペースが提供される必要があります。近々、しっかりと食事もとれるホテルのような施設に宿泊できるようになるでしょう。

　都市の設計と同様に大学キャンパスの設計デザイン要素は往々として異質なものの集合体となりがちです。ここでの命題はさまざまな要素があるなかでいかに統一感を保つかということでした。そのために重要なのは外部空間を適切なスケールで設計することで、利用者に憩いの場を与えるということも必要です。

Fumihiko Maki

Fumihiko Maki was born in Tokyo, Japan in 1928, and studied at the University of Tokyo and Graduate School of Design, Harbard University. Since 1965, he has been the principal of Maki and Associates, an international architecture firm based in Tokyo. He taught at both Harvard and Tokyo University. His achievements have been recognized by many prizes, including the Pritzker Architecture Prize, the Union of International Architects Gold Medal, the AIA Gold Medal and the Premium Imperiale from the Japan Arts Association.

槇文彦

1928 年の東京都生まれ。東京大学工学部建築学科を卒業し、ハーバード大学 GSD の修士課程を修了する。1965 年より、槇総合計画事務所の代表取締役として、数々のプロジェクトを手掛ける。また、1989 年まで東京大学の教授を務める。その業績は国内外で高く評価され、プリツカー賞、国際建築家連合 (UIA) ゴールドメダル、AIA ゴールドメダル、高松宮殿下記念世界文化賞などを受賞している。

Today, I would like to talk about my architectural works first and then the disaster relief projects that I have been working on around the world for 23 years.

Though architecture plays an active part in the process of reconstruction, human injuries due to collapse of buildings occur during natural disasters. In other words, it is a natural and man-made disaster at the same time and the responsibility of architects is very big. Victims have to live for months and years in a very poor environment such as shelters and temporary housing. It is one of the responsibilities of architects to improve such an environment. I have been involved in volunteer works with Keio students in the disaster-affected areas. I am really looking forward to seeing the collaboration of the Faculty of Science and Engineering and SFC as Keio Architecture

Exhibition of Alvar Aalto

I wanted to express the uniqueness of Aalto with free curves, trees, and the sunlight. The budget was not enough to use wood, and I thought it was a waste to throw away valuable wood after a short-term exhibition. So I started considering to use paper tubes of tracing paper and fax paper left in the office as an alternative of wood. Using small tubes on the ceiling, large tubes on the partition, I realized that they were stronger than I thought.

I asked Professor Gengo Matsui of Waseda University to conduct strength tests so that it could be used as a structure.

Odawara Pavilion

In 1990 when no one was interested in buildings of paper, I used paper at a temporary pavilion in Odawara City. It was necessary to obtain the Minister's approval to use unusual materials in construction. So I used total of 330 hollow paper tubes of 8m long, 55cm in diameter, 15mm thick for outer and interior curtain walls independent from a steel structure. A large paper tube with a diameter of 120cm was placed in one corner as a toilet. When you run out of toilet paper, peel off the inner wall.

Paper House

I designed my weekend house experimentally, and over for about a year, I received a certification of Minister of Construction. I constructed a paper tube building as a permanent structure. It was designed to bear all vertical loads and seismic forces in paper tube columns and walls.

In the 2000s, ecology and environmental issues started to draw attention all over the world. The theme of the World Expo 2000 in Hannover, Germany, was environmental issues. Countries built pavilions for the event in six months and after another six months they were dismantled to produce large amounts of waste. Even though it was an expo to think about the environment, it would leave a lot of industrial waste in the end. My goal was set in the time when the building was demolished where a design goal was usually achieved when the building completed. The design and construction method was selected based on the criteria that materials would be reused and recycled. All the paper tubes used here were made in cooperation with a local German manufacturer. as part of the contract with the manufacturer, After dismantling the building all the building materials were collected and recycled. It is very difficult to recycle concrete so I made wooden boxes filled with sand to replace the concrete foundation. Sand and wood can be recycled as well. The joints of the paper tubes were all cloth tape. It was a very simple joint that can be tightened with a buckle on an incombustible cloth like a seat belt. We didn't want to use PVC membrane because it is not good for the environment, though it's a common material of the roof. We experimented in Germany to use non-flammable paper.

Odawara Festival Main Hall
小田原パピリオン

photo: Hiroyuki Hirai
写真：平井広行

今日は前半に建築の作品の話、後半は23年ほど活動している世界中の災害支援活動の話をしたいと思います。

地震時には建築が崩れることで死傷者が生じることから、たとえ自然災害でも人災と言うことができます。自然災害において、建築家の責任は非常に大きいのです。被災者は避難所や仮設住宅という貧しい環境で、何ヶ月も何年も生活しなくてはならず、そういう環境を改善するのも建築家の一つの仕事と考えています。慶應の学生とは被災地に出向きボランティア活動を今も続けています。今回、慶應アーキテクチャということで、念願叶って理工学部とSFCがこれから少しずつ一緒に活動していくことをとても楽しみに思っています。

アルヴァ・アアルト展の会場構成
自由な曲線や木や太陽光をふんだんに使うアアルトらしさを表現したいと考えました。木を使う予算的な余裕は無く、また短期的な展覧会の後に捨ててしまうのはもったいないと思いました。そこで当時事務所に余っていたトレーシングペーパーの紙管やファックスの芯を見て、木の代わりに使えないかと考え使い始めたのがきっかけです。小さい紙管を天井に使ったり、大きめの紙管を間仕切りに使ったり、いろいろな使い方をしてみて思った以上に強度があることに気付きました。

そこで、早稲田大学の松井源吾先生にお願いして、強度実験を経て建築の構造として使えないかと考えました。

小田原パビリオン
1990年に、まだ紙で作る建築に誰も興味を持ってない頃、小田原市に仮設のパビリオンを依頼され、始めて紙を使いました。ただし、建築で普通にない材料を使う場合は大臣認定が必要となり、当時はそれが取れず構造としてではなく内装として使いました。構造は鉄骨の柱で、それとは完全に独立した壁として合計330本、長さ8m、直径55cm、厚み15mm中空の紙管を外壁、内壁に使っています。一部大きな紙管があり直径は120cmで中はトイレになっています。いざトイレットペーパーがなくなった時は内壁をむしって使ってください。

紙の別荘
自分で自分の別荘を実験的に設計して、1年くらいかけて当時の38条認定建設大臣認定を取得し、初めてパーマネントな構造として紙管の建物をつくりました。紙管の柱と壁で全ての鉛直荷重と地震力に対して持つような設計になっています。

ハノーバー万博日本館
2000年代になると世界中がエコロジー、環境問題に関心を示すようになり、ドイツのハノーバー市で行われた万博では環境問題がテーマでした。ただ、環境のための博覧会といっても、世界中の国がパビリオンを作り、半年後にそれを解体して大量の産業廃棄物を出すわけです。結局、多くの産業廃棄物を出すのが万博です。普通、デザインのゴールは建物が完成した時ですが、この日本館は、建物を解体した時をデザインのゴールにしています。つまり、解体された建物の建材がリユース・リサイクルされるということをクライテリアとしてデザインや工法の選択をしています。ここで使われた紙管は全てドイツの地元のメーカーと協力して作りました。そのメーカーとの契約の一部として、建物を解体した後、建材を全て引き取ってリサイクルすることにしています。コンクリートというのはリサイクルするのが非常に難しい材料ですので、木で箱を作り、中に砂を詰めてコンクリートの基礎の代わりにしました。砂も木もまた利用することができます。紙管同士のジョイントは全部布のテープです。不燃化した、シートベルトに使われるような生地をバックルで締めるだけの非常に簡単なジョイントになっています。屋根の膜材ですが、塩ビというのは環境にとって良くないと考え、不燃性を持った紙を屋根材としました。

Japan Pavilion, Expo 2000 Hannover
ハノーバー国際博覧会 2000 日本館

photo: Hiroyuki Hirai
写真：平井広行

I would like to talk about disaster relief works now. In 1994, over 2 million people became refugees in Africa. I was surprised to see the photo showing that people were wrapped in a blanket trembling with cold because I thought Africa was a warm place. Tents provided by the UN were poor and it got freezing during the rainy season according to the magazine I read. I wondered how it would make any difference to provide medical activities in such a poor environment. So I felt I had to do something to improve their shelter. I visited the Office of the United Nations High Commissioner for Refugees in Geneva, Switzerland without an appointment. Fortunately, I was able to meet a German manager who was in charge of shelters and I was hired as a consultant after my presentation of the paper tube shelters.

A typical shelter used in Africa had a frame made of wood cut down by refugees themselves and a tent provided by the UN. As many refugees cut down trees, forests were disappearing. A refugee camp caused deforestation and it became a serious environmental problem. The UN once supplied aluminum pipes, which were very expensive in this region. The refugees cut trees again for money and the problem was not solved at all. My proposal to use paper tubes was accepted because people would not likely to sell them.

Swiss furniture manufacturer Vitra worked with us to create a prototype and set it up in Runda, Rwanda. I wanted to make something more comfortable to stay, but offered a minimal shelter instead at the request of the United Nations who feared the refugees wouldn't return to their home village.

Great Hanshin-Awaji Earthquake occurred in 1995. I went to the disaster area every Sunday and saw a tent with a blue tarp in the park used for temporary refuge. When it rains, it will be flooded, and when it is fine, it gets as hot as 40 degrees Celsius. Moreover, people in the neighborhood were trying to get rid of them from the park. I decided to make comfortable shelters to live in with a double roof where hot air can flow out in summer.

I wondered what a definition of temporary architecture was and what of permanent luxury architecture. If it's loved by people, even a paper building made by students can be permanent luxury architecture. Kenzo Tange's Akasaka Prince Hotel was demolished after less than 30 years. Commercial architecture constructed by a developer for making money could be temporary. Even if it is made of paper, beloved architecture can be permanent. I think that was the difference between temporary and permanent architecture. I would like to continue to create a place loved by people in the world.

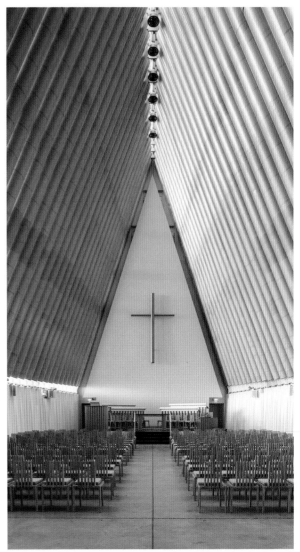

Cardboard Cathdral
紙の大聖堂

photo / 写真 : Stephen Goodenough

Paper Log House - Kobe
紙のログハウス　神戸

photo: Takanobu Sakuma
写真 : 作間敬信

Paper Emergency Shelter for UNHCR
国連難民高等弁務官事務所用の紙のシェルター

photo: Shigeru Ban Architects
写真: 坂茂建築設計

　ここから災害支援の話になります。1994年にアフリカで200万人以上が難民となり、その写真をみて驚きました。アフリカは暖かいところだと思っていましたが、写真を見ると毛布にくるまって震えている人がいました。国連のテントが貧しい物ですから雨季の間は皆寒くて震えていると雑誌に書いてありました。これじゃいくら医療活動しても意味がないため、もっとシェルターを改善しなければならないと思いました。スイスのジュネーブにある国連高等難民弁務官事務所にアポなしで飛び込み、運よくドイツ人のシェルター管理担当に会うことができました。そこで紙のシェルターについてプレゼンテーションしたところ、コンサルタントに雇って頂きました。

　アフリカで使われている典型的なシェルターは、難民の人たちが自分たちで切った木でフレームを作り、国連からもらったテントをかけたものです。難民の人たちが大量の木を切ったものですから、元々森だったところの全ての木が無くなってしまいました。難民キャンプを作るといっても大変な森林伐採が起こって環境問題に発展したのです。そこで国連側は一度アルミのパイプを支給しましたが、この地域ではアルミは高価なために売られてしまい、結局木が切られるため、全く問題は解決しませんでした。そこで、紙管だったら売らないだろうということで紙管を使ったシェルターのプロジェクトが始まりました。

　運がいいことに、スイスの家具メーカーのビトラが色々と協力をしてくれて、まずルワンダのルンダというところに試作品を設営しました。本当はもっと居心地のいいものを提供したかったのですが、難民が村に帰らなくなってしまうので、国連の要請で最小限のシェルターを提供しました。

　そして、95年に阪神・淡路大震災が起こります。毎週日曜日に被災地に通いましたが、被災者は公園にブルーシートのテントを張っていま

した。雨が降れば水浸しになるし、晴れれば中は40度を超える高温になります。しかも、近隣住民が公園から追い出そうとしていたわけです。そのため、仮設でもっと住み心地の良いものを作ろうと考えました。テントの屋根は二重にして夏は暖かい空気が流れるようにしました。

　定義として、仮設建築とはなにか、パーマネントな高級建築とはなにかと考えています。たとえ学生の手で作られた紙の構造物でも、皆が愛してくれればパーマネントな高級建築になります。ところが、丹下健三作の赤坂プリンスホテルは30年持たずに解体されてしまいました。デベロッパーが金儲けのために作った建築は仮設的と言えます。たかが紙で作ってもみんなが愛せばそれはパーマネントになれます。それが仮設とパーマネントの定義の違いなのではないかと思います。これからも世界中にみんなに愛される場所を作っていきたいと思います。

Paper Partition System
避難用間仕切りシステム

photo: Voluntary Architects' Network
写真: ボランタリー・アーキテクツ・ネットワーク

Shigeru Ban

Born in Tokyo in 1957. Graduated from the Cooper Union School of Architecture in the United States. Established Shigeru Ban Architects in 1985. In early 90s, he developed Paper Tube Architecture and provided paper tube shelters in the areas affected by the Great Hanshin-Awaji Earthquake and the 2011 Great East Japan Earthquake. In addition, he designed many cultural facilities including Centre Pompidou-Metz in France and temporary facilities in disaster areas in Japan and abroad, and was awarded the Pritzker Prize in 2014.

坂 茂

1957年、東京都生まれ。米クーパー・ユニオン建築学部卒。85年に坂茂建築設計を設立。90年代初頭、紙管（紙の筒）を用いた紙の建築を開発。阪神・淡路大震災、11年の東日本大震災の被災地で紙管による仮設住宅などを提供した。この他、フランスのポンピドー・センター分館など国内外で文化施設や被災地の仮設建築などを多数設計。14年に「建築のノーベル賞」とも呼ばれるプリツカー賞を受賞した。

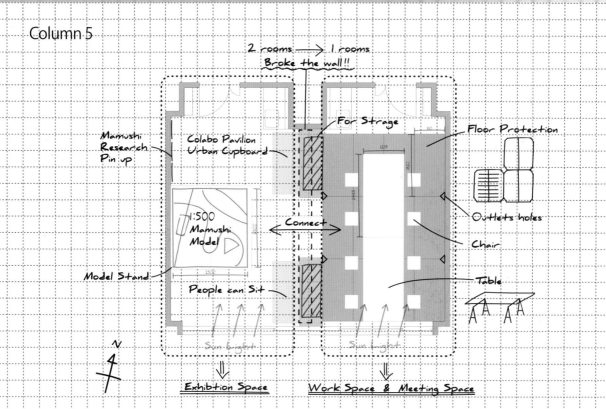

2 rooms ⟶ 1 rooms
Broke the wall!!

Mamushi Research Pin up
Colabo Pavilion Urban Cupboard
For Strage
Floor Protection

1:500 Mamushi Model
Connect
Outlets holes

Model Stand
People can Sit
Chair

N

Table

⇓ Exhibition Space   ⇓ Work Space & Meeting Space

R

The snapshots from production of Keio Architecture

ROOM 1

Room to be the base for research
リサーチの拠点となるまむし部屋

The interior of the room which is the base of the CDW activity was made by the student's hand. Yagami Campus It connects two rooms of 34 buildings, one of which is used for work and meetings, the other is used as an exhibition space,

CDWの活動の拠点となる部屋のインテリアを学生の手によって製作した。矢上キャンパス34棟の2部屋をつなぎ、片方は作業やミーティングができるスペース、もう片方は展示スペースとして活用している。

cc labo

Chapter 5
Studio A 2019
Designing of Mamushi Center

第 5 章　2019 年度　スタジオ A　慶應義塾大学まむし谷センターの設計

This subject was coordinated by Prof. Kishimoto in Spring 2019, with the support of Jorge Almazán and Professor Darko Radović. There were also three teachers visiting teachers, Motoo Chiba, Katsuhito Komatsu, and Satoshi Sano. A total of 13 students attended divided into three groups: Chiba Studio (with an assignment entitled "Association between element and space"), Komatsu Studio ("Layering Context"), and Sano Studio ("Playground of Sensory Spaces").

　本科目は 2019 年春学期に実施、主担当となった岸本達也教授と共にアルマザン・ホルヘ教授とダルコ・ラドヴィッチ教授で授業が行われました。さらに千葉元生先生、小松克仁先生、佐野哲史先生にご協力いただきました。参加した 13 名の生徒は 3 つのグループに分かれ、作品制作に取り組みました。千葉スタジオ (要素と空間の連携)、小松スタジオ (コンテクストのレイヤー化)、佐野スタジオ (感覚空間の遊び場)。

Interview ———————————————————————————————— p.86-97

Sano Studio

Mamushi-indeterminate Direction | Norimi Kinoshita ——————————————— p.98-99
マムシに交わる不定軸 | 木下規海

Student Education, Sport and Research Center | Zan Krivec ——————————— p.104
慶應学生教育、スポーツ、調査センター | ジャン・クレヴィック

Platforms | Gabriel Chatel ———————————————————————————— p.105
プラットホーム | ガブリエル・チャテル

The Node of Continuity | Shinichi Nishibori ——————————————————— p.106
マムシ谷における連続性のツボ | 西堀槙一

Komatsu Studio

Sequence of Mamushi Public Space | Hiroki Shigemura ———————————— p.100-1
マムシ谷における公共スペースのシークエンス | 重村浩槻

Multiple Exposure Architecture | Junpei Kawamoto ——————————————— p.107
多重露光する建築 | 川本純平

Intervention37 | Manca Kosir ——————————————————————————— p.108
インターベンション37 | マンカ・コシール

CO-LIVING:nature, sporting and dwelling | Francisco Javier Celaya Moron —— p.109
共生する建築：自然、スポーツおよび大学寮 | フランシスコ・ハヴィエール・セレヤ・モロン

Chiba Studio

Avalanch-scape | Shohei Yamashita —————————————————————— p.102-1
雪崩を生み出すランドスケープ | 山下翔平

Do it by Your Sense | Amami Iwata ——————————————————————— p.110
蝮谷における自発的空間形成 | 岩田あま美

All Stairs Lead to Mamushi-dani Valley | Shun Kato ———————————————— p.111
階段が創る活動空間 | 加藤旬

MAMUSHI SPORTS CUBE/2 | Sanja Zonja ———————————————————— p.112
マムシスポーツキューブ/2 | サーニャ・ゾーニャ

Connecting Nature and Sports | Yuki Wada —————————————————— p.113
自然と運動の接続 | 和田雄樹

Overview of the Studio A
スタジオ A の課題概要

Overview of this Studio

The task for the Studio A, 2019, titled "Sports, Body, Space (everyday life and special events)" was to propose an environmentally and culturally responsible design of sports and recreation facilities at the Keio Hiyoshi Campus. The students were divided into 3 groups led by 3 visiting teachers, practicing architects with relevant practical and academic expertise. In each groups, the students were given detailed tasks, and were required to define the relationship between the site and their project.

スタジオの概要

2019 年スタジオ A の課題は「スポーツ、体と空間（日々の生活と非日常体験）」と題し、環境と文化について考えられたスポーツとレクリエーション施設を慶應義塾大学日吉キャンパスにデザインすることである。生徒は 3 つのグループに分かれ、各グループは実用的かつ学術的専門知識を有し、現役で活躍する 3 名の建築家によって指導された。各グループでは更なる詳細な課題が与えられ、製作したプロジェクトと敷地の関係性について注意して取り組むよう求められた。

Although they play Kendo & Judo basically in the interior space, the new space should have exterior/semi- exterior spaces integrated into the interior space so that their activities would be expanded to the exterior and its surroundings.
1. Kendo/Judo are played in bare feet. Propose the building programme based on the consideration of the difference in bare feet/indoor shoes(socks)/outdoor shoes. Note that the programme should be beneficial to visitors too.
2. Design spaces and the scenery considering haptics & audiology
3. Design a place for meditation

　基本的には内部空間で剣道と柔道をしますが、新しい空間では、外部 / 周辺空間に活動を拡大するために、内部空間に外部 / 半外部空間を統合する必要があります。
1. 剣道と柔道は素足で行われる。素足・屋内靴（靴下）・屋外靴の違いを考慮した建築プログラムを提案する。プログラムは訪問者にとっても有益であるものとする。
2. 触覚と聴覚を考慮した空間と景色の設計。
3. 瞑想の場所を設計する。

Satoshi Sano / 佐野哲史

1999-2003	Waseda University
2004-2006	Waseda University (Master Course)
2006-2009	Kengo Kuma & Associate
2009	Eureka
2014	Keio University part-time lecturer

1999-2003	早稲田大学　卒業
2004-2006	早稲田大学大学院　修士課程修了
2006-2009	隈研吾建築都市設計事務所
2009	Eureka 共同主宰
2014	慶應義塾大学理工学部非常勤講師

1. Policy of studioA スタジオの進め方について

First, what did you think was the most important thing in this studioA at every esquise?

エスキスにおいてどのようなことを軸として毎週進めていましたか？

　We focused on designing not only within the scope of the plan but also considering the relationship with the surrounding environment outside the scope. As a result, there was also a proposal that was designed by expanding the planning target area specified in the issue.
I don't give detailed instructions on how to proceed, because I think each person has a different method of study. At Esquisse, after listening to the proposal, we presented examples that could be helpful, and exchanged opinions with everyone to find the possibility of developing the proposal.
I think that the idea often swells when students discuss with each other rather than unilaterally saying something on the teacher side. In that sense, rather than setting an axis, I tried to present topics and examples that would spark discussions.

　計画対象範囲内だけでなく、範囲外の周辺環境との関係について考察し、デザインすることを重視しました。その結果、課題で定められた計画対象地を拡張して設計を行った提案もありました。

　具体的なスタディの進め方は人それぞれ違うと思うので、進め方については細かい指示はしませんでした。エスキスでは、まず提案を聞いた上で、参考になりそうな事例を提示したりしながら、僕だけでなく全員で意見を交わしながら、案を発展させる可能性を模索しました。

　教員側が一方的に何かを言うよりも、学生同士で議論したほうがアイデアが膨らむことが多いと思います。そういう意味で、軸を設定するというよりも、議論のキッカケになるような話題や事例を提示することを心がけました。

What was your impression of the students as the studio progressed?

スタジオが進んでいく中で、学生の印象はどうでしたか？

 Japanese students and foreign students had different impressions. Japanese students tended to make concrete shapes immediately, and international students tended to build forms and programs before shapes. It's not about which is better, but each has its strengths and weaknesses. If you want to make a concrete shape immediately, you can study and develop variations of the shape and space each time you esquisse. When thinking about formats and programs, ideas are ordered and spatialized, so it can be summarized as a clear proposal.

 Disadvantages are that there is a gap between the concept spoken and the specific space in case of the morphological type, so it tends to fall into a study of only morphological operation. As a result, there is a tendency that ideas and studies to dramatically develop the space shape do not come out.

 However, these two trends can make up for their shortcomings if you can study each trend alternately. In case of the morphological precedence type, you can develop a plan without falling into only morphological operations by finding the format from the shape you have created and developing a study to develop the format. In the case of the format-preceding type, once the form has been reached in order, it is possible to find a direction to develop the idea by creating a variation of the morphological operation away from the premise and verifying it.

 By repeating the study of morphology and form alternately, you can develop without any bias to either types. I think Japanese students and international students have noticed and absorbed each other's characteristics at this studio, so it would be nice to practice esquisse that incorporate their strengths in the future.

日本の学生と海外（今回のスタジオではヨーロッパ）からの留学生には、それぞれ異なる印象を持ちました。日本の学生は、具体的な形をすぐに作る傾向があり、留学生は形の前に形式やプログラムを積み上げる傾向がありました。どちらが良いという事ではなく、それぞれに長所・短所があります。具体的な形をすぐに作る場合は、その形や空間のバリエーションをエスキスの度に検討して発展させることができます。形式やプログラムを考える場合は、考えを順序立てて空間化していくので、明快な提案としてまとめることができます。

短所としては、形態先行型の場合は語られるコンセプトと具体的な空間との間にギャップがあるために、形態操作のみのスタディに陥りがちであり、形式先行型の場合は、順序立てて進めてきているがために空間形状を飛躍的に発展させるアイデアや検討が出てこない傾向があります。

しかし、これらの2つの傾向は、それぞれの傾向のスタディを交互に行うことができれば互いの短所を補うことができます。形態先行型の場合は、とりあえず作った形から形式を見出して、その形式を発展させるスタディを展開することで、形態操作のみに陥ることなく、案を発展させることができます。形式先行型の場合は、順序立ててたどり着いた形態について、一旦その前提から離れて形態操作のバリエーションを作り、それを検証することで、案を発展させる方向性を発見できます。

形態と形式のスタディを交互に繰り返すことで、どちらかに偏ることなく発展させることができます。今回のスタジオで、日本の学生と留学生とが互いの異なる特徴に気付いて吸収し合っていると思うので、今後はそれぞれの長所を取り入れたエスキスを実践してくれると良いと思います。

2. Design and teching 設計と教育

What is your consciousness in designing and what are the features of the design?

ご自身が設計をする上で意識していること、設計の特徴はどのようなものですか？

In this studio project, all students formulated the Urban Design Strategy, and then they individually designed each building. When designing architecture, I think it is important to design it with consideration of its position within a large context.

On the other hand, I think it is necessary to have an approach that does not just assemble a design in order from a large context. Even if we can't clearly explain why the shape came out, we are conscious of finding a space where the space is one of the appropriate solutions, and in addition, it brings a unique quality. It is also related to what I wrote as " the student impressions" (morphology-first vs. form-first).

今回のスタジオ課題では、アーバンデザイン・ストラテジーを履修者全員で策定し、その上で各々が個別の建築設計を行いました。建築を設計するにあたって、大きな文脈の中での位置付けを考えて設計するのは、まず大切なことだと思います。

一方で、大きな文脈から順序立てて設計を組み立てるだけではないアプローチも必要だと思います。その形が何故出てきたのかを明確に説明できなかったとしても、その空間が適切な解のひとつであって、それに加えてユニークな質をもたらす、というような空間を発見することを意識しているのだと思います。それは、「学生の印象」として書いたこと（形態先行型 vs 形式先行型）に関連することでもあります。

Was the core of your studio based on your experience?

スタジオでの軸はご自身の設計での経験に基づくものですか？

I wouldn't say that I had a "core", but I intended to ask the students questions that bring discussions. So through my esquiesse, I made opportunities for discussion by considering several things. This comes from my own experience.

　「軸を設定するというよりも、議論のキッカケになるような」投げかけをしていたので、「軸」というわけではないのですが、設計の進め方ということでいうと、さまざまな種類の検討から議論のキッカケをつくっていく進め方は、自身の設計の経験・進め方に基づくものだと思います。

What have you experienced through teaching your students?

学生に教えたことはご自身にとってどのような経験になりましたか？

Rather than one-way teaching to students, I used a method similar in my office where we proceed together through discussion. Therefore, for me, working on the studio was also an experience of practicing the usual design method with a person (= student) who is not a regular member of my office. I think I was able to verify my way of designing objectively.

　学生に対して一方通行で教えるというよりも、一緒に議論しながら進めていくという自身の事務所での進め方に似た方法をとりました。そのため、僕にとって、スタジオ課題に取り組むことは、普段の設計の進め方を自分の事務所のいつものメンバーではない人（＝学生）と実践するという経験でもあったので、自身の設計の進め方を客観的に検証できたように思います。

3. For the future architects　将来の建築家に向けて

Please give a message for the students.

最後に学生へのメッセージをお願いいたします。

I hope the students make use out of, not only specific things we achieved through drawings and models, but also the different ways of thinking and advancing of other students who worked on the same task.

　図面や模型などの課題を通して達成した具体的な事柄だけでなく、共に課題に取り組んだ他の学生達の考え方・進め方との違いや、課題に取り組む中で気付いたこと、感じたことを今後に活かしてもらえたら良いと思います。

Renovation and adaptation of Taniguchi Legacy for sports and recreation
1. Analyze the legacy of Taniguchi's dormitory and delayering the context
2. Add a new layer to the context by designing and renovating the legacy, with an emphasis on linkages with sport and recreation resources
3 . Make the new relation of everydaylife (sleep, study, bath etc.) and sports in the dormitory.
4. Propose how the urban design integration of the broader project behave in the urban scale, whole Mamushi-Valley area.

スポーツとレクリエーションのための谷口レガシーの改修と適応
1. 谷口の寮の遺産を分析し、文脈を遅らせる。
2. スポーツおよびレクリエーションリソースとの連携に重点を置いて、レガシーを設計および刷新することにより、コンテキストに新しいレイヤーを追加する。
3. 寮での日常生活（睡眠、勉強、お風呂など）とスポーツの新しい関係を作る
4. より広範囲なプロジェクトの都市デザインの統合が、より大きな都市規模やまむし谷地域全体で、どのように機能するかを提案する。

Katsuhito Komatsu / 小松克仁

2007-2011	Keio University
2011-2013	Keio University (Master Course)
2013-2018	Kengo Kuma & Associate
2018	Fukei laboratoy
2019	Keio University part-time lecturer

2007-2011	慶應義塾大学　卒業
2011-2013	慶應義塾大学大学院　修士課程修了
2013-2018	隈研吾建築都市設計事務所
2018	風景研究所　設立
2019	慶應義塾大学理工学部非常勤講師

1. Policy of StudioA スタジオの進め方について

First, what did you think was the most important thing in this studioA at every esquisse?
エスキスにおいてどのようなことを軸として毎週進めていましたか？

 We carefully read the environment around the site and aimed to creat a project that matched to the environment. Since it was a challenge to renovate the dormitory, I considered the existing building as a part of the environmental elements and thought together with the students how the space imagined by the students could behave and color the environment. Usually, students tend to challenge making new projects, so I think this project was their first experience of renovation. At the beginning of the project, we were contemplating about details and renovations. But since the students were treating the existing building as equivalent to the surrounding trees and environmental elemtents, we aimed to propose something that was in between construction and renovation. Renovation, which has accounted for a large proportion of architects' work in the era of population decline and left over homes, shouldn't be limited indoors, but should influences the surrounding environment. This is how we explored a new environment.

　課題敷地周辺の環境を注意深く読み込み、その環境に即したプロジェクトになることを目指しました。寄宿舎をリノベーションする課題であったので、既存の建物を環境要素の一部としてとらえ、その中で学生の想像する空間がどのようにふるまい、環境を色付けすることができるかを学生と共に思考しました。学生の時は新築のプロジェクトがほとんどで、リノベーションは初めての経験であったと思います。プロジェクトの開始当初はよりディテールと向き合い、リノベーションを提案することも考えていました。しかし、学生の提案を見て、既存の建物を周辺の樹木などと等価に扱い、ひとつの環境要素として扱うことで、新築とリノベーションの間のような提案をつくることを狙いました。人口減少、家余り時代において、建築家の仕事の多くの割合を占めてきているリノベーションを、室内だけにとどめるのではなく、周辺環境までを射程にいれたプロジェクトとすることで、新たな環境とのかかわり方を模索しました。

What was your impression of the students as the studio progressed?

スタジオが進んでいく中で、学生の印象はどうでしたか？

　There is a period for study and a period for creating a presentation. Since this studio was for master students, I thought that it was important to spend a lot of time in the study and thinking period rather thanb than the presentation. A study is a stack, and various plans are created, compared, and decisions are made. The plans are more personal to the designer, and the combined personality makes the architecture interesting. This time, I felt that personality was weak overall. Many students could not jump up from the idea that they thought in the first three weeks. Nowadays, a lot of information is available on SNS and the internet, and it is easy to search for architectural images. I want you to do the reverse, and build up the work of finding personality that doesn't appear on the internet.

　設計にはスタディをする期間とプレゼンテーションを作成する期間があります。今回のスタジオは修士のスタジオであったので、後者のプレゼンテーションの指導は少なく、スタディに多くの時間を割き、思考を突き詰めることが重要だと考えていました。スタディとは積み重ねであり、さまざまな案を作成し、比較検討し、決断を積み重ねることで案はより設計者の私性を帯び、その纏わりついた私性が建築を興味深いものにしていきます。今回は全体的にその私性が弱かったように感じました。多くの学生がはじめの3週間くらいで考えた案からあまりジャンプアップをすることができなかった。今はSNSやインターネットで多くの情報が出回っており、建築のイメージを探すことも容易です。それを逆手にとり、ネット上には出てこない私性を見つける作業を積み重ねていってほしいです。

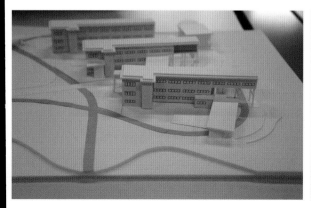
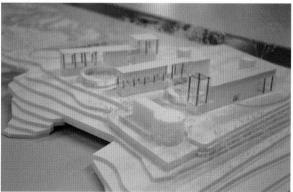

2. Design and teching 設計と教育

What is your consciousness in designing and what are the features of the design?

ご自身が設計をする上で意識していること、設計の特徴はどのようなものですか？

I design with constant consideration of dialogue between the site and architecture.
There are never two same sites for architecture, and the conditions are different each time. The best part of the design is to step on the land, feel the air, and to put what your thoughts into the space. In addition, clients and craftsmen differ from project to project, so I would like to find out what we can do only in that project while talking with them. In the near future, once the site condition and the design condition is given, it will be an era where AI automatically performs design to estimation. OYO is currently using AI to dominate the real estate industry. To live as an architect in such a time like this, it is necessary to perform activities that only humans can do. As the starting point of creation, I would like to create a building that can interact with various conditions and ultimately interact with the environment.

　敷地と建築との対話を常に考えて設計しています。
　建築には同じ敷地は 2 つとなく、毎回条件は異なる。その土地を足で踏み、空気を感じ、それを空間に落とし込むことが設計の醍醐味です。またプロジェクトごとにクライアントや職人さんは異なるので、その方々と対話をしながら、そのプロジェクトでしかできないことを見つけていきたいと考えています。近い将来には敷地条件や設計条件を与えれば、AI が自動で設計から見積まで行う時代になるし、現に OYO などは AI を活用して不動産業界を席捲しています。その時に建築家として生きていくためには、人間にしかできない活動を行う必要がある。創造の原点としてさまざまな与条件と対話を重ね、最終的には環境と対話をできる建築を作りたいと考えています。

Was the core of your studio based on your experience?

スタジオでの軸はご自身の設計での経験に基づくものですか？

Yes.

そうです。

What have you experienced through teaching your students?

学生に教えたことはご自身にとってどのような経験になりましたか？

It was a good opportunity to objectively view my design philosophy and explain it externally. By explaining my project and sharing my thoughts with students, my thoughts became clearer, and I was able to know what students were thinking and what they like.
I had the impression that, for better or worse, the students had not changed much since I was a student. In the last decade, social conditions and technology related to architecture have changed significantly. Architects in the future need to have a strong personal style and the ability to communicate as a team to the society. I thought that we also had to take on new challenges and impress students.

自分の設計思想を客観視し、対外的に説明をしていく良い機会となりました。自身のプロジェクトの説明をし、また学生と思想を共有することで、自身の考えもよりクリアになったし、今の学生が何を考えて何が流行っているのかを知ることもできました。

学生は良くも悪くも自分が学生のころとあまり大きくは変わっていないという印象を持ちました。ここ10年で社会状況も建築に関わるテクノロジーも大きく変わっています。これからの建築家はより自分のスタイルを強く持ち、社会にチームとして発信する力が必要となります。自分たちも新しい挑戦をして、学生たちに大きな刺激を与えていかなければいけないと思いました。

3. For the future architects 将来の建築家に向けて

Please give a message for the students.

最後に学生へのメッセージをお願いいたします。

Architects can only work with the society. There is a client, a contractor, and an architect. It is very important to have an image of how you are involved in the society as an architect. There are many architects who are just good at designing. However, there are not so many architects who project their ideas into their design and try to change the society. Through architecture, my goal is to combine technology and design, add value to the land and products, and enrich people's lives. I want you to find your way to the future society through the precious time of studying architecture as a student without being bound by the framework of an architect.

建築家は社会との関わりを持って、はじめて仕事ができます。建築には施主がいて、施工者がいて、建築家がいます。社会に建築家としてどのように関わるのか、そのイメージを持つことは非常に大切です。ただ単に設計の上手な建築家はたくさんいます。しかし、設計に自分の思想を投影し、社会に変化を起こしていく建築家はそう多くはありません。私は建築を通して、技術とデザインを結び付け、土地や製品に付加価値をつけ、人々の生活を豊かにすることを目標としています。建築家という枠組みにとらわれることなく、建築の勉強と学生という貴重な時間を通して、自分の将来の社会への関わり方を見つけてほしいと思います。

Design a large space by assembling small elements.
1: Students will analyze the relationship between architectural elements and behavior of people with an emphasis on sport and recreation facilities which can be found in the Campus and Mamushi-Valley area. After that, choose one element (for example the roof, the ceiling, the stairs, the window, the void etc.) and study the characteristic of the element in relation to specific sport and 2: Design buildings containing the above facilities by using the chosen element. The proposal should have an idea for human scale and large scale.

　小さな要素から大きな空間をデザインする。
1. 建築要素と人々との関係をキャンパスとまむし谷エリアに存在するスポーツ施設とレクリエーション施設から分析する。一つの要素（例えば屋根・天井・階段・窓・ボイドなど）を選んで、その特性を特定のスポーツやレクリエーションのニーズに関連して学ぶ。
2. 選択された要素を用いてテニスコートと拳法道場を含む建物を設計する。提案は人間サイズのスケールと大きな規模のスケールの考えを含む。

Motoo Chiba / 千葉元生

2009	Tokyo Institute of Techonology
2010	Eidgenössische Technische Hochoschule Zürich
2011	Jonathan Woolf Architects London
2012	Tokyo Institute of Technology (Master Course)
2013	Established Tsubame Architect
2019	Keio University part-time lecturer
2009	東京工業大学　卒業
2010	スイス連邦工科大学　卒業
2011	Jonathan Woolf Architects London
2012	東京工業大学大学院　修士課程修了
2013	ツバメアーキテクツ設立
2019	慶應義塾大学理工学部　非常勤講師

1. Policy of StudioA スタジオの進め方について

First, what did you think was the most important thing in this studioA at every esquise?

What was your impression of the students as the studio progressed?

エスキスにおいてどのようなことを軸として毎週進めていましたか？

スタジオが進んでいく中で、学生の印象はどうでしたか？

In order to tackle this task, firstly, students need to think about the urban strategy of the Campus from a macro scale. And then, they need to work on to their own project, considering what they learned from it. In our studio, I asked each member to extract architectural elements through the observation of the campus, such as windows or the roof, which were creating a rich relationship among people. I asked the students to develop their project from whole to detail, and recapture the whole from the part at the same time. I expected them to discover an idea by repeating this process. So, I asked everyone to make a model in 1 to 200 and also another in 1 to 10.

The members tried hard with this, but I also thought their pace was pretty slow. So, it took time for the project to develop. Don't hesitate, and give form to your idea. Once you do it, criticize what you made and break it. And then rebuild it. It would have been nice, if the students could repeat this in a nice tempo.

今回の課題はキャンパスの urban strategy というマクロなスケールを考えることから始まり、それに沿って個々のプロジェクトに取り組むというものでした。一方でスタジオでは、キャンパスの観察から人と豊かな関係性を生み出している建築エレメント（窓や屋根など）を学生ごとに抽出してもらい、その部分を考えるということに取り組んでもらいました。全体から部分に落とし込んでいくと同時に、部分から全体を捉え直すこと、その思考の往復を繰り返す中でアイデアを発見してもらいたかったからです。そのためにスタジオでは 1/200 といったスケールと同時に 1/10 の模型での検討も要求しました。学生もこのような方法に前向きに取り組んでくれましたが、スタディの速度がゆっくりで、なかなか発展しない印象がありました。まず恐れずに一度アイデアを形にし、自分でそれを批評して壊す、その批評をもとにつくりなおすというサイクルをテンポよく進めて案を発展していけるようになると良いと思います。

2. Design and teching 設計と教育

What is your consciousness in designing and what are the features of the design?

Was the core of your studio based on your experience?

What have you experienced through teaching your students?

ご自身が設計をする上で意識していること、設計の特徴はどのようなものですか？

スタジオでの軸はご自身の設計での経験に基づくものですか？

学生に教えたことはご自身にとってどのような経験になりましたか？

Of course, the core idea that I wrote in the previous question comes from my own design experience. For example, we architects often work on renovation projects where we only change or redesign one part of the building. When I work on such projects, I make sure that my partial design will change the entire building. Furthermore, one new project is a part of one city, so I try to influence the entire city by designing a new building. The filed that we design is a society where the modern planning concept has collapsed, syllabizing the whole to parts. Our mission is to create a network among the small works that we make in a city or architecture that already exists, and to consider what is necessary for the future society. So I think it is important to keep this idea in mind when you design. I was happy to share this with the students through this task.

　上述した様なスタジオの軸は、もちろん自身の設計経験に基づくものです。例えばリノベーションの仕事で建物のほんの一部にだけ手をつけるといったことは少なくありません。そんな時は部分の変更で全体の価値を変えてしまえるような方法を意識して取り組んでいます。もっと言えば新築のプロジェクトであっても一棟は街の部分であり、一棟であっても街の価値が変わる様な建築のあり方を考えます。私たちが設計をするフィールドは、全体を部分へと分節していく近代の計画概念が崩れた社会であり、すでに出来上がった街や建物に対する部分的な取り組みをネットワークさせることから社会を考える時代だと感じています。ですから、設計をするときにもそういったことを意識化した上でとりくむことが大事だと思っています。今回はこうした考え方を学生たちと共有して、一緒に課題に取り組む貴重な機会になったと思います。

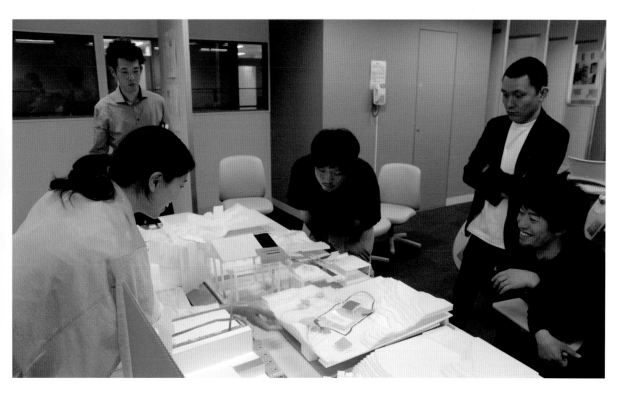

3. For the future architects 将来の建築家に向けて

Please give a message for the students.

最後に学生へのメッセージをお願いいたします。

 The biggest message I would like to give is to keep on thinking about what excites you, and to pursue it. And another thing. There are tons of things that only student can do, who have plenty of time to spend. I recommend you to experience many things by traveling, meeting people, and reading books. Be ambitious.

　自分の興味がわくことを信じて考え続けること、それを突き詰めていくことが大事だと思います。あとは、学生の時間のあるうちにしかできないことがたくさんあります。旅行していろんなものに触れたり、人と会ったり、本を読んだりなど積極的に動くことが大事だと思います。

Mamushi-indeterminate Direction
マムシに交わる不定軸

Norimi Kinoshita
木下規海
Sano Studio

The design created by many axes from Mamushi-valley makes boundary ambiguous where axes of artificial design and nature context are merging. Those transition space between boundaries mixed by various direction find new unexpected relationships with education, residence, commercial, taking in the context of Mamushi nature.

　キャンパスから抽出された人為的方向性を無秩序なまむし谷の地形に伸ばすことで、日常行為と経験が自然の中に溶け込む。さまざまな方向性で形成される境界は自然の中に予期せぬ関係性を生み出す。

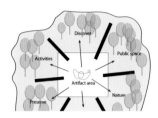

Perspective

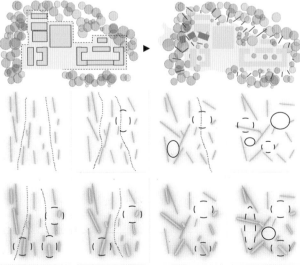

Diagram

Site Plan S=1/4000

0　　40　　80m

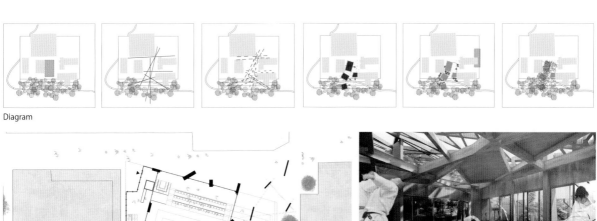

Diagram

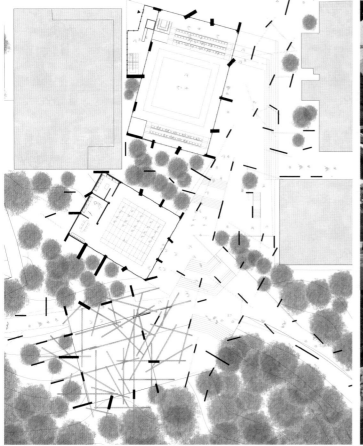

Plan S=1/1500

0   10   20m ◯

Perspective

Longitudinal Section S=1/1000

0   10   20m

Sequence of Mamushi Public Space
マムシ谷における公共スペースのシークエンス

Hiroki Shigemura
重村浩槻
Komatsu Studio

The Hiyoshi Domitory provides hints for finding various public space for visitors by designing the rhythm or the density of the space along the path. This is an architecture to create the new public space of Mamushi Valley that leads people to their own way of using without designing program.

　日吉寄宿舎は、道に沿った空間のリズムを設計することにより、訪問者にさまざまな公共空間を見つけるためのヒントを提供する。これは、プログラムを設計せずに人々を独自の使い方に導く、まむし谷の新しい公共空間を作成するための建築である。

Site Plan S=1/1500

0　10　20m

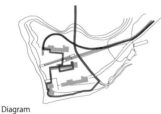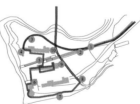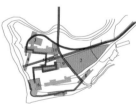

Diagram

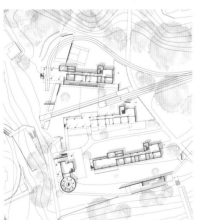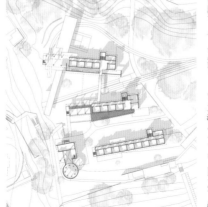

Plan S=1/2500

0　10　20m

01. Entrance
Enter the site along the track from the university.
It branches and leads to the north wing.

02. Outside Playground
Pass thorough under the gate, which also makes the chance for sports.
Along with the continuous cor-ten, people's perception will come to space gradually.

03.Observation Platform
Look at the same continuously branced space from the 02, Gate.
A sequence of material leads people to the space.

04. Work Space
Long space along the sequence.
Low density space design and mirror make people aware of exisiting facade.

05. Connecting Corridor
Open the view for outside nature closed at 04, Work Space.
It offers a view that extends radially along the existing building, PictureFrame.

06. Meditation Space
Rooms repeated at equal intervals gradualy open to outside.
It makes a preparation period to go out and see the surrounding nature.

07. Hotel/Public Dining
Guide people to a quiet space from the open, lively outdoor terrace.
Emphasize the changing of liveliness of space.

08. Space in Bamboo
A space in the bamboo forest that is separate from the other places.
A closed space that you can feel only nature.

09. Entrance form Southside
Tour the site along the sequence and enter again to for the center of the site.
The same material eith 02,Gate reminds the entering again.

Elevation S=1/1000

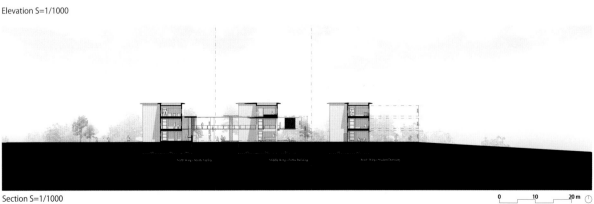

Section S=1/1000

0   10   20 m

03 Avalanche-scape
雪崩を生み出すランドスケープ

Shohei Yamashita
山下翔平
Chiba Studio

Avalanche-scape is a metaphor of a new landscape approach oriented to enhance the transition of human activities in Mamushi valley, chosen as the proposed site becoming a sports Lynchpin. Tennis courts and Kenpo dojo become parts of the proposal placed as main functions to active activities with running path.

「Avalanche-scape」はまむし谷における人々の活動の移動を強化するために用いられる新しい景観的アプローチのメタファーである。主としてテニスコートと道場をその活動の中心として据えている。

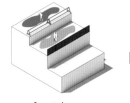
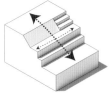
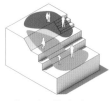

Perspective

Only 2D Connection	Separated spaces	3D Design for Activities	Happening of Avalanche
二次元的なつながり	独立した空間	アクティビティのための３次元的デザイン	雪崩的空間の創出

Diagram

102

The idea derived from presences of partitions limiting human circulations with rigid boundaries, where Avalanche design is applied to root on site with the centrality of the bottom of the valley, creating seamless landscape integrating voumes and voids. The approach results in functional diversity, vernacular, and sustainability towards a lively village.

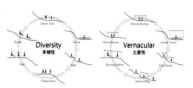

この「Avalanche」デザインでは谷底部の中心と山中腹に設定されたルートに適用され、それら 2 つの地点をシームレスにつなぎ新たな風景を提供する。

Diagram

Plan S=1/1500

0 10 20 m

Section Perspective S=1/500

0 5 10m

By opening the middle part of the existing sport and office building, I created an outdoor extension of the inner spaces. The new "street" of the building creates a horizontal and vertical interaction between different programs. By opening the existing basement floor and designing a sloped entry plaza, a new ambience appears in the campus.

設計された内部の「道」はさまざまな用途を垂直、水平につなぐ。既存の地下室を開放し、そこへ地上と連続性を持った広場を設けることで従来に無かった雰囲気を持つ公共空間を計画した。

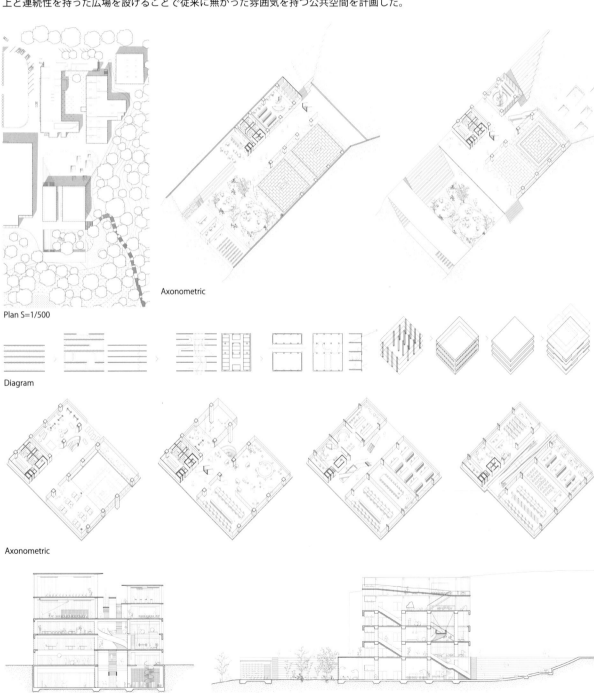

Plan S=1/500

Axonometric

Diagram

Axonometric

Section 1

Section 2

Platforms
プラットホーム

Gabriel Chatel
ガブリエル・チャテル
Sano Studio

We noted two main problems on the Hiyoshi campus: circulation between the high and low part of the campus, and lacking space for students. Platforms are very effective for managing topographies. This project uses this system at the campus level and at the scale of the dojo building. The different platforms create spaces of different sizes, responding to specific function

　キャンパス内の高低差、学生のための憩いの場の不足という問題に焦点を当てる。地形をうまく利用できる「プラットホーム」システムを利用し、特定の機能に応じたさまざまな空間を設計した。

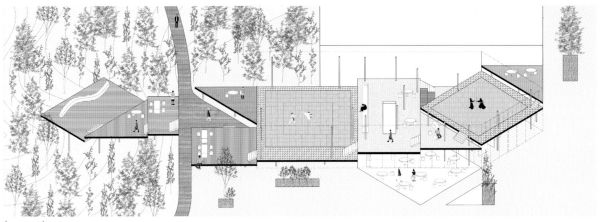

Axonometric

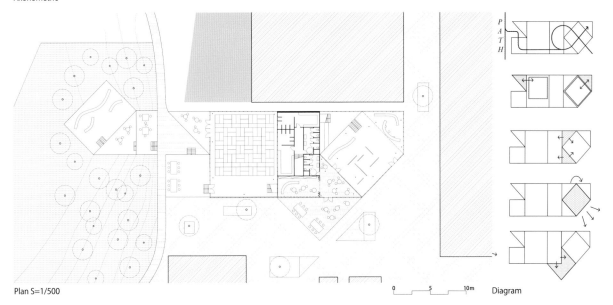

Plan S=1/500

0　　　5　　　10m

Diagram

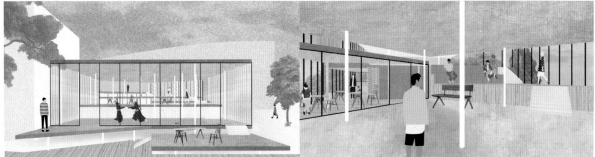

Outside View　　　Inside View

The Node of Continuity

マムシ谷における連続性のツボ

Shinichi Nishibori
西堀槇一

Sano Studio

 The clear, but obstructive boundary are existing between Mamushi and Hiyoshi campus. It's created by high dense planning of large buildings.　It cut the continuity to the Mamushi Valley where plenty of greenery and some sports facilities are there. So, in this project, designing the path and nodes on this boundary to create continuity.

　まむし谷と大学キャンパスの間に存在する境界。これは高密に計画された大学施設によってもたらされ、連続性を遮断している。本提案では連続性をもたらす「路とツボ」を境界上に計画した。

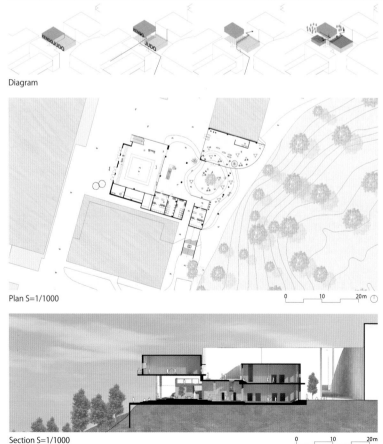

Diagram

Plan S=1/1000

0　　10　　20m

Section S=1/1000

0　　10　　20m

View

07 Multiple Exposure Architecture
多重露光する建築

Junpei Kawamoto
川本純平
Komatsu Studio

This proposal want to do the renovation that scenery which is new to be multi-layered by adding sports facilities as a public place on the background of the view to the southwest direction which Yoshiro Taniguchi respected..

　谷口吉郎が大切にした南西方向への眺望を背景に、パブリックな場としてのスポーツ施設を加えることであたらしい景色が多重に重なるリノベーションをおこないたい。これを建築的「多重露光」と定義し、この空間演出を目指す。

Model

View 1

View 2

View 3

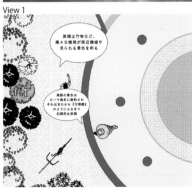

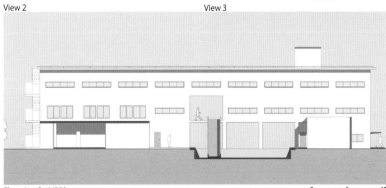

Elevation S=1/500

0   5   10m

Manca Kosir
マンカ・コシール
Komatsu Studio

The project is based on the analysis of the most obvious qualities pres- ent in the extremely interesting project of Taniguchi's. Designing the concepts started of the decision not to radically interfere with the object itself.

このプロジェクトは、谷口の非常に興味深いデザインに存在する、最も明白な品質の分析に基づいている。オブジェクト自体に根本的に干渉しないという決定から始まった概念の設計。

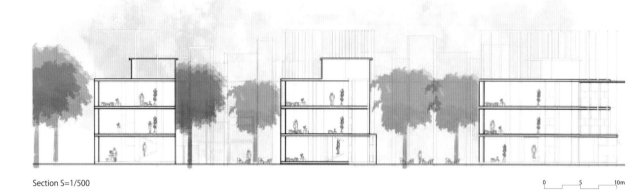

Section S=1/500

0   5   10m

Section S=1/200

0   2   4 m

Perspective

09 CO-LIVING: nature, sporting and dwelling
共生する建築：自然、スポーツおよび大学寮

Francisco Javier Celaya Moron
フランシスコ・ハヴィエール・セレヤ・モロン
Komatsu Studio

For this renovation work, we take into consideration two preexisting elements: three university dormitories and the natural environment that surrounds the site. Additionally, we want to introduce a new element, sports facilities to help for the activation of the area.

この設計では、3 つの大学寮と敷地を取り巻く自然環境の 2 つの既存の要素を考慮した。さらに、地域の活性化に役立つスポーツ施設などの新しい要素を導入したいと考えている。

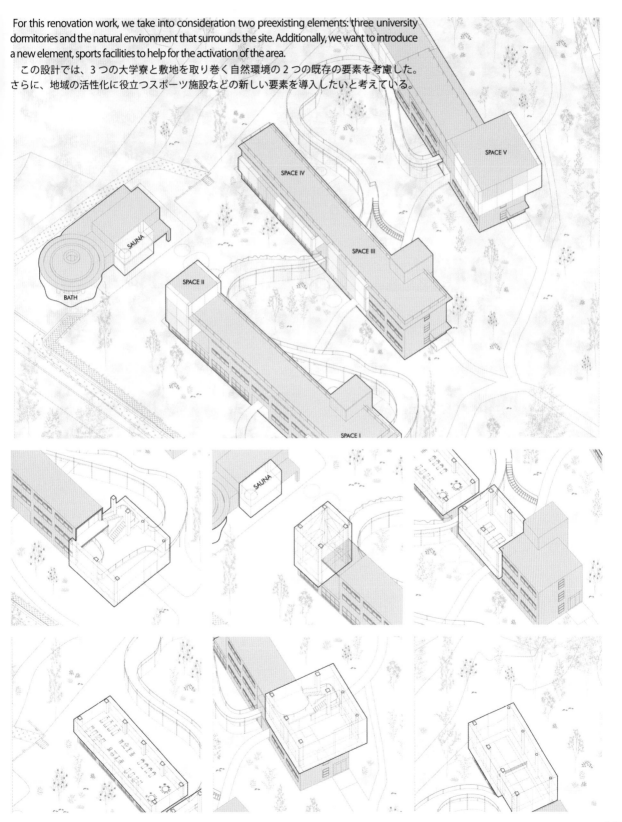

10 Do it by Your Sense
蝮谷における自発的空間形成

Amami Iwata
岩田あま美
Chiba Studio

The bottom of the Mamushi Valley is adjacent to all of them and has a direct connection. However, they exist without mixing. Intervene an element of one roof in such a place. The element is created by people spontaneously, and new space is created. The place created in this way will also created the formation of a new place, and the entire valley will gradually be marged and become one.

　周囲にさまざまな要素を持ちながらも断絶されているむむし谷に、各々を繋ぐような屋根空間を挿入することで利用者による自発的な要素・使われ方の混合をもたらし周辺と敷地の一体化を目指す。

Model

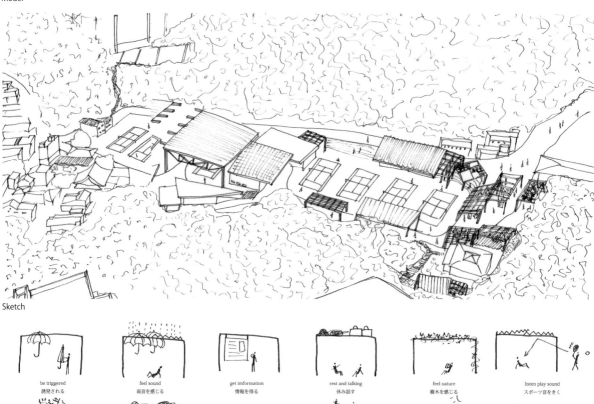

Sketch

be triggered 誘発される	feel sound 雨音を感じる	get imformation 情報を得る	rest and talking 休み話す	feel nature 樹木を感じる	listen play sound スポーツ音をきく
feel season 季節を感じる	watch history 歴史を感じる	listen steps 足音をきく	play sport 運動をする	evy covered 覆う	watch movie 映画をみる

Diagram

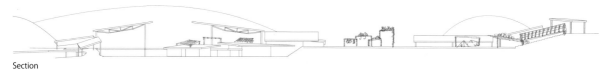

Section

110

11 All stairs Lead to Mamushi-dani Valley
階段が創る活動空間

Shun Kato
加藤旬
Chiba Studio

Dating back, people used to live with the forest. Nowadays, the forest disappeared from people's daily life due to urbanization. This proposal aims to offer a space which triggers people to interact with the forest by designing a roof , covering the natural atmophere of the forest in Mamushi valley.

　昔から人々は、森とともに住んでいた。しかし、人口増加によって土地が開発されると、人々の生活から森が消えた。このプロジェクトでは人々が再び森と関わり合いを持つきっかけとなる空間を、まむし谷の森に大きな屋根をかけることで実現することを目的とした。

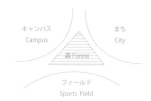

キャンパス Campus　　まち City
森 Forest
フィールド Sports Field

Zoning according to height

Each function was arranged according to the elevation of the valley. The lower part of the valley is the active sports activities, and the upper part of the valley is a relaxing space surrounded by trees.

Gathering
Cafe
Terrace
Watching space
Sports

Perspective

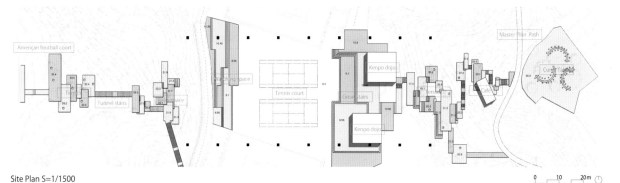

Site Plan S=1/1500

0　10　20m

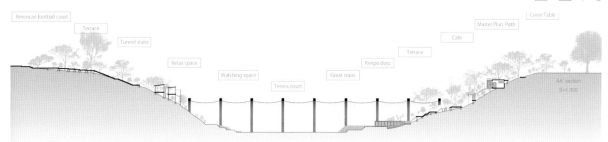

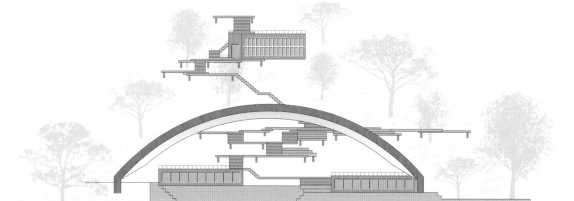

Section Perspective S=1/100

111

MAMUSHI SPORTS CUBE/2
マムシ スポーツキューブ /2

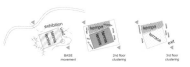

Sanja Zonja
サーニャ・ゾーニャ
Chiba Studio

The main idea was to question the porosity and transparency of the roof and the duality between the roof and the wall. Main structure of the building is elevated from the ground level and is supported by strong perpendicular walls and the set of columns. The roof grid is broken by openings which introduce movement and by sport fields that slide through the beams and vreate holes in them.

大屋根とそれに伴う構造グリッドについて、多孔性と透明性、そして壁との二重性という点からさまざまなスポーツや動きを誘導するような施設の設計を行った。

Perspective

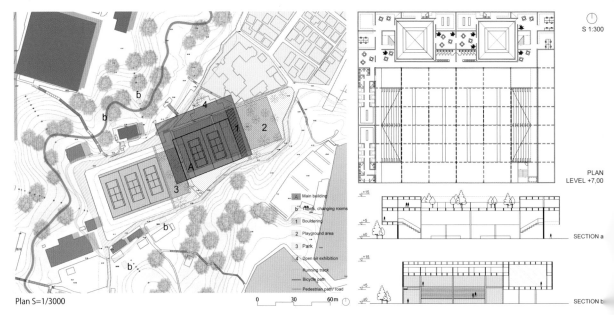

Plan S=1/3000

A Main building
b Toilets, changing rooms
1 Bouldering
2 Playground area
3 Park
4 Open air exhibition
— Running track
— Bicycle path
— Pedestrian path/ road

0   30   60m

S 1:300

PLAN
LEVEL +7,00

SECTION a

SECTION b

13 Connecting Nature and Sports
自然と運動の接続

Yuki Wada
和田雄樹
Chiba Studio

In Mamushi valley, human activities including sports, and the existing natural environment are cut off. So, as a connecting element of these, I introduce a shell structure that imitates trees to the boundary space, and create spaces for students and local residents by interspersing spaces that allow a small number of people to rest under the trees.

まむし谷で切り離されたスポーツなどの活動エリアと自然環境を繋ぐために、それらの境界空間に木々を模したシェル状の構造体を点在させ、学生と地域住民のための休憩スペースを設ける。

Perspective

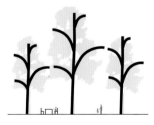

Tree trunks and branches are dense

Concrete shell structure with integrated pillar and ceiling supports each other

Diagram

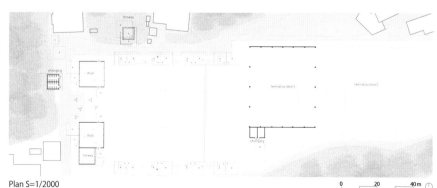

Plan S=1/2000

0   20   40m

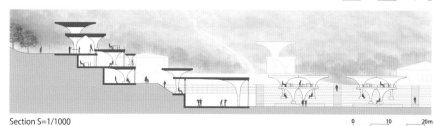

Section S=1/1000

0   10   20m

P

The snapshots from production of
Keio Architecture

POSTER2

Exhibition & Lecture Poster 2019
展示会とレクチャーのポスター2019

Keio Architecture Ehivition and guest lecture was held. A lecture was given that will be a hint of investigation and design of the target area from a wide viewpoint, such as domestic architects and overseas researchers.

慶應アーキテクチャエキシビジョンが開かれ、その一環としてゲストレクチャーが行われた。国内の建築家や海外の研究者など、幅広い視点から対象地域の調査、設計のヒントとなるような講演が行われた。

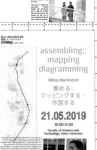

慶應 アーキテクチャ展示会
CDW COMPREHENSIVE DESIGNWORKSHOP

2019/07/19
|
2019/07/22

来 往 舎 1F

第 6 章　2019 年度　製図 3　慶應義塾大学まむし谷センターの設計

This subject coordinator was Professor Darko Radovic, the Spring Semester of 2019. A total of 8 students attended, divided into three groups lead by one instructor. Jorge Almazán's group continued the previous topic on "Urban Acupuncture", this time centered on Hiyoshi Campus. Kishimoto's group assignment was entitled "The Proposal of the Masterplan and Architecture program that improves the Space System of Hiyoshi, Yagami, and Shimoda". Radović's group focused specifically on designing a karate dojo for 2020, a space for an ancient art which became a modern sport.

本科目は 2019 年春学期に実施、ダルコ・ラドヴィッチ教授が主担当となりました。参加した 8 名の生徒は 3 つのグループに分かれ、各グループは担当教授によって指導されました。アルマザン・ホルヘ班では去年に引き続き、都市の鍼治療について考え、今回は日吉キャンパスを主軸としました。岸本達也班の課題は、日吉・矢上・下田の空間システムとそれを改善するマスタープランおよび建築プログラムの提案でした。ラドヴィッチ班は 2020 年にむけた空手道場の設計に着目し、現代スポーツとなった古代芸術のための空間を考えました。

Interview ——————————————————— p.120-12

Radović Studio

Born in Mamushi | Koki Suzuki ————————————— p.128
マムシに生まれる｜鈴木浩貴

Rolling into Mamushi | Yuki Mori ————————————— p.128
マムシにコロがる｜森祐樹

Mamushi-Healing | Muxi Yang ————————————— p.128
まむ治癒　｜楊沐渓

Almazán Studio

HIYOSHI Stadium | Shunsuke Shimizu ———————————— p.124-1
日吉スタジアム｜清水俊祐

Chain of Mamushi-Valley | Ryota Ibaraki ———————————— p.126-1
まむし谷の鎖｜茨木亮太

Nothing Comes out of Nothing | Daiki Sekiguchi ——————————— p.128
境界を開く｜関口大樹

Activity Mixed Forest | Maroya Harigaya ————————————— p.129
活動混交林｜針谷円

Field's Intervention | Yoshitomo Yonamoto ————————————— p.129
介入する畑｜要名本義朋

Overview of this competition

This competition was organized for senior students from department of System Design Engineering. As a collection of undergraduate architecture studies, 8 students from architecture design laboratories participated in this competition. The final question and answer session took place in Raiousha, Hiyoshi Campus.

コンペの概要

この設計競技会は、理工学部システムデザイン工学科の建築を学んでいる四年生を対象としたものである。学部の集大成として、意匠系の 2 つの研究室から計 8 人が参加した。 最終の質疑応答は慶應義塾大学日吉キャンパスの来往舎にて行われた。

Final Presentation　　　　最終プレゼンテーション

Jury	Estanislau Roca	審査員	エスタニスラウ・ロカ
	Neno Kezić		ネノ・ケジック
	Gabriele Masera		ガブリエル・マゼーラ
	Tadej Glažar		タデイ・グラザール
	Takumi Saikawa		齋川拓未
	Takashi Suo		周防貴之

Takashi Suo / 周防貴之
2004 Graduated from the Department of   2004 慶應義塾大学理工学部
      System Design Engineering at Keio University   システムデザイン工学科卒業
2006 Graduated from Keio University (master Course) 2006 慶應義塾大学大学院　修士課程修了
      Kazuyo Sejima & Associates and Sanaa   妹島和世建築設計事務所・SANAA
2015 SUO   2015 SUO 設立

1. Please tell us about the characteristcs of the site Mamushi-Valley and impression of theme for this class.

まむし谷の敷地と課題テーマの印象について教えてください。

 I think that it is interesting to regard Mamushi valley as one sports facility. I believe that it is possible to create a unique environment not only by scattering facilities for only sports in Mamushi but also making them gather integrating its topography. Students are required to clarify the close relationship between the body and the environment by designing the facillteis. I think that projects will be more intriguing if you can design the place where the embodiment expands with the surroundings.

　まむし谷全体をスポーツ施設と捉えるという視点はおもしろいと思いました。単に色々なスポーツのための施設がまむし谷に分散されるのではなく、それらがユニークな地形と一緒になって集合することで一つの独自の環境を作り出すことができるのではないかと感じました。スポーツという全身を使ったアクティビティによって、身体と環境がより密接な関係であることを求められているのだと思います。身体性が環境によって拡張されてるような設計ができるとおもしろいと思いました。

2. What was your impression of the the students' work in the exhibition?

学生の展示作品についての印象をお聞かせください。

 I think that there were many interesting proposals, but some seemed to spend little time on their presentations. I think there is a deference between how to express your ideas when you have a client and you can do a presentation in person, and when you need to stand out in a lot of ideas such as the competition type. Students should be conscious about the approach or expressions they use in their presentation, according to what they have proposed.

　たくさんのおもしろい提案がありましたが、人に見せるためのアウトプット（プレゼンテーション）に十分な力を注げていない案も少なくなかった印象があります。クライアントがいて一対一で自分の提案を聞いてもらえる場面に求められる表現と、コンペ形式でたくさんの提案がある中で自分の提案を主張するような表現は違うのだと思います。自分の提案の内容に合わせて、その提案自体が求めるアウトプットの方法、表現はないだろうかと意識できるといいのだ思います。

3. When looking at the students' work, do you have any advice for their presentations?

学生の作品、展示の表現の向上について学生にアドバイスをお願いします。

A lot of students took an approach of solving current issues from elaborate research. While it is required for architectural design to solve the problems functionally, research itself should be creative in order to do good design. Not enumerating obvious problems but exploring an original view and perspective based on diverse and deep insight about the culture and environment of a site will lead to an original design.

　リサーチを入念に行い、現状の問題点を解決するというアプローチが多かったように思います。機能的に解決すべきことは建築の設計に求められる一方で、それだけでは物足りないのかもしれないと感じます。機能や価値観は時代によって移り変わりやすいものなのだと思います。よい設計をするためには、リサーチ自体にも創造性が必要なのだと思います。見えやすい問題点の列挙ではなく、その場所の歴史や環境について、多角的で深い洞察をもとに、独自の視座と視点を見つけることが独自の設計につながるのではないかと思います。

4.What do you keep in mind throughout your design project?

ご自身が設計をする上で意識していること、特徴はどのようなものですか？

I am still exploring, but I want to be able to look at things from various measure. We need to think about how to comply with our clients' request. And at the same time, I would like to design in a wider perspective, considering where to put my design position on architectural history in the current era, even after I am finished with the initial client. What I am interested in is to figure out flexible architectures that are adopted as a part of the society, and that can be adopted to each situation. I feel that it is required to design and construct architecture, not only as a physical thing, but as system or as a cycle (in other words, environment).

　私自身も手探りですが、いろいろな尺度でものごとを考えられるようになりたいと思っています。目の前のクライアントが望むことにどう応えるかを考えると同時に、もっと大きな視点でいまの時代にとって、あるいは建築史の中でどう位置づけることができるのかを考えながら設計したいと思っています。時間が経ち、当初のクライアントから手が離れたとしてもです。社会の一部として受け入れられ、その時々に応じたあり方ができるような柔軟な建築とはどのようなものか興味があります。それは物としての建築を美しく設計するのではなく、もう少し大きな建築を含めたシステムやサイクル、一言でいうと環境となるのかもしれませんが、そういった形のないものも同時に美しく組み立てられるかが問われるのではと感じています。

5. May we have one last comment for the studesnts?

最後に学生へのメッセージをお願いいたします。

I also studied architecture in Keio University and got my bachelor and masters degree. Looking back to my school life, I think that it was a huge advantage that I was in an environment where there were different types of people who major in not only architecture but other subjects. When it comes to design architecture, we must put emphasis on economic, cultural, and historical aspect as well as engineering, and also cannot help but recognizing that we all are connected in this world. In this complex and diverse world, I myself always would like to see things as simply as possible and from as different view as possible. Students can cultivate how to perceive things by making the most of any resource from the university and putting yourself in a diversitive, extreme, and intense environment as much as possible. It is the privilege of school days to spend much time to be in such an environment without hesitation.

　私自身も慶應の理工学部、理工学研究科で建築を学びました。いま振り返ると、学内の身近な所に建築以外を専門とした尖った人がたくさんいる環境にいられたことのメリットは大きかったように思います。実際に建築を作るとなると、もちろんエンジニアリング的なことの比重は大きいですが、経済のこと、文化のこと、歴史のことについても考えるようになるし、そして世界と繋がっていることを意識せざるを得ません。複雑で多様な世界において、ものごとをできるだけ単純に、かつ、できるだけさまざまな角度で見たいと私自身常々思っています。大学のあらゆるリソースを活用して、できるだけたくさんの、エクストリームな環境に身をおくことによって、ものの見方を養えることができるのではないかと思います。そのようなことに時間を惜しげなく使えるのは学生時代の特権だと思います。

Takumi Saikawa / 齋川拓未

1993-1997	Shibaura Institute of Technology
1998-2001	Massimiliano Fuksas Architect
2002-2004	Keio University (Master Course)
2004	Kengo Kuma & Associate
2016	Takumi Saikawa Architects

1993-1997	芝浦工業大学　卒業
1998-2001	Massimiliano Fuksas Architect
2002-2004	慶應義塾大学大学院　修士課程修了
2004	隈研吾建築都市設計事務所
2016	齋川拓未建築設計事務所

1. Please tell us about the characteristcs of the site Mamushi-Valley and impression of theme for this class.

まむし谷の敷地と課題テーマの印象について教えてください。

Since Mamushi-Valley has diverse potential from the aspect of history and place, students can reflect those potential on the program and design of each project. In addition, what is required is an environment which expands human relationship and the community for not only students and teachers of Keio University but also Keio University itself, its neighbors and world-wide people who will involve with this university. Those attempts will not only bring about the benefits of Keio University's new activity (such as comfortable training environment and activation of sports education and research), but also allow this university to lead the society. In such a large framework, the site and ambitious theme were set up this time, and the more I think, the more challenging this task is.

　まむし谷は、歴史的にも場所的にも多様な可能性があり、それをプログラム、建物のデザインに反映できます。また、慶應義塾大学の学生、教員だけでなく、慶應義塾大学と周辺地域、また、そこに関わる可能性がある世界中の人々に対して、コミュニティや人と人のつながり、広がっていく環境が必要になります。それによって、慶應義塾大学の新しい活動によるメリット（快適な練習環境、スポーツ教育・研究の活発化など）が生まれるだけでなく、社会を先導していくような大学を目指すことにつながると考えられます。そのような大きな枠組みの中で今回の敷地とテーマの設定があり、とても野心的で考えれば考えるほど難しい課題であったと思います。

2. What was your impression of the students' work in the exhibition?

学生の展示作品についての印象をお聞かせください。

Overall, the quality of students's presentation skills physical model, drawings, etc.) were high. However, it was ambiguous how new ideas and values were found in all the proposals for universities, students, teachers and neighbors. Some were finished with interesting and cool-looking architecture, but I think it would have been nice if the students could clearly show who enjoies the benefit of their proposal, and not to finish just by designing. Also, I think that Yoshiro Taniguchi's student dormitory / spa renovation project is a very good approach. However, I think that a more polite proposal was desired. Since it is not an ordinary old building in the city, it must be respected. I think it was important to think what to leave and what to renovate from the research of the concepts, designs and details.

　全体的にプレゼンテーションのスキル（模型、パースなど）は、高かったと思います。しかしながら、どの案も大学、学生、教員や周辺住民などに対して、どれぐらい新しい活動や価値を見出しているかが曖昧でした。おもしろい、かっこよさそうな建築で終わっているものも見受けられましたが、デザインだけで終わるのではなく、どのようなメリットを誰に与えてくれるのか明確にプレゼンで表現できるとよかったと思います。また、谷口吉郎の学生寮・スパの改修プロジェクト案については、とてもよいアプローチだと思います。ただ、もう少し丁寧な提案のほうが望ましかったように思います。普通に街中にある古い建物ではないので、建物へのリスペクトが必要です。コンセプト、デザイン、ディテールなどを調査した上で何を残し、何をリノベーションするのかも大切であったと思います。

3. When looking at the students' work, do you have any advice for their presentations?

学生の作品、展示の表現の向上について学生にアドバイスをお願いします。

 I think almost all the students gave a presentation mixing various methods such as drawings, models, perspectives, and sketches, and that was nice. However, I think that there were many proposals which were a little difficult to understand at a glance. Students explained to me about their works, but I felt that I didn't understand what the main theme of the project was. They might know it, but they seemed to follow unconsciously the habits of architectural expression, and the matters to be explained faded and their concepts became difficult to understand. There may be a desire to make a cool architecture and design, but rather than creating something that has already been seen, it may be useful for the future to think and express something that is original, even if it is dull.

　図面、模型、パース、スケッチなどいろいろな方法を上手く混ぜながらプレゼンができていたと思います。ただ、一目で何を提案しているかが少しわかりづらい提案が多かったように思います。作品の説明をしてもらったのですが、プロジェクトの核心が何であるか本人がわかっていないようにも感じられました。おそらくわかっているのですが、建築表現の習慣に無意識に従ってしまい、説明すべき事項が薄れ、わかりづらいものになっているのだと思います。かっこいい建築、デザインをしたいという思いがあるのかもしれませんが、それによって既視感のあるものがつくられるよりは、ダサくてもオリジナリティのあるものを考え、表現したほうが将来に役立つのではないかと思いました。

4.What do you keep in mind throughout your design project?

ご自身が設計をする上で意識していること、特徴はどのようなものですか？

 I try to find the optimal solution for various conditions such as requests from clients, site conditions, laws and regulations, and costs. In many cases, the resulting shapes and materials used are not very specific. However, I always want the experience there to be very beautiful for those who use it. In that sense, I always think that it would be nice to create an architecture that cannot be verbalized.

　施主からの要求、敷地条件、法規、コストなどの多様な条件に対して最適な解を探すようにしています。結果的にできてくる形や使用する素材にあまり特異性はないものになることが多いです。しかし、そこにある体験が利用する人にとって、とても美しいものでありたいといつも思っています。その意味で言語化できないような建築を作れたらよいなといつも考えています。

5. May we have one last comment for the studesnts?

最後に学生へのメッセージをお願いいたします。

 The answers to the above questions are also words for myself by telling students.
Since architecture is very deep and never ends, I hope to continue to think about the events related to architecture and architecture itself with you.

　上記の設問にたいする返答は、学生を通じて自分に向けた言葉にもなっています。
建築はとても奥が深くて終わりがないので、皆さんと一緒に建築や建築に関わる事象について考えていくことができればと思います。

Concept

I made the new stadium around the existing athletic field. That field has a great potential, such as rich nature, good location, sophisticated field and tradition. We often hold a big sports event or use as a rest place. However, we can't make good use of those. This proposal integrates the function as a bridge into stadium by cantilever system which avoid the position of trees. This system will form a various space controlled by nature and contribute to revitalizing of Hiyoshi. That's why this will be a "bridge" between university and local city.

Main Perspective

設計趣旨文

豊かな自然、恵まれた立地、洗練されたフィールド、受け継がれた伝統。そんな可能性を秘めたキャンパス内の陸上競技場に針治療を行う。競技場の周りに広がる自然から木を避けるように伸びてきた腕（キャンチレバー）が屋根を支え、橋と一体型のスタジアムを形成する。自然に支配された多様な空間によって、塾の伝統、あるいは塾と日吉の街との間に橋渡しが行われることで2つの場所の魅力を再確認し、森と暮らしが寄り添いあっていく。

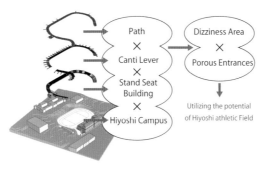

Concept Diagram

Path × Canti Lever × Stand Seat Building × Hiyoshi Campus → Dizziness Area × Porous Entrances → Utilizing the potential of Hiyoshi athletic Field

Kyoseikan

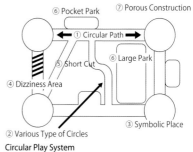

⑥ Pocket Park　⑦ Porous Construction
① Circular Path
⑤ Short Cut　⑥ Large Park
④ Dizziness Area
② Various Type of Circles
③ Symbolic Place

Circular Play System

1) Searching the position of trees

2) Making cantilevers among trees

3) Combining cantilevers & putting decks

Structure Diagram

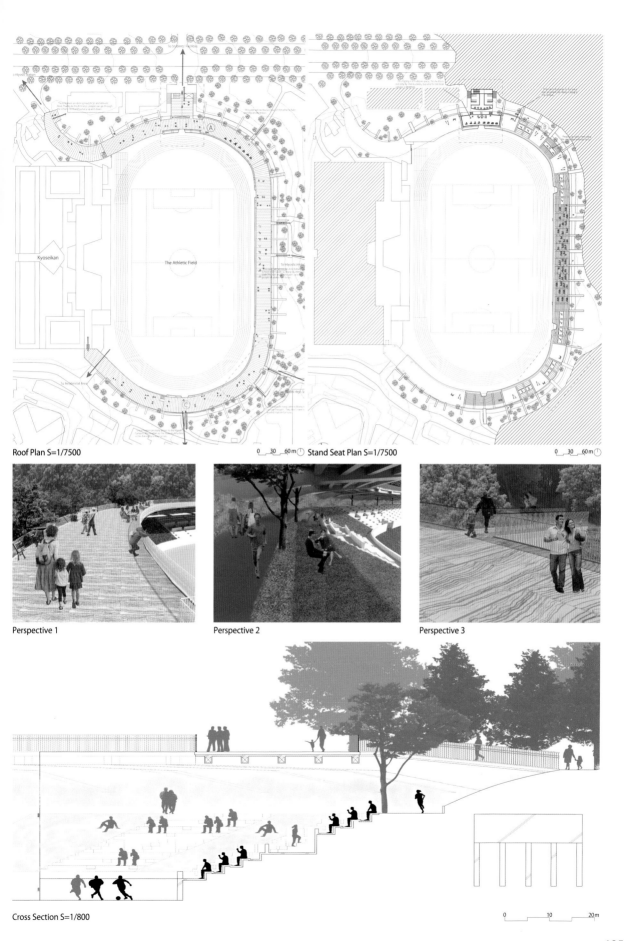

Roof Plan S=1/7500

Kyoseikan

The Athletic Field

0 30 60 m

Stand Seat Plan S=1/7500

0 30 60 m

Perspective 1

Perspective 2

Perspective 3

Cross Section S=1/800

0 10 20 m

125

Chain of Mamushi-Valley
まむし谷の鎖

Ryota Ibaraki
茨木亮太
Almazán Studio

Concept

My concept is to make paths to connect the valley to connect the history in the site, and make a trail that can go around the valley. However, it should not be the shape of directions or paths. Because the history covered in this project is apart of his tories of the valley that still exist. It must bea ble to pick up and update them. Therefore, we will make paths flexible by creating an architecture that incorporates the great history about the valley and paths that incorporates the small history, and think that it will eventually expand throughout the valley.

設計趣旨文

敷地にある歴史を繋げるようにまむし谷を繋げる道を作り、まむし谷を一周ぐるっと回れるようなトレイルを作る。しかし、それは道順が決まり切ったものであってはいけない。なぜなら、今回この課題で取り上げる歴史はまむし谷の歴史の一部であり、まだまだ、まむし谷に関する歴史は存在する。それらを取り込んでアップデートできるようなものでなくてはいけない。そこで、まむし谷に関する大きな歴史を取り入れた建築と、小さな歴史を感じるような事物を取り入れた道を作ることで、道を柔軟なものとし、やがてさらにまむし谷全体に波及していくことを考える。

Concept Diagram

Large and small buildings created by pinpointing the history of the valley
蝮谷の歴史を拾ってピンポイントで作る大小の建築

These are connected to form a chain around the valley
これらが繋がり、蝮谷を一周する鎖となる

Activate the entire Mamushi-Valley as a great chain of history
蝮谷全体が大きな歴史の鎖として活性化される

I hope a larger chain of history could be made in other places
蝮谷以外の土地でも歴史の鎖ができることを願う

An overview of the designed trail　設計したトイレの全貌

Sketch of the present condition of site A,B,C,D　敷地 A,B,C,D 現状のスケッチ

Sketch of the path and landscape I want to make in site A,B,C,D　作りたい道と風景のスケッチ

Path Through Baths
水浴場の道

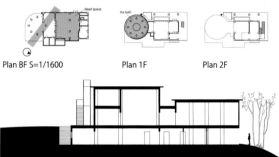
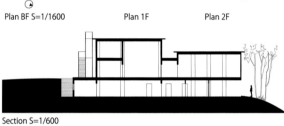

Plan BF S=1/1600   Plan 1F   Plan 2F

Section S=1/600

Underground Museum
地下の展示部屋

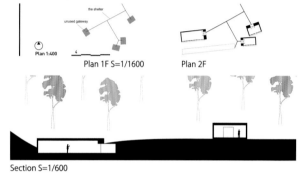

Plan 1:400

Plan 1F S=1/1600   Plan 2F

Section S=1/600

Dormitory of Village
集落の合宿所

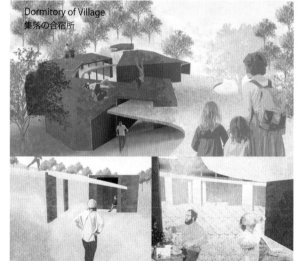

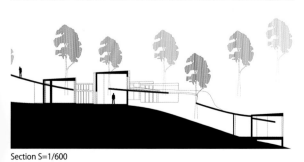

Section S=1/600

Observatory Moth
櫓の展望台

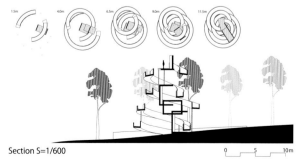

Section S=1/600

0   5   10m

Born in Mamushi
マムシに生まれる

Koki Suzuki
鈴木浩貴
Radović Studio

This project focuses on the new interaction between Keio students and local residents, utilizing a Karate Dojo. In order to revitalize the Mamushi valley, a new Karate Dojo ringed with two slopes are expected to be a node allowing multiple local activities, as well as offering a comfortable space for practicing.

　まむし谷地域はその豊かな自然環境にもかかわらず、活用が十分とはいえない。本提案では、空手道場をその結節点として位置付けた 2 本のスロープにおいて、学生と地域住民が空手を中心として多様な形の活動・交流を可能となる空間の設計を目指した。

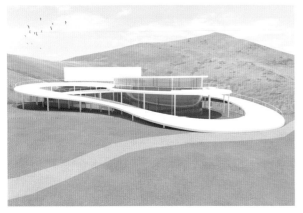

Rolling into Mamushi
マムシにコロがる

Yuki Mori
森祐樹
Radović Studio

The aim of this project is to induce human activities on the slope and deisgn new sports culture. The architecture inserted into the existing slope allows a valley road which will be in the center of the new exercise trail connecting Hiyoshi station and Yagami river.

　日吉駅と矢上川を繋いだトレイルのコアの設計。建築を既存の斜面に挿入することにより斜面をスケールダウンし、建築と地形が融合した空間が人の活動をまむし谷の微地形に誘発することで、新たなスポーツ文化を創る。

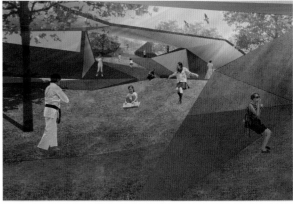

Mamushi-Healing
まむ治癒

Muxi Yang
楊沐渓
Radović Studio

Mamushi Valley is a historically valuable place that is not well known. By applying an acupuncture treatment to the athletics stadium located at the entrance of this valley, it will lead to the activation of the entire Hiyoshi Campus.

　貴重な自然、歴史が残るまむし谷を知る人は少ない。このまむし谷のエントランスに位置する陸上競技場に屋根をかけるという鍼治療を施すことでまむし谷はもちろん、日吉全体の活性化につなげる。

Nothing Comes out of Nothing
境界をひらく

Daiki Sekiguchi
関口大樹
Almazán Studio

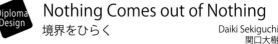

In Hiyoshi, where Keio University is located, there is a path called "Rikozaka" that links campus and Yagami's residential area. This time I propose an attractive space where students and local residents intervene together by placing new path along Rikozaka and placing fields and facilities on three sites.

　慶應義塾大学がある日吉には、大学のキャンパスと矢上の住宅街を結ぶ「理工坂」と呼ばれる道が存在する。理工坂に沿って新たなパスを通し、選定した 3 つのエリアに畑を介する施設を配置することで、学生と地域の方々が集まる魅力的な空間を提案する。

Activitiy Mixed Forest
活動混交林

Maroya Harigaya
針谷円
Almazán Studio

Field's Intervention
介入する畑

Yoshitomo Yonamoto
要名本義朋
Almazán Studio

Riko Zaka connects Hiyoshi Campus and residential area. Into mixed forest of Riko Zaka, I weave architecture and human activity. Lots of tiny buildings between existing nature are diversified into club rooms, rest space etc. Through varios activities there, students, region peolple and nature interact.

日吉キャンパスと住宅街を繋ぐ理工坂。その自然がなす混交林に、建築と人間の活動を織り込む。既存の木を守り、その間を多量の極小建築で縫う。極小ユニットを部室や休憩所へと多様化させる。そこでの多様な活動を通して学生・地域・自然が交流する。

In my design, I want to make dojo a mental purifying space for University students and residents living nearby. In the buildings, people could feel they are surrounded by nature, and outside buildings, people could also take a rest look into Dojo through layered holes and windows.

道場の設計を通じて学生及び近隣に住む人々が日常生活から離れ、落ち着けるような場所を提供することを目指す。道場では人々は自然に囲まれていることを認識し、またその周りの連続した壁は内にある道場を眺めながらさまざまな活動を生み出す場となる。

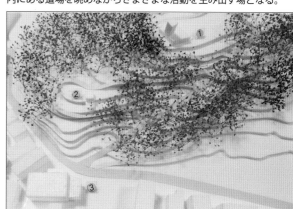

The snapshots from production of
Keio Architecture

MODEL2
Mamushi-dani 1：500 Model
蝮谷1：500モデル

It was the site model of the Mamushi Valley area. We made a m
with a scale of 1/500 on a 1.25-square area and exhibited the same
archtecture models which were designd by students.
敷地となるまむし谷エリアの敷地模型である。1.25㎢四方のエリアを1/500スケールにした模
作し、学生の設計した建築模型も同じスケールで展示された。

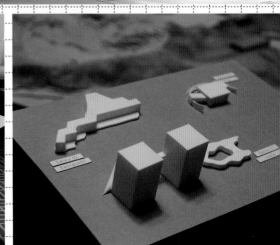

Chapter 7
SFC Studio 2019
Designing of Mamushi Center

第7章　2019年度　SFCスタジオ　慶應義塾大学まむし谷センターの設計

At the bachelor's design studio "City and Architecture", students examined to maintain the local environment, thinking about health promotion through sports activities in Hiyoshi Mamushi-Valley and the residents. The theme was "The City Edge and The Connector / To Create a form of a healthy town development, stepping into the sports facilities and neighboring residents that exist between the Mamushi-Plateau and Valley". (Instructor: Hiroto Kobayashi, Yutaro Muraji, Yoshiki Mishima).

At the Applied Environment Design Studio of the Graduate School, the task was to "Design a large roof over the tennis stadium that allows the athletes to practice in any kind of weather condition, and something that also works as a venue that functions as an event space during the Olympics". Students learned about structure and materials beforehand and were required to propose something feasible. (Professor: Shigeru Ban, Yasunori Harano, Rumi Okazaki, Ryuta Kidokoro)

　学部のデザインスタジオ「都市と建築」では、「都市のエッジとコネクター／慶應日吉まむし谷台地と谷が織りなす大学スポーツ施設群と近隣住区に介入し、健康なまちづくりの形を創出する」をテーマに日吉まむし谷およびその周辺地域を巻き込んだスポーツによる健康づくりを目指した地域環境整備を検討しました。（担当教員：小林博人、連勇太朗、三島由樹）

また大学院の応用環境デザインスタジオでは、「競技場（テニス場を想定）に大屋根をかけることで，全天候型の練習が可能となると同時に、オリンピック期間中におけるイベントスペースとして機能するものを設計する」を主題としました。設計には構造や材料について学習したうえで、実現可能な提案が求められました。（担当教員：坂茂、原野泰典、岡崎瑠美、城所竜太）

Studio Works
作品一覧

Ban Studio

HP Shell Structure | Ilham Ras — p.136
HPシェル構造 | イルハム・ラス

Mamushi-Valley Tennis Court | Gabriel Chatel — p.136
まむし谷テニスコート | ガブリエル・チャテル

Minimal Timber Truss | Yusuke Nakagawa — p.136
ミニマル木トラス | 中川雄介

Green Architecture Design | Deric Low Seong Hee — p.137
緑の建築デザイン | デレク・ロウ・セオン・ヒー

Mamushi-Valley Tensile Bamboo Roof | Francisco Javier Celaya Moron — p.137
まむし谷　竹引張屋根 | フランシスコ・ハビ・セレヤ・モロン

Mamushi-Valley Roof | Ayano Yasunaga — p.137
まむし谷の天井 | 安永彩乃

Kobayashi Studio

Crave | Hiroshi Ohara — p.137
クレイブ | 小原寛史

Creating Multiple Sense of Place in Multilayer Slab by User Definition | Sekiguchi Daiki — p.138
様々な味のある場を利用者が多層スラブ上に創造する | 関口大樹

"Mamushi" Road | Mayu Masuda — p.138
まむしロード | 増田真由

Flow | Yuko Yamashita — p.138
流れ | 山下裕子

Overview of this Ban Studio

This studio is for students who have completed the basic practice of architecture, and this time the focus is on Hiyoshi Campus. Through the studio, students will learn how to organize the conditions required for proposing, and will acquire the techniques how to design logically.

Hiyoshi Campus has been selected as a pre-camp site for the UK Olympic athlete team and will serve as a hub for sports and cultural interaction. By putting a roof on the tennis field located in Mamushi Valley, the task is to design a place where people can interact in various applications during and after the tournament period. Based on site analysis and case studies, student should propose a design with unique structural ideas. At the end, students are required to present there ideas using diagrams, drawings, and models etc...

坂スタジオの概要

建築の基礎演習を終えた学生に対して日吉キャンパスを敷地とした設計課題を課す。提案のために求められる諸条件を整理し、論理的に設計プロセスを組み立ててデザインを行う手法を習得する。

日吉キャンパスは英国の事前キャンプ地に選定され、スポーツや文化交流の拠点となる。本課題は、まむし谷にあるテニス場に屋根をかけることで、大会期間中やそれ以外でも人々がさまざまな用途で交流できる場を設計する課題とする。敷地分析や事例研究を踏まえ、構造を十分に検討した上で意匠設計を行い、最終成果としてダイアグラム・図面・模型を用いたプレゼンテーションを行う。

Overview of this Kobayashi Studio

Urban Edge and Connector/Keio Hiyoshi Mamushi-Valley intervene sports facilities in University campus and its neighborhood, and create health-oriented town for the future.

There is a valley called "Mamushi-Valley" in Keio Hiyoshi Campus where many sport club's facilities are concentrated in. Going down into a deep forest from the Hiyoshi Plateau, a large field composed of tennis courts, gymnasium and other sports facilities opens in front of you. This is the valley where many sports clubs and their facilities are located, which is going to be used as the official sports training ground for the Great Britain team in 2020 for the Olympic and Paralympic Games of Tokyo. This opportunity can be a start to establish a sports-based healthy and sustainable city including the Mamushi-Valley and its neighborhood community. We try to propose a holistic and strategic plan for health based well connected district between the university and local community.

In this studio, we as future architects, landscape architects, and urban designers, faced a series of spatial issues such as university campus planning, infrastructure, vernacular culture, economy, ecology and natural topography, and envisioned a large scale scope in order to tackle these issues. We would like to develop and propose a new space typology to bridge the gap between the university and its neighborhood.

小林スタジオの概要

都市のエッジとコネクター / 慶應日吉まむし谷台地と谷が織りなす大学スポーツ施設群と近隣住区に介入し、健康なまちづくりの形を創出する。

慶應日吉キャンパスには体育会関連の施設の集中するまむし谷がある。日吉台地から深い森に覆われた急な坂を下りると、そこには広々としたテニスコートや体育館、その他のスポーツ施設があり慶應義塾大学の体育会それぞれの活動拠点としている。また、この場所は 2020 年のオリンピック・パラリンピックの際、英国チームの事前キャンプや大会期間中のトレーニング場として利用されることが決まっている。これらを一つの契機とし、まむし谷およびその周辺地域を巻き込んだスポーツによる健康でサステナブルな街づくりが可能となる。大学とその近隣との健全な関係を構築するとともに将来に向けて、健康に根ざした街づくりの提案を目指す。

本スタジオでは、学生が未来の建築家・ランドスケープアーキテクト・都市デザイナーとして、大学キャンパス、インフラ、地域文化、経済、エコロジー、自然地形などを含んだ複雑な都市を取り巻く環境に向き合い、そこから大きなビジョンを構想しさまざまな課題に取り組んだ。これらを通して新しい大学と都市の関係のタイポロジーを構想し提案がなされた。

HP Shell Structure
HPシェル構造

Ilham Ras
イルハム・ラス
Ban Studio

Mamushi-Valley Tennis Court
まむし谷テニスコート

Gabriel Chatel
ガブリエル・チャテル
Ban Studio

This project explores the structural details of the HP Shell Structure* to create a curved shaped building only from individual linear structural elements inspired by the Concrete Shell wooden formworks. *Hyperbolic Parabloid Shell

本プロジェクトは、コンクリートシェルの木型枠からヒントを得た線状の構造部材を用いている。この部材のみで曲線状の建築を造るため HP シェル構造（ハイパボリックパラボリックシェル）の詳細を参考にした。

The Mumashi-Valley is one of the lowest part of the Hiyoshi Campus, so is difficult for trucks to come in. This project was designed from the size of a standard Japanese semi-trailer. Its extensible structure allows a fast and clean construction. The diamond shape provide light effects for the tennis player. On the top of the structure, a polycarbonate roof is hanged with a slope of 5% for the rain.

まむし谷は日吉キャンパスの中でも標高が低いため、トラックの搬入には不向きである。本プロジェクトは一般的な日本のセミトレーラーの寸法を基に設計された。伸縮する構造が早くてクリーンな建設を可能にする。ダイアモンドの形状はテニスコートに自然光をもたらす。構造体の上にはポリカーボネートの天井が張られ、雨を流す目的で 5%の傾斜がつくられている。

Minimal Timber Truss
ミニマル木トラス

Yusuke Nakagawa
中川雄介
Ban Studio

This is an attempt to design a minimal timber truss roof out of small handheld elements, for simple logistics and construction. Each span is constructed on the ground, then lifted for connection from both sides of the court. All elements which compose each span are specific lengths of 2 by 4 timber, a low cost and simple production material.

本プロジェクトは、物流と建設の簡略化を目指し、携帯可能な要素から小さな木トラス屋根をかける提案である。木トラスのユニットは地上で作られ、テニスコートの両端から徐々に連ねられていく。各スパンを構成する部材はツーバイフォーという安価で生産性に富んだものを使用している。

Green Architecture Design
緑の建築デザイン

Deric Low Seong Hee
デレク・ロウ・セオン・ヒー
Ban Studio

This is a design proposal for the upcoming Olympics and in way to withstand any kind of weather condition. The site is connected with the narrow path, causing it a challenge to access to the site. This causes limited options for building materials too. So, this study implemented bamboo as its primary material. Bamboo is versatile, inexpensive, light weighted and easy to move, and its large span does not need conventional support.

　本プロジェクトはオリンピックを視野に入れ、どのような天候条件にも対応できる設計となっている。本敷地への通路は非常に狭く、建材に用いられる材料は限られているため主要材として竹を用いた。竹は凡庸性が高く、安価で軽いことから移動や運搬には最適であり、部材の間隔を広くとれ補助部材を必要としない。

Mamushi-ValleyTensile Bamboo Roof
まむし谷
竹引張屋根

Francisco Javier Celaya Moron
フランシスコ・ハヴィエール・セレヤ・モロン
Ban Studio

This project is to desing a roof cover the tennis fields in the Mamushi-Valley area by the tensile properties of bamboo. Most of the resources are used stiff wooden rings, and adopting a saddle geometry that would allow for the roof, made of overlapped bamboo flooring pieces, to behave tensile. Scaffolds economize material and time for construction. The roof is covered with tent for natural light to filter through it.

　本プロジェクトはまむし谷にあるテニスコート上に、必要最小限のマテリアルを用いて天井をかけることであり、今回は竹の引張特性に着目した。大半の資源は非常に硬い木製のリングを使い、天井はサドルの形状により重なり合う竹の床材で創られた屋根が引張動作する。柱の足場材は材料費・建設時間が抑え、天井のテントからは太陽光がこぼれる。

Mamushi-Valley Roof
まむし谷の天井

Ayano Yasunaga
安永彩乃
Ban Studio

The Mamushi-Valley site contains narrow roads and many elevation differences, making it difficult for transporting large materials and preparing open construction spaces. For this reason, this proposal utilizes the scissor structure so that it can be folded while it is getting transferred. The expandable frames become a roof when it is combined with the membrane system.

　まむし谷は道が狭く、起伏が激しいことから、大きな建材や建設スペースの確保が難しい。これらの理由から、ハサミの構造を利用した屋根を提案している。伸縮可能な部材が膜構造と合わさって完成する。

Crave
クレイブ

Hiroshi Ohara
小原寛史
Kobayashi Studio

"Carve" interconnects the three separate programs of sports, research, and local areas.

　本プロジェクト「クレイブ」は、スポーツ・リサーチ・地元という、別々の3者の関係を強固なものにする。

137

Creating Multiple Sense of Place in Multilayer Slab by User Definition
様々な味のある場を利用者が多層スラブ上に創造する

Daiki Sekiguchi
関口大樹
Kobayashi Studio

"Mamushi" Road
まむしロード

Mayu Masuda
増田真由
Kobayashi Studio

 In this Architecture, there are various height of slabs connected by stairs. By dividing the slabs by height, it is possible to create various spaces. Each slab has its originality and generates incidental interaction when people move around the building. The slab and stairs serve as a place to perform something,The users define the space as a sensory place by using it. We create various sensory places in multilayer slabs.

　この建築にはさまざまな高さのスラブが階段によって繋がれている。スキップフロアのようにスラブを分けさまざまな空間を作り出した。各スラブは独特の個性を持ち、利用者の間に偶発的な出会いを生み出す。スラブと階段は演出の舞台となる。利用者はその場を感覚的な場として捉える。言い換えると、我々は多層スラブ上にさまざまな感覚的な場を創造する。

 "Mamushi Road" in the "Mamushi-Valley". It is a place where locals learn each other, a place where students stroll, a place where people see campus athletes, and a place where campus athletes also chat. This road will become a part of the users' lives, and as the year passes by, the people relaxing on the bench or enjoying sports will change, and so will the "Mamushi Road".

　「まむし谷」にある「まむしロード」。そこは地元の人々が会い、生徒が集い、スポーツに励むアスリート達を観戦し、アスリート達も休憩がてら会話を楽しむところである。利用者にとっての日常となり、時が経つにつれて、安らぐ人が変わり、スポーツを楽しむ人々が変わる。それに伴いまむしロードも変化するだろう。

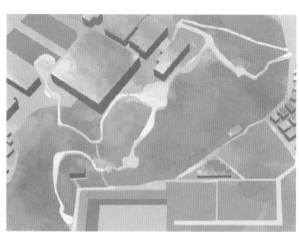

Flow
流れ

Yuko Yamashita
山下裕子
Kobayashi Studio

 At the site Keio Hiyoshi Campus, there is an edge between students, athletes, and the local residents, due to landscaping and planting. This project proposes a connector to repair this edge. The program are public baths, tennis seats, changing rooms, and a footbath. All of these facilities have different entrances, for students, athletes, and the locals, facilitating more interaction with others within the building.

　日吉キャンパスでは、そのランドスケープと植栽から、人々の間に距離がある。本プロジェクトはこの隔たりを埋める提案を行う。提案するプログラムは、公衆浴場・テニス鑑賞ベンチ・更衣室・足湯である。施設への入り口を、学生・アスリート・地元の人々、それぞれ専用に設けることで、3者の間で交流を生む。

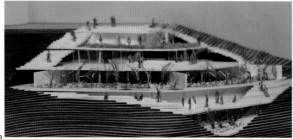

Column 8
The snapshots from production of
Keio Architecture

P PAVILION 2
colabo Pavilion 2019
colabo パビリオン2019

eated a new pavilion. A three-dimensional Japanese-style twill was
eated by a nearby hanger and put on the exhibition.

なパビリオンを実施製作した。身近にあるハンガーが織り成す3次元の日本的な綾を空間
し、展示会場に設置した。

綾織り   3次元が織りなす綾

Hanger   Plane   3-dimensional unit   Hang

In a square   In a alley

[Study Process] [Design Process]

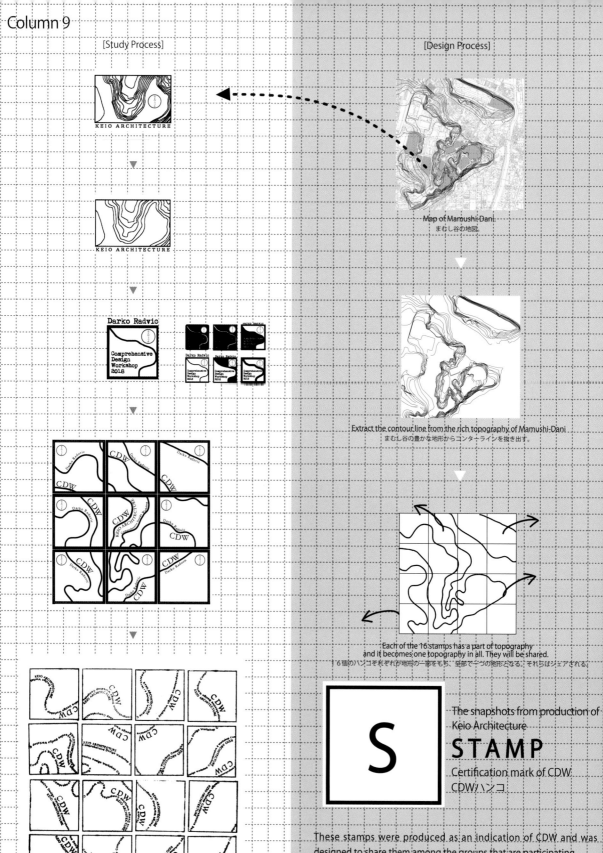

Map of Mamushi-Dani.
まむし谷の地図。

Extract the contour line from the rich topography of Mamushi-Dani.
まむし谷の豊かな地形からコンターラインを抜き出す。

Each of the 16 stamps has a part of topography
and it becomes one topography in all. They will be shared.
16個のハンコそれぞれが地形の一部をもち、全部で一つの地形となる。それらはシェアされる。

The snapshots from production of
Keio Architecture

S

STAMP

Certification mark of CDW
CDWハンコ

These stamps were produced as an indication of CDW and was
designed to share them among the groups that are participating.
CDWを示すものとして、ハンコが制作された。CDWに参加するグループがハンコ
を共有できるようにデザインされた。

Complete!

第 8 章　2019 年度　慶應アーキテクチャ展示会

The theme "Hiyoshi Mamushi-Valley sports activities that unites the university and the region", strongly connects to the problem of how universities can create an open relationship with the society. Continuing from last year, this exhibition envisioned the future of Keio University through sports, which is something we all learn from our physical body.

「日吉まむし谷におけるスポーツが繋ぐ大学と地域」というテーマは、大学が社会に対してどのように開けた関係を作れるかという大きな課題に直結する問題でもありました。本展示会では昨年に引き続き、スポーツという身体を伴った学びを通して、これからの大学のあるべき姿を構想しました。

Continuing from last year, the CDW Keio Exhibition 2019 was held at Hiyoshi Campus in July. Many visitors came to see the exhibits; works designed by graduate and undergraduate students in SFC and Faculty of Science and Engineering, the pavilion and model of Mamushi-Valley, which they have been working on from the previous term.

昨年に引き続き 7 月の日吉キャンパス来往舎にて CDW 慶應展示会 2019 が実施された。前期から取り組んでいた理工学部と SFC の院生と学部生の設計作品およびパビリオンやまむし谷全体模型などが展示され、多くの来場者が訪れた。

During the exhibition period, the competition of studio A and undergraduate Architectural space planning and design 3, a lecture by Kengo Kuma, a symposium by professors invited from abroad and the Institute of Physical Education, and a talk by Fumihiko Maki and Yoshio Taniguchi were held.

　展示会では、修士によるスタジオAと学部生の製図Ⅲのデザインコンペ、隈研吾氏による講演、海外から招聘された教授と体育研究所によるシンポジウム、そして槇文彦氏と谷口吉生氏による対談が行われた。

Day 1

CDW 展示会開会
CDW Exhibition Door Open

デザインコンペティション
CDW Design Competitoin

対談：槇文彦先生と谷口吉生先生
Conversation by Maki and Taniguchi

Day 2

シンポジウム[スポーツ、体と空間]
Symposium [Sport, Bodies and Spaces]

隈研吾氏による講演
Lecture by Kengo Kuma

テーブルディスカッション
Table Discussion

Day 3

展示会
Exhibition

訪問者賞発表
Students and Visitors Awards

展示会閉会
Closing Down

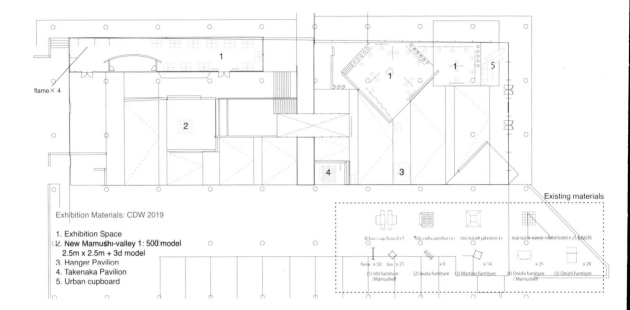

flame × 4

Exhibition Materials: CDW 2019

1. Exhibition Space
2. New Mamushi-valley 1: 500 model
   2.5m x 2.5m + 3d model
3. Hanger Pavilion
4. Takenaka Pavilion
5. Urban cupboard

Existing materials

Urban cup board x1　Tokonoku pavilion x1　Tea house pavilion x1　Mamushi valley 3d model x 25 places

flame　x 50　box x 21　　　x 0　　　　　x 14　　　　　x 25　　　　x 20

(1) Ishi furniture /Mamushell　(2) Iwata furniture　(3) Martino furniture　(3) Onishi furniture / Mamushell　(5) Onishi furniture

1. Exhibition Space

Same as last year, original wooden furniture without joints such as nails were placed at the exhibition. Many visitors came to see 34 architecture works designed by undergraduate and graduate students. On the first day, the CDW design competition was held. It was a good opportunity to show the potential for the relationship between architecture and sports in Mamushi-Valley. After the exhibition, the furniture will be dismantled and will be reused for the next time.

1.展示会場

　去年に引き続き、釘などのジョイントを使わないオリジナルの木家具で展示会場のレイアウトが行われた。今年は修士と学部を合わせて34作品が来往舎に並び、多くの来場者が訪れた。1日目にはCDWデザインコンペティションと学部部門と修士部門でのコンペが行われ、まむし谷における建築とスポーツ施設の在り方の可能性を示す良い機会となった。展示会後、家具は折りたたんでまた再利用する予定である。

2. Mamushi Model

A 1:500 wooden model of Mamushi-Valley was exhibited. Around the model, 3D-printed models were exhibited. This space was made for visitors to understand how the design works which are proposed by students benefit Mamushi-Valley.

2.まむし谷模型

　まむし谷全体の木製模型が1：500のスケールで展示された。周りには、スタジオと製図の授業における作品を3D印刷したものが展示され、提案された作品がまむし谷でどう機能するか、来場者の皆さんが想像できるような展示空間とした。

3. Hanger Pavilion

The idea was to make an exhibition space by using materials in daily life, so this pavilion was made by hangers. This is a flexible pavilion which can be folded and resized easily to fit in to different spaces. Some exhibits can be hanged on the pavilion itself. The combination of the white line of the hangers and the unique shape creates a beautiful pattern.

3.ハンガーパビリオン

日常生活で使われている部材を組み合わせて展示空間を作ることを目指し、ハンガーによる自立型パビリオンを製作した。折りたたみ可能で、場所によって大きさを自由に変えられるフレキシブルなパビリオン。また、物を引掛けて展示できるモニュメントでもあり、ハンガーの白いラインと特有の形が合わさり、きれいな模様を映し出す。

4. Children's Play House

The Children's Playhouse is designed according to the size of children to create a place where kids can gather and enjoy playing. The furniture which was created by the parts taken away from walls and roofs can be easily made by the children themselves. The holes on the playhouse are also designed to make a familiar shape for children.

4.子供プレイハウス

子供プレイハウスは子供たちが楽しく集い、遊べる場所となるよう、子供の寸法に合わせてデザインされたミニ・ベニアハウス。家具は壁と天井から切り出したパーツで子供たち自身がつくれるように工夫されており、切り出した後の穴はさまざまな表情の顔を描き、子供たちからも親しまれるデザインになっている。

5. Urban Cupboard

A movable and foldable pavilion. A famous urbanist Yang Gael's techniques were used for the design, and it is used for fieldwork. This pavilion gives an opportunity to create an open space in the city. During the exhibition, visitors were reading books and posters inside.

5.アーバンカップボード

移動可能な折りたたみ式のパビリオン。都市デザイナーのヤン・ゲール氏の手法を解釈して作られたパビリオンはフィールドワークを実施する際に使われ、街の中でオープンスペースを生み出すきっかけとなる。展示会でも来場者が本やポスターを手に取り、中で読んだり休憩する場面が見られた。

6. Original CDW Bag

An original tote bag given to the visitors. Its aim was to advertise the existence of Keio Architecture to the society. The logo was designed based on the plan of Mamushi-Valley. During the exhibition, many people carried the bag all over Hiyoshi Campus.

6.CDW手提げバッグ

来場者にプレゼントした、オリジナルのトートバッグ。使用してもらうことで慶應建築の存在を世間に広めることを目的に、まむし谷の図面を基にしたロゴがプリントされている。展示会期間中、日吉キャンパスではバッグを持ち歩く人の風景が広がった。

In collaboration with the institute of physical education in Mamushi-Valley, research about the relationship between sports, human body and space were reported. There was a discussion about how sports facility should be opened to the society in the area of Mamushi-Valley.

日吉まむし谷で活動している体育研究所と共同し、今回のテーマである「スポーツと体と空間の関係性」について、建築と体育の分野での報告会が行われた。今後まむし谷という敷地において、スポーツ施設が社会にどう開かれるべきか意見が交わされた。

Yamashita Shohei, Renan Prandini Tan, Olena Kopytina

山下翔平、レナン・プランディーニタン、エレーナ・コピティーナ

Students studying architecture explained that the design of sports facilities and its surroundings can generate interaction with neighbors in urban spaces. From holistic and multicultural views, several analysis were carried out among students studying architecture in Mamushi-Valley. Then students proposed architectural ideas to enhance sports and recreational activities. During the survey process, the students figured out that Mamushi-Valley was divided into 5 areas due to its topography, and roads were paved along the boundary, leading to university faculties. Despite the rich nature and its spatial uniqueness, the nature has become a boundary that weakens the relationship with the valley floor. Thus, one of the projects, Avalanche-scape, proposed to integrate sports facilities with the topography in order to facilitate human activities. The idea also included ideas to minimize environmental burdens and turned out to be a proposal rooted to the region. In order to understand the sustainability of architecture better, another design proposal "Re-stadium" in New York was introduced. This idea is based on the adaptive reuse of the World Cup stadium against the housing crisis. With the contextual survey, the form was inspired by city blocks in Brooklyn, designed to handle high-density environments, maintaining daily activities. After the events, the stands will turn into residential spaces. These approaches help building strong relationship between neighbors and could be a system introduced in Mamushi-Valley also.

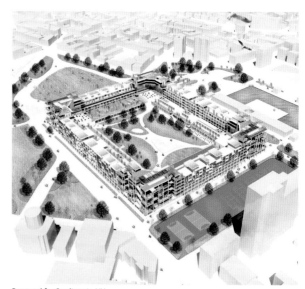

Proposal for Stadium in NY
ニューヨークにあるスタジアムのワールドカップ後の利用提案

建築を学ぶ学生側からは、都市空間におけるスポーツ施設とその周辺へのふるまいをデザインすることが、周辺住民との交流を生み出す機会に繋がるということが説明された。全体的かつ多文化的な視点から、まむし谷において数多くの調査が行われた。その後学生は同敷地において、スポーツとレクリエーション活動発展のための建築提案を行った。調査を進めていくうえで、まむし谷は地形の違いから5つのエリアに分かれており、その間に大学の施設へと繋がる道が舗装されていることがわかった。自然が多く、空間的な面白さが点在しているにも関わらず、その自然が境界となって谷底との関係性を弱めている。それゆえに、一つの提案としてAvalanche-scapeは、スポーツ施設と地形の特徴につながりを持たせ、利用する人々の活動を促す提案となった。そのほかにも環境的負荷を減らす工夫も組み込み、土地に根差した提案となった。より建築における持続可能性を理解するために、ニューヨークで提案された「Re-stadium」という作品の紹介があった。このアイデアはワールドカップスタジアムの適応型再利用という考えをもとに行われ、住宅危機に対する提案となっている。コンテクスト調査から、建築形状はブルックリンの街区からインスピレーションを受け、日常の活動を保ちながら高密度の環境に対応できる設計がなされている。イベント後に取り外されたスタンドは住宅として使われ、周辺との関係構築に寄与する。こういった考え方はまむし谷にも適用可能であると考えられる。

StudioA Proposal in Mamushi-Valley
スタジオ A におけるまむし谷スポーツ施設の提案

History of Mamushi-valley sports

Monya Kazuma   Waki Marumi   Yusuke Maruyama

From the institute of physical education, the history of the gymnasium at Keio University and the fundamentals of Yukichi Fukuzawa's philosophy, "developing human bodies first and minds later" was explained. Currently, Mamsushi-Valley has several facilities all over the nature and has a wonderful environment for sports. However, the facilities built in the 1950s are getting old, leading to bad practicing environment. Another problem was the insufficient barrier-free facilities that apply to the level difference of Mamushi-Valley. Moreover, since each clubs are physically isolated, students in different clubs lack mutual recognition. As a solution, facilities like Kyoseikan (shared facility) are expected to be built in Mamushi-Valley, the facilities consolidating items like shower rooms, cafes, and canteens. Since facilities need more space due to the increase of members taking part in sports, the institute is facing several issues like how to establish a funding source, how to use the existing facility in the future, whether there should be a facility where all activities can communicate.

Discussion   Chairman : Sakai Toshiaki

For discussion about the utilization of a slope in Mamushi-Valley, there has never been a successful precedent building that was built by destroying the topography. Therefore, in Mamushi-Valley without exception, a new core should be designed making full use out of the slope. And of course, athletes shouldn't suffer from the lack of not only design but facilities and rules. Many people mention about opening the facilities to the public during hours when the activities aren't held. This will definitely help increasing the relationship with Mamushi-Valley. Athletes also expect stronger relationship with others, because they want their sports to become more famous. Many discussions focused on how to design facilities that can satisfy both the athletes and the locals by using the lopes.

まむし谷スポーツの歴史

門矢和真　脇成美　丸山優佑

慶應義塾体育研究所からは体育会の歴史と、福沢諭吉先生の教えである「先ず献身を成して後に人心を養う」精神についての説明があった。現在まむし谷には自然の中にいくつかの施設が点在しており、スポーツをするのに適した環境ではあるものの、1950年代に建設された施設を中心に老朽化が進んでおり、練習環境の質が悪化している。また、まむし谷特有の段差によりバリアフリー設備が不十分である。そしてなによりも、各部活が孤立していることから互いの認識が足りていないことも挙げられた。これらに対する解決策としてまむし谷に協生館（共有施設）のようなものができ、シャワールームやカフェ、食堂などの設備が一つに集約されることが望まれている。体育会に所属する部員数も増加しているため、施設の増築が迫られている体育研究所は、資金源の確保、今ある施設を今後どう使っていくのか、全部活が意思疎通できる施設の必要性について考えさせられている。

ディスカッション　司会：坂井利彰

まむし谷の坂を利用して何かできないかという議題に対し、既存の環境を壊して建造物を設計してうまくいった事例はない。まむし谷も既存の坂を十二分に活かす、中核施設の設計が必要である。またデザイン的要素だけなく、設備やルールの関係で選手に負担がかることは絶対に避けなくてはならない。スポーツ施設が使われていない時間帯は施設を公開して地域の人々に使ってもらえると、まむし谷との関係性は強化されるという意見もよく出た。選手にとっては競技の知名度を上げたいこともあって、周りとの関わりを求めている。坂と上手くからめて、スポーツをする側・見る側関係なくスポーツを楽しめる施設が議論の対象となった。

Sports, Bodies and Spaces, convened by Keio Architecture

Neno Kezic, Gabriele Masera, Tadej Glažar, Estanislau Roca

スポーツ、体と空間 建築部門

ネノ・ケジック、ガブリエル・マゼーラ、タディ・グラザール、エスタニスラウ・ロカ

Small Sport facilities of Global Standard

Neno Kezić, University of Split

Professor Neno Kezic introduced some examples of sport facilities used not only for sport events, but also for community sapces. One example was the sport ski center "Podi u Dugopolje", which is a project opened to a small and quiet town. It incorporates not only sport activities, but also other functions such as pedestrian streets for the town and event spaces. The interior design focused on the visual connection in order to facilitate the interaction among the visitors. Another project was a student community center. Keeping the topography, the project connects the buildings with the sport facility, encouraging student activities to occur. The visual connection inside the building also helps the students to find other activities and increases the chance for them to learn something new. At the end, Professor Neno mentioned the importance of designing by thinking how the users will use your project, and the most interesting part is that sometimes, something un-expecting happens. These projects are interesting because of this.

グローバルスタンダードの小規模スポーツ施設

ネノ・ケジック、スプリット大学教授

コミュニティの場としても利用されているスポーツ施設の例を示した。1つはスポーツスキーセンター「Podi u Dugopolje」で、非常に小さく静かな町に開いた施設である。この施設にはスポーツ活動だけでなく、街のための通路やイベントスペースが組み込まれている。内部は視覚的繋がりを意識した設計となっており、人々の間で交流が生まれやすくなっている。もう一つ、学生施設についての紹介があった。既存の地形を残して設計されたプロジェクトは、スポーツ施設と建物を接続しながら学生による活動を誘発する。建物内の視覚的繋がりにより学生は互いの活動に触れ合い、新たな発見のチャンスをもたらす。最後にネノ氏は他の人が使用することを想像してデザインすることの重要性を語った。その上で予期しない活動が発生するからデザインは興味深い。紹介したプロジェクトではそのような経験がみられて面白い。

Sustainable Campus and Recreation

Gabriele Masera, Politecnico di Milano

Professor Gabriele Masera made a presentation about the sustainable campus in Politecnico di Milano and the activities by the university. Due to the deterioration of the campus, a new proposal is coming up. The idea is to have a forest, one level under the ground in the middle of the court yard, and the people walking along the pedestrian can see the students doing something. This kind of design came up because nowadays, students bring their laptops to the terrace or public space for studying. 50 years ago, this scene was unimaginable and the professor mentioned how important it is for designers to change previous recognitions. Professor Masera introduced another project held in Lecco campus. The task was to design the canoe facilities which are one of the most traditional and historical sports facilities in this area. The main problem was that people has forgotten those places since the facility closed to public. The interesting part of this workshop was to connect the lake, the rowing club, and the city by organizing ideas from students who participated from different backgrounds. In the end, each proposal was presented to the people living in the city. This workshop was a great opportunity to share the ideas of the students to the locals and to connect sports culture and the city.

サステナブルキャンパスとレクリエーション

ガブリエル・マゼーラ、ミラノ工科大学教授

ガブリエル・マゼーラ氏はミラノ工科大学の持続可能なキャンパスとそれに基づく活動に関するプレゼンテーションを行った。キャンパスの老朽化に伴い新たに建設される建物は、コートヤード内の一段下がった部分に森林が生い茂り、公共道路からもそこで活動する学生の姿が認識されるよう創られている。この提案では学生がテラスや公共スペースにPCを持って活動に励む光景を想定しており、50年前には到底想像できないものである。設計者は日々変わる常識に合わせて認識を改めなければならない。他にもレッコキャンパスで行われたワークショップが紹介された。レッコにおいて伝統的であるカヌー施設のリノベーションが課題であり、施設が公共から閉鎖されたことを機にカヌー施設の認知度が下がったことが問題として挙げられた。本ワークショップの面白さは異なる文化を持つ学生がアイデアを整理することにより、湖、地元クラブ、街を繋ぐことであった。これらの提案は地元の人々に紹介され、スポーツ文化と都市を繋ぎ、市民と建築学生が交流する良い機会となった。

Sport in Architectural Education

Tadej Glažar, University of Ljubljana

Professor Tadej Gražar made a presentation about the "Bežigrad Stadium" which opened in 1935 and closed in 2008, after the club broke up in 2004. The stadium was deeply related to the urban design in the city, which means the stadium was considered as one part of the city. The stadium is surrounded by trees and has a tower as a symbol which make us imagine the city. However, this wonderful project is about to be demolished due to a private company's idea to build a commercial complex. The neighbors made a strong protest against this competition, and a young architect proposed the idea to reuse the stadium. She did an analysis about the greenery in the stadium and proposed a new master plan for it. The idea is to create various public spaces in the stadium by controlling the density of the plants. Some spaces can be used for picnics, and some work as stages. Professor Tadej also introduced the reuse of a ski field that is opened only for 2 month a year. In this case, a learning center was designed under the ski jumping table that is available during summer. The professor showed the possibility of young architects coming up with wonderful ideas.

Sport Events and Quality of Public Space

Estanislau Roca, UPC Barcelona

Professor Estanislau Roca talked about the history of Barcelona, how the city expanded its range from the seaside to the mountain area, and then also explained the public spaces in Barcelona by showing some example of projects related to the Olympics. Most of the projects had to consider the context of urban design in Barcelona which has unique characteristics. This is because there are possibilities to lose the culture of Barcelona due to the design of the architecture, and also it is necessary to prevent the disaster from the sea. So almost all of the projects had to consider the proper direction from the urban context and had to design the public space following that direction. Professor Roca also mentioned the importance of the urban transportation system by showing the road hierarchy in a super block model, and insisted that all elements should be urban in order to be universal.

慶應教育におけるスポーツ活動

タディ・グラザール, リュブリャナ大学教授

タデイ・グラザール氏は1935年にオープンして、2004年のクラブの解散後、2008年に閉鎖された「ベジグラードスタジアム」についてプレゼンテーションを行った。スタジアムは都市デザインに深く関係しており、都市の一部として捉えられる。スタジアムの周辺には木々が生い茂り、都市を連想させるモニュメントとしての塔がある。しかし、民間企業による総合施設建設のためにスタジアムが取り壊される事態となっていた。この計画に抗議する住民が現われ、ある若い建築家がスタジアムを再利用する計画を提案した。彼女は緑についての分析を行い、スタジアムの新たなマスタープランを提案した。スタジアム内に植物を植え、その密度に変化を加えることでさまざまな空間を作ることができる。それらのスペースは時にピクニックをする場として、時にはステージとして機能する。タデイ氏は他にもスキー場を再利用する計画を紹介した。年に2ヶ月間しか使用されていないスキージャンプ台の下に学習センターを作り、夏期間でも人々が施設を利用できるよう意図されたものだった。こういった事例を通して、若い世代の建築家が活躍する可能性について語った。

スポーツ行事と公共空間の質

エスタニスラウ・ロカ、カタルーニャ工科大学教授

エスタニスラウ・ロカ氏はバルセロナが海辺から山岳地帯へと範囲を拡大していった歴史について話した。そしてオリンピックを背景としたプロジェクトの例に示すことで、バルセロナにおける公共空間についても論じた。ほぼ全てのプロジェクトにおいて、独自の特性を備えたバルセロナの都市デザインについて考慮がなされていた。これは建築デザインによってはバルセロナの文化を失う可能性があり、また海からの災害を防ぐ必要性もあったからである。そのため都市文脈から適切な方向性を抽出し、軸に従って公共空間を設計する必要があった。ロカ氏はスーパーブロックモデルの道路階層を示すことにより都市交通システムの重要性についても言及し、常に普遍的であるためにすべての要素が都市的であるべきだと述べた。

Yoyogi National Stadium by Tange Kenzo

 Today is an important day for Keio and I'm much honored to speak to you on this day. The topic of my speech is "What happened after Tokyo Olympic." Let's go back to the time of 1964 Tokyo Olympic, when I was at the age of ten. My father brought me to the Yoyogi Stadium and I was impressed by the building. That was the first time when I heard the name of Kenzo Tange from him. I decided to become an architect though I wanted to be a veterinarian before. Tange knew what kind of buildings were required at the time when people hoped for the rich and higher quality of life through the economic growth. There were only buildings with two or three stories in Shibuya at the time and tall buildings were not in demand. But, Tange designed a symbolic monument with a unique structural system that two concrete columns suspended the roof and beams. The shape was monumental and he also tried to combine the landscape smartly. Moreover, the period of construction was as surprisingly short as six months and people worked for 24 hours a day. The interior was also amazing and I remember that a swimmer looked up the ceiling and said "wow, it's like heaven. " As I said, Tange is a representative of 1964, the age of concrete and steel, industry and economic growth. I tried to go in the opposite direction in design of the New National Stadium.

丹下健三氏による代々木体育館

　今日は慶應義塾大学にとって重要な日であり、講演する機会をいただき大変光栄です。今日のトピックは「東京オリンピック後」についてです。ちょうど私が10歳だった、1964年、東京オリンピックに時を戻しましょう。私は父に連れられ代々木競技場に訪れ、その建物を見て感銘を受けました。そこで初めて丹下健三の名前を聞いた私は、獣医になりたかった夢を変えて建築家になることを志しました。高度経済成長期を背景に人々が豊かな生活を望む中で、丹下先生はどのような建物が求められているか理解していました。当時、渋谷には2、3階建ての建物しかなく、高い建築物の需要はありませんでした。しかし、彼はコンクリートでできた2本の柱を用いて屋根と梁を吊り下げるというユニークな構造で、象徴的なスタジアムを設計したのです。ランドスケープも上手く調和させました。さらに驚くべきことに工事期間はたった半年で済んだのです。当時施工関係者は24時間体制で働いていたそうです。インテリアも素晴らしく、ある水泳選手の一人が天井を見上げ「素晴らしい。まるで天国のようだ」と言っていたのを覚えています。丹下先生は鉄とコンクリート、経済成長、産業を擁する1964年の代表者です。それに対し私は新しい国立競技場で全く反対の方向で設計しようと思いました。

Yoyogi National Stadium
国立代々木競技場
KENGO KUMA AND ASSOCIATES
隈研吾建築都市設計事務所

New National Stadium Development Project

 Kezo Tange built the stadium of 60m in height, but I managed to design the New National Stadium with 49 m height as a result of a thorough discussion with structural engineers. While Tange was an expert in steel and concrete, we used natural materials as much as possible because I thought the environment was one of the most important issues in 2020. The facade is covered by wood from 47 Prefectures in Japan, which means every community throughout the country is participating in this project. The color and grain of each wood were various and I wanted to show the diversity of Japan in terms of the culture, the climate and the environment. Another important thing is a hint from Japanese historical buildings. This is Houryuji Temple Pagoda, the oldest wooden building in the world. I thought about why this survived more than 1400 years. This is because wood is replaceable, unlike concrete. Most of the units have already been replaced since it was built in the 7th century. Modern engineers recognize the importance of sustainability and replaceability, The Houryuji Temple already represented the idea. Then, the idea was applied to the stadium. Soffits are protected by replaceable wood and small PC which integrate the greenery on the balcony.
 On the top of the building, there is a sky corridor which is open to the public every day throughout the year. The stadium should be open to the community every day even though the sport events

新国立競技場

　丹下先生は60mの競技場を作りましたが、私は構造家の方々と議論を重ねた末、なんとか高さ49mの新国立競技場を設計しました。丹下先生は鉄骨とコンクリートの専門家ですが、2020年の最重要課題は環境問題にあると思った我々は、できるだけ自然素材を使用するよう心掛けました。ファサードに使われている木材は47都道府県から集められたものであり、日本全土のコミュニティがこのプロジェクトに参加していることを示しています。用いられた材の木目と色はさまざまで、日本の文化、気候、環境などの多様性を示したいと思いました。もう1つの重要なことは歴史的な建物からヒントを得ている点です。私は世界で最も古い木造建築である法隆寺が1400年以上生き残った理由を考えました。これはコンクリートとは異なり、木材には交換

Fcade Design
ファサードデザイン
KENGO KUMA AND ASSOCIATES
隈研吾建築都市設計事務所

place only 20-30 times a year. I used natural ventilation instead of air conditioners. The angle and density of the soffit allow good environment in the stadium. We designed landscape like this picture on the terrace which can be used as the public space. The dimension of wood is 100mm, 5mm, and 30 mm, which are the least expensive sizes. In some stadiums, timber with glue gun which is as large as two meters are used, but the size of wood we used in the new national stadium is the same with those in Japanese normal houses. The human scale is very important for even as large buildings as this.

Inside perspective
競技場の内部風景

KENGO KUMA AND ASSOCIATES
隈研吾建築都市設計事務所

できるという性質があるためです。法隆寺は7世紀に建ってから、ほとんどすべての部材が交換されています。現代のエンジニアはサステナビリティと柔軟性の重要性を認識していますが、法隆寺はすでにこれを発見していました。梁は交換可能な木材と小さなPC板によって保護されており、バルコニーの緑とも調和します。建物の上部には年中無休で一般開放される空廊下があります。スポーツイベントが年に20〜30回しか開催されない場合でも、競技場は毎日地域に開放されるべきです。また人為的な空調を避け、自然換気を使用し、梁の角度と密度により、スタジアム内の環境が心地よくなるような設計にしました。写真のように公共に開放されているテラスで風景をデザインし、木材の寸法は最も安い100mm、5mm、30mmものを使用しました。スタジアム建築では、2ｍくらいある巨大な接着剤付き木材を使用する場合がありますが、新国立競技場では日本家屋に用いられる寸法の材を使用しました。このような大きな建物においても、ヒューマンスケールは非常に重要です。

Sky corridor
外周に沿った憩いのスペース「空のテラス」

JR Takanawa Gateway Station

Next year, Takanawa Gateway Station will open before the Olympic. We also use wood for the big station buildings. Some stations were built with wood in my childhood. They were very small but I felt intimate with them. So we decided to use timber for the station as a symbol of the age of ecology and sustainability. Most of the existing station buildings are so big that the space inside is separated from the community. At Takanawa Gateway Station, people can feel the activities of the town which are invited through the station building.

高輪ゲートウェイ駅

来年、東京オリンピックが開催される前に、高輪ゲートウェイ駅が新しく建てられます。このような大きな駅舎にも木材を使用しました。私が子供の頃、いくつかの駅は木造で建てられていて、規模が小さいながらもなにか親しみやすさがありました。そこで私たちは、エコロジーとサステナブルの時代の象徴として木材を使用したのです。既存の駅は大きなものが多く、内部空間が街と分断されがちですが、この駅では街の活動を感じることができます。

Inside Perspective
内観パース

KENGO KUMA AND ASSOCIATES
隈研吾建築都市設計事務所

Nagaoka city hall Aore

These ideas started with Nagaoka City Hall. Nagaoka is relatively a small city with the population of 280,000. We proposed "Doma" space as a city hall. "Do" means earth and "Ma" means space. The competition's requirement was to design "a plaza", but my answer was "Doma" which is a small semi-outdoor space of a farmer's house. People eat, drink and work at doma as part of their daily life, while tatami space is for the ceremony. Materials of the floor were also important. Many plazas in Europe are covered by stone and ceramic tiles which feel very hard and cold. On the contrary, wood feels warm and humid, and people like the texture. The city hall has become a very active space. City halls are usually only for offices, but this works as a community space. It has attracted more than five million visitors since it completed four years ago. The city has hosted an event every day. The arena is a part of the building and open every day to the public including children and Japanese traditional dancers. People can see what is happening in the assemble hall from the Doma space. I remember there was one time when a brass band played in the hall. The assembly hall was used for a different purpose from the city council. This is a good example of the public space in the future. Local materials are reused for every part of the building and some of the furniture and walls are made by locally-produced rice paper. Beautiful silk made by local farmers are used in the design of the entrance counter.

Saint Denis Pleyel Station Paris, France

I have been trying to apply those ideas to some projects in Europe. This is a proposed design of a station which we won the competition of in 2014. You can find it in the today's poster. Saint Denis Pleyel is located in the north of Paris, where most residents are immigrants. It was not a safe neighborhood and a guide even advised me not to walk on the street when I visited there for the first time. He wanted to warn me about danger of terrorism. The city wanted to build a new station in the area and our proposal was a station as a park full of greenery. We wanted to create a park on the roof top with wood, but the client feared that the wood panels would be taken away. The city of Paris appointed an art director for the project, who was a rap musician. I was so surprised because an art director is usually a famous person who has an insight for contemporary architecture. He turns out to be a very strong personality and we are now working with him in an effort to create the station for the community. It was a very good experience for us.

Inside Perspective
内観パース

KENGO KUMA AND ASSOCIATES
隈研吾建築都市設計事務所

シティホールプラザアオーレ長岡

こういったアイデアはアオーレ長岡から始まりました。長岡の人口は約28万人で、比較的小さな街ですが、ここに市庁舎としての「土間」スペースを提案しました。市の要求は「広場」を設計することだったのですが、私はあえて農家によくある小さな半屋外空間を提案しました。畳はお祝い事などに使われる一方、土間というのは、人々が食べたり・飲んだり・仕事したりをする、きわめて日常的な場なのです。素材にも非常にこだわりました。ヨーロッパの広場は石やセラミックタイルで覆われていることがほとんどで、硬くて冷たく感じてしまいます。これに対して、木や土というのは温もりと湿気があるので人々が寄り付きやすい。市役所は普通オフィスとして機能しますが、このホールはコミュニティスペースとしての機能を果たしており、竣工して4年の間に500万人もの訪問者を迎えました。市は毎日イベントを開催しており、建物の一部であるアリーナも、子供や日本舞踊といった活動のために毎日開かれています。土間空間からは会議室の様子を見ることでき、一度吹奏楽の演奏に使われたのを覚えています。会議室が全く想定外の用途として使われたこの事例は、未来の公共空間の良い例であると思います。建物のあらゆる部分には地元の素材が再利用されており、家具や壁にいたっては地元のライスペーパーで作られています。案内カウンターには地元の農家の方が創られた絹も飾られています。

Inside Perspective
内観パース

KENGO KUMA AND ASSOCIATES
隈研吾建築都市設計事務所

サンドニ・プレイエル駅、パリ、フランス

私はヨーロッパでも似たようなアイデアを実践しようと試みています。これは2014年のコンペティションで勝った案件ですが、みなさん今日のポスターで見ていますよね。場所はパリ北部にあるサンドニ・プレイエルという移民のための地区です。私が初めてそこを訪れたときは、案内人から通りを歩かないように忠告されるくらい治安の悪い場所でした。テロの危険性もあるくらい危険だったのでしょう。しかし、市はそこに新しい駅を作りたいと考えており、私たちは緑豊かな公園のある駅を提案しました。当初、屋上に木材を使用した公園を作りたかったのですが、施主はそれらの木製パネルが盗まれるのではないかと恐れていました。またパリ市は、この建物のアートディレクターにラップミュージシャンを任命したのです。アートディレクターというと、現代的な建物にある程度知識を有しているものに依頼するのが普通です。これにはさすがの私も驚きを隠せませんでした。でも蓋を開けてみると、非常に強い個性の持ち主であることがわかって、コミュニティのため、駅の完成を目指して一緒に頑張っています。これは非常に良い経験となりました。

V&A Dundee, Scotland

In Scotland, we designed V&A Dundee inspired by a sea cliff. Before the project started, a community of Dundee was not active at all. People wanted to bring the feeling of the city into the project. What we did is to create a gate which invites people to the water front. The water front used to be totally abandoned and nobody was seen walking along the sea. I came up with an exact idea from the "Torii" Japanese traditional gate in front of a shrine. "Torii" is a kind of a magnet bringing people from the gate to mountain. The concept for the interior design is to create the living room of the city. Museums are usually only for display of the art, but this museum has exhibition rooms on the 2nd floor and spaces for the community, a cafe, shops, and the concert space are on the ground floor. It is covered by wood and the design is different from a white cube which was typical in the 20the century.

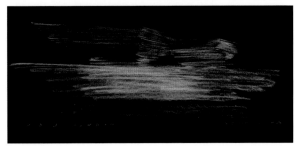

Image Sketch
イメージスケッチ

KENGO KUMA AND ASSOCIATES
隈研吾建築都市設計事務所

The H.C. Andersen's House of Fairy Talies in Odense

In Denmark, we designed the H.C. Andersen's House of Fairy Museum. Odense is also a very small and quiet town. We didn't want to create concrete walls in the town. We tried to integrate the town and the museum, and we didn't build the fence in the border of the museum. The main architectural vocabulary for the museum is a green hedge. Instead of concrete fence, we used a green hedge to integrate them. The main part of the building is a wooden structure. We worked with a landscape designer. The final achievement is that the museum overflows and connects with the city integrating the community.

Facade Design
ファサードデザイン

KENGO KUMA AND ASSOCIATES
隈研吾建築都市設計事務所

ヴィクトリア＆アルバート・ミュージアム、スコットランド

スコットランドでは、海の崖から発想を得てＶ＆Ａダンディー博物館を設計しました。プロジェクトが始まる以前、ダンディーの街は暗く機能していませんでしたが、地元の人々は都市の雰囲気を博物館に取り入れたいと考えていました。そこで私たちは、人々を水辺へと誘うゲートのようなものを設けました。設計する前、ウォーターフロントは廃れていて、海沿いを歩く人は見受けられませんでした。そこで神社の正面に置かれている「鳥居」を思い浮かべました。「鳥居」は人々を門から山に誘う磁石のようなものです。内部デザインのコンセプトは、街のリビングルームを作ることでした。通常の美術館は芸術作品を展示するためだけに機能しますが、この美術館は2階に展示室があります。1階にはコミュニティの場として、カフェ、ショップ、コンサートスペースが設けてあります。意匠としては木で全体を覆い、20世紀に流行ったような白い箱とは異なるものが完成しました。

Facade Design
ファサードデザイン

KENGO KUMA AND ASSOCIATES
隈研吾建築都市設計事務所

ハンス・クリスチャン・アルデルセン美術館、オーデルセン、デンマーク

デンマークではハンス・クリスチャン・アンデルセン美術館を設計しました。オーデンセの街もまた、非常に小さくて静かな町でしたので、街中にはコンクリートの壁を建てたくはありませんでした。街と博物館の統合を図り、博物館の敷地には柵を設けませんでした。このプロジェクトのコンセプトは"緑の生垣"です。コンクリートフェンスの代わりに、緑の生垣を通して街と美術館を統合しようと試みました。建物は主に木造で、ランドスケープデザイナーと協力して外部空間も設計しました。美術館は現在、街にはみ出すようにして繋がることで統合されつつあります。

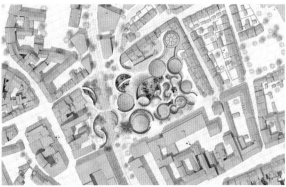

Plan
平面図

KENGO KUMA AND ASSOCIATES
隈研吾建築都市設計事務所

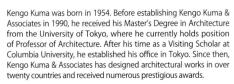

Kengo Kuma

Kengo Kuma was born in 1954. Before establishing Kengo Kuma & Associates in 1990, he received his Master's Degree in Architecture from the University of Tokyo, where he currently holds position of Professor of Architecture. After his time as a Visiting Scholar at Columbia University, he established his office in Tokyo. Since then, Kengo Kuma & Associates has designed architectural works in over twenty countries and received numerous prestigious awards.

隈研吾

1954年生。東京大学大学院修了。1990年隈研吾建築都市設計事務所設立。現在、東京大学教授。コロンビア大学客員研究員を経て、1990年、隈研吾建築都市設計事務所を設立。これまで20か国を超す国々で建築を設計し、(日本建築学会賞、フィンランドより国際木の建築賞、イタリアより国際石の建築賞、他)、国内外でさまざまな賞を受けている。

小林博人
槇文彦・谷口吉生対談「慶應建築の系譜」からの学び

This is a summary of the talk between two notable architects, Fumihiko Maki and Yoshio Taniguchi, held in 2019, with comments and responses from Professor Hiroto Kobayashi who teaches architecture and urban design at Keio University SFC.

The first half of the talk started from how the two architects were inspired and interconnected by Yoshiro Taniguchi, Yoshio Taniguchi's father. Spending a lot of their time under the roof designed by Yoshiro Taniguchi, the two young architects aspired to become architects.

Progressing their career in their own way, Maki and Taniguchi met for the first time at Harvard University Graduate School of Design as a teacher (Maki) and a student (Taniguchi). They learnt a lot from each other and again cut their way open to a new world. Maki traveled all over the world, and Taniguchi worked in Boston.

The latter half of the talk focused on their significant body of work. The two architects have both designed several buildings related to Keio University. The "New Library in Mita", "SFC Campus" were shown by Maki, and the "New Gym of Yochisya, Keio's elementary school", "Mid and High School Complex of SFC" were shown by Taniguchi. It was amazing to see the high quality of study spaces they both shaped for the professors and students at Keio University.

After more elaboration of other works, the talk concluded with their future expectations towards Keio Architecture. They both mentioned the importance of the special bonds that surround us. The two architects met by chance in Harvard, and the buildings we study in are a production of a series of coincidences. These unexpected relationships are what makes us strong.

Though Keio does not have an architecture department, something is about to start through such talks, lectures, and Keio Architecture itself. We have learned a lot from this talk. Now we need to carry on what they have left for us, and to find our way towards the future.

本稿は、2019年初夏に慶應義塾の建築に関わりの深い二人の建築家、槇文彦さんと谷口吉生さんに「慶應建築の系譜」というテーマで対談いただいた内容から私たちが学ぶことを、筆者なりに解釈し、その意味を考えてみたものである。両氏には、ともに慶應義塾の出身であるとともにハーバード大学デザインスクールに学び、また丹下健三先生との関係も非常に深いという共通点がある。両氏と、そして慶應の建築にとって欠かせない存在である谷口さんの父親、谷口吉郎さんの話に触れながら、両氏の今までの建築設計活動、あるいは交遊、そして建築家としての人生について、自らの言葉を交えて紹介していく。この考察が慶應アーキテクチャに限らず建築教育に携わる人たちの一助となれば幸いである。

対談はまず槇さんの曾祖父にあたる槇小太郎さんから始まり、谷口吉郎さんと槇家との関係、そして慶應における吉郎先生の作品へと展開する。

槇・谷口・慶應のつながり
槇小太郎さんは長岡藩の藩士であったが、戊辰の役で負けて会津に行ったそうだ。小太郎さんはもう侍の時代ではない、これからは学問の時代だということで、福澤先生の門をたたいた。その息子が槇武さんで槇文彦さんの祖父にあたる。武さんには五人の男の子がいて、長男が槇智雄さんで、小泉信三塾長のもとで常任理事をやっていた。槇さんの父親は三番目である。
槇さん曰く、
「武は本郷の真砂町に住んでいました。真砂町は本郷三丁目の角から西へ少し行った高台で、東京大学から遠くなかった。それで谷口吉郎先生が、まだ東大の学生のときに時々そこ遊びにきていたときいています。当時からこのようなお近づきがあったのではないかという気がします。」

このことが縁で幼稚舎が天現寺に移転する頃に常任理事の槇智雄さんが谷口吉郎さんに、現在の幼稚舎本館の設計を依頼したそうである。槇・谷口・慶應の繋がりがここから始まった。(幼稚舎本館写真①)。

谷口吉郎さんが最初に設計した仕事は槇本家のお墓だそうだ。氏はお墓とか記念碑の類を、生涯で70件ぐらい設計したので「お墓ばかり設計するので、『博士』より『墓士』と書いた方が合うと言われる」と本人が話していたという。
槇さん曰く、
「私も谷口先生のつくられたお墓に入るはずだったのですが、男の父は子どものいない同じ家系の別の槇家に養子に行ってしまったので、私は私自身が設計したお墓に入ることになっています(笑)。」

谷口吉郎建築に育つ
そして幼稚舎に入った頃の空間の体験を槇さんはこう述壊している。
「私が幼稚舎に入ったのは、まだ幼稚舎が三田にあった頃で三田の門を入りますと坂道になっていて、上って行くと左に旧図書館、右に塾監局がありました。その前が中庭で、私が子どものときはそこから海が見えて、ゆっくりと船が走ったりしていました。非常に印象的な丘でした。その後、二年の三学期に天現寺に移りました。新しい幼稚舎本館は素晴らしい建物で、残りの四年間、大変エンジョイさせていただきました。「君たちはこれから東洋一の学校に行くのだ」と言われました。当時「日本一」の上に「東洋一」という表現があ

①幼稚舎本館写真

②幼稚舎工作室

③幼稚舎理科室

④学生ホール(三田キャンパス)

ったんですね。やはりここに慶應義塾としていい建物をつくろう、という意志が非常にあったのだと思います。

これは工作室②で、先生が上のほうにいて、下のほうで生徒が作業ができる。理科室③もあり、当時としては珍しい机です。このように非常に印象に残るものがあったのが天現寺の幼稚舎です。一番うれしかったのは二階から階段で直接運動場に出られることで、皆、元気に駆けずり回っていました。谷口先生のおかげで非常に幸せな建築環境で小学校時代を過ごさせていただいた。このことは後年建築家になってからも、とてもよかったと思っています。」

槇さんの幼少期が谷口吉郎建築の中で育まれ、それがその後の槇さんの建築設計に少なからず影響していたということは、日本における近代建築の一つの流れがここで形成されたといってもいいのかもしれない。槇さんの記述にある幼少期の空間体験の詳細な記憶が80年経った今でも鮮明に語られるということに驚きを隠せないが、それだけ一人の人にとって幼少期における空間体験がいかにその人の人格形成に関わっているかをも物語っている。

アーティストとのコラボレーション

谷口吉郎さんはよく芸術家とコラボレーションをした。氏が設計した戦後に建てられた三田キャンパスの学生ホール（1949年）④は後に北門付近に移築されたが、1990年代のはじめに撤去された。この建築には猪熊弦一郎さんが壁画「デモクラシー」⑤を描き、現在は壁画だけ移設されて、三田キャンパスの西校舎の生協食堂の中にある。

片や息子の谷口吉生さんは、四国の丸亀にある猪熊弦一郎現代美術館を設計し（1991年）、親子二代の猪熊さんとの協働となった。ちなみに、猪熊さんは有名な画家であると同時に建築家や芸術家のパトロン的な存在であって、丹下健三先生を高松や広島に紹介したり、イサム・ノグチさんを谷口吉郎さんに紹介したのも猪熊さんであったとのことである。

アーティストとの協働ということで顕著なのはイサム・ノグチさんと谷口吉郎さんとのコラボレーション、万来舎（ノグチ・ルーム）である（万来舎と吉郎、イサムの写真、⑥⑦）。慶應ではこのような建築家とアーティストとの協働が様々な場面でされてきた。

谷口吉郎による慶應の建築

谷口吉郎さんは慶應の建築を26棟設計している。慶應病院の病棟（臨床研究棟）や、建築以外では「慶應義塾発祥の地記念碑」という碑が築地明石町にある。

谷口吉生さん曰く「私には3件しか依頼がありませんでしたけど（笑）。」

槇智雄常任理事は、慶應の施設関係のことをやっていて、東急から土地を譲り受けて日吉キャンパスをつくることにも尽力したので、谷口吉郎さんの建築の中の何件かは日吉にある。

日吉の寄宿舎（大学予科寄宿舎）⑧は学生の新しい住まい方を提案している建築で、これができたのは幼稚舎のちょうど一年後、1938年のこと。戦後、進駐軍に接収された。

槇さんは、自身の日吉の校舎との関わりについて
「終戦の年に藤原工大の予科の一年生で日吉に行っていた縁で、非常に思い出がある。（中略）海軍の施設があったので、時々アメリカ軍の艦載機が飛んできて、皆で逃げた覚えがあります。8月15日も学校に行きましたら、先生が「今日は天皇陛下の話があるから君た

ち、帰りなさい」と言われた。そして、友達の家で陛下の玉音放送を聞いたのです。」
と回想している。

敷地の中にはローマ風呂⑨と呼ばれた、丸い大きな風呂がある。そこが戦後は進駐軍のバーとして使われ、そこでダンスが踊られていたという歴史がある。

ハーバードでの出会い

槇さんは、ある日、谷口吉郎さんに呼ばれ、「槇さん、実は息子の吉生が今年からハーバードの建築学科に行く。会ったらよろしく頼む」と言われた。槇さんはちょうどその頃ハーバードでも教鞭をとり始めていたので、実際に教員として赴任したら谷口さんが生徒の一人でいたそうである。1926年のことである。

その当時のことを谷口吉生さんは振り返って
「槇先生とお会いしたのです。英語で話すのが照れくさかったものだから、ずっと日本語で話していたら、授業が終わった後、「なぜ日本語で話すのか。ここはアメリカだから英語で話せ」とクラスメートに怒られた。

もう一つ、「日本人の男性で、あんなハンサムな人がいるのかね」と言われ、僕はだいぶ傷つけられたことを覚えています（笑）。1960年に出て、1964年に帰るまで四年半の間、一度も帰ってきませんでした。当時は今と違って夏休みに気軽に帰ってきたり、ネットや電話で話せませんでした。慶應の工学部の機械工学科を卒業していたので、共通する学科は取らなくてよかったのですが、建築の歴史から法律まで全部やらされて。二年間バチェラーのコース、二年間マスターのコースと、計四年間行きました。寄宿舎は、グロピウスが設計したグラデュエートセンターに住んでいました。」

槇さんも学生時代同じワルター・グロピウスの設計した寄宿舎の二人部屋に住んでいたという共通点も見つかった。

奨学金を得て建築行脚へ

谷口吉生さんはハーバードの大学院修了のときにアップルトン賞という最優秀設計賞を授与され、その賞金で、ニューヨークの、氏が後に設計することになるＭＯＭＡ（ニューヨーク近代美術館）へ友達と回ったという。

一方槇さんは、1968年に、シカゴのグラハムファウンデーションからフェローシップを受け、2年間アジア、中近東やヨーロッパを周った。

谷口さんは卒業後、半年間ほどボストンの建築事務所で働き、帰国。氏曰く、
「一級建築士で日本の建築の大学を出ていない第一号のようです。日本に帰国後、一級建築士の試験を受けようと思ったら、外国の大学の卒業資格ではダメだと言われた。「デザインスクール」という名前だと、日本ではインテリアデザインかファッションデザインなので、建築士の試験を受験できない。「大学のカタログを全部訳して持ってこい」と。それを出したら、「今度は卒業証書を持ってこい」と。持っていったら、当時のハーバードの卒業証書は全部ラテン語で書いてあって読めないので怪しまれましたが、どうにか建築士の試験を受けさせてもらえました。」
と述べている。それに応えて槇さん「私も、もしかしたら幼稚舎にコネで入った第一号かもしれない（笑）。」

日本とアメリカの経済状況が大きく異なる時代の米国での生活は、今の時代とは比べものにならないほどの異文化体験であったことと思う。そこに自ら身を投じ確かな成果を上げてきた両氏が、その後日本の近代建築の発展を支えてきた。世界で活躍する建築家が若い時代にどのような体験を通してその道を進んだか、今の時代の若き建築家の卵たちにも知ってもらいたい体験談である。

現在の慶應義塾の建物を作る

慶應の三田の新図書館⑩が槇さんの初めての慶應における仕事である。建築家の黒川紀章さんが慶應の図書館の設計をやりたがっているという話を聞き

「慶應は自分の縄張りだと思って。ヤクザと同じですね、生まれて初めて営業をしました（笑）。」

と話している。

「石川忠雄塾長のところに行き、「新図書館をやらせていただけますか」と言うと、快く「うん、やりたまえ」と言っていただき、新図書館を設計することになりました。新図書館は大きい建物ですが、プログラムではもっと大きかった。地下５層を書庫にすることで、このくらいで済ませることができたんです。入り口に飯田善國さんの彫刻、それから、宇佐美圭司さんの版画、保田春彦さんの彫刻といろいろなものがあります。ジェニファー・バートレットの大きな壁画もあります。旧図書館は東京大学１期生の曽禰達蔵さんがおやりになった。これが慶應の50周年のときで、僕が新図書館を頼まれたときは、125周年ですから75年たっています。東大の名簿を調べましたら、もちろん曽禰さんは第１期生で、僕は74期生。ほとんど同じ年ぐらいのときにそれぞれ慶應の図書館を設計したんですね。」

幼稚舎の新体育館⑪（1987年）は、谷口吉生さんの設計である。

「これは、私がいちばん初めに慶應の建築に関わらせていただいたものです。どういうご縁かと申しますと、『三田評論』の1976年12月号に、当時の幼稚舎長、川崎悟郎先生と父が幼稚舎の建築について対談している。そして、「次は谷口先生に体育館をお願いすることになるかもしれません」という話で終わっています。それが、父が亡くなったので私のところに回ってきたということです。（中略）これは幼稚舎の設立50周年記念でした。1937年、私が生まれた年に父が幼稚舎本館をつくり、50年後にこの体育館ができました。

次に私が設計させていただいたのが、幼稚舎新館21⑫です。けやきホールという食堂があります。父の幼稚舎の建築（本館、自尊館、百年記念棟など）にはいろいろな様式がありますが、私はできる限り父の初期、1937年当時のモダニズムスタイルでいこうと思い、真っ白な感じの建築をつくったわけです。」

槇さん、谷口さんが慶應義塾の建築の設計を始めたきっかけはそれぞれに異なるが、両氏の慶應に対する思い、そして既に建っている建築やその設計を行った先達に対する尊敬の念を感じ取ることができる。慶應義塾の時代の変遷とともに育まれていった建築の系譜はまさにこのような世代間の意識の継承にあるように思う。

ＳＦＣの建築

槇さんは、

「日吉の図書館をつくってしばらく後、石川塾長に呼ばれ、「今度、藤沢にキャンパスをつくるのでやってくれないか」という依頼がありました。（中略）その頃、他の大学では、何万平米もある大きな建物をつくるのが流行ったのですが、石川塾長から、ビレッジのようなキャンパスをつくってほしい、と言われ、できたのがＳＦＣのキャンパス⑬です。非常に野趣の豊かなところで、正面性はあったほうがいいだろうということで、キャンパスに来る人は正面から入ってくる。また、図書館は、すべての大学の活動の中核的なところです。

キャンパスの南側にある大きなコンプレックスが谷口吉生さんの設計された湘南藤沢中高等部⑭です。」

谷口さんが続いて、

「槇先生が設計なさった大学のキャンパスの中に、中高一貫の六年制の学校として、独自の領域をつくろうと思い、コートハウス的というか、周りを一般教室で囲む構想にしました。そして、中心部分に共用で使う図書館、特殊教室や体育館を置き、教室との間に広場をつくりました。生徒たちが六年間を過ごすために、小さな街のような学校をつくろうと考えたのです。

ただ、問題なのは、コートハウス的にすると増築が難しいことです。「増築はしなくていいのですか」と聞くと、「増築はあり得ない。アセスメントでも法律的にも困難だから」という話だったので、そのようにしたのですが、それから二度増築しています（笑）。校舎の中に広場や路地のような場所をたくさんつくり、休み時間に先生と生徒が話あったり、友達同士が出会ったりできるようにしました。藤沢というところは周りに街がないですから、学校の中で楽しい空間、いろいろな出会いの場をつくりました。

教室⑮の配置は大きなチャレンジでした。通常、学校は全部東南に向いた一列の建築ですが、なるべく賑わいのある空間をつくろうと思い、コートハウス（中庭形式）にしたわけです。そうすると、オリエンテーションがみんな変わってしまうので、教室を一対にして、その間に光庭を設け、そこから自然光を間接的に取り入れている。これは賛否両論があったのですが、あまり大きな問題は聞こえてこなかったので、安心しました。」

と述べている。

ＳＦＣにおける大学と中高の計画は、この二人の建築家のそれぞれの思いが形になった独立した作品の集合であると同時に、二人のコラボレーションの結果としての一つのキャンパスでもある。建設から約25年経った今、このキャンパスのユーザーの一人として感じることは、それぞれの個性は現在でも際立っているものの、それをつなぐモダニズムの律を共有し、そしてそれに大きく育った自然が介入して、キャンパス全体が一つのユニークな世界を作っているということである。そこに後に葉祥栄さんや池田靖史さんらの建築も加わっていくが、それらも包含したSFCの建築文化が醸成されていったのだと思う。

⑤デモクラシー

⑦イサム・ノグチ（左）と谷口吉郎

⑨「ローマ風呂」（日吉寄宿舎）

⑪幼稚舎新体育館

⑥万来舎

⑧日吉大学予科寄宿舎

⑩三田図書館新館

⑫幼稚舎新館21

金沢建築館

金沢市に新しく谷口吉郎・吉生記念　金沢建築館⑯というものができた。金沢市には加賀藩の時代からの歴史的建造物や明治時代のレンガ建築など様々な近代建築もある。谷口吉生さんも鈴木大拙館を設計した。当日対談を聞かれた妹島和世さんも21世紀美術館を市内に設計されている。

「谷口吉郎・吉生記念　金沢建築館」は、谷口吉郎さんが育った家であり、吉生さんも戦争中に疎開した土地に、金沢市が建築の美術館として2019年に建設、オープンした。

常設展示室には吉郎さんの設計した東京の迎賓館の赤坂離宮の和風別館の中の和室と茶室をそのまま復元してある。親子の合作とも言える建築博物館には世代をつなぐ建築への思いが込められている。

槇さんと馬

スライドの最後に槇さんは、自身が90歳になり親しい方々をお呼びしたときに渡したという一枚の絵（この絵⑰）を披露した。

「いちばん左上はハーバード時代の25歳、その下はイランのペルセポリスでの国際会議のときに建築家アルド・ロッシ、ジェームズ・スターリング、ヴァン・アイクとともに。右下が70歳です。上が現在です。

「なぜ、まだ仕事をしているのですか」という質問に対し、「いや建築家はニンジンがあれば追いかけているんです」と答えているんです（笑）。これは谷口さんも、建築家の方は皆、同じだと思うのですね。何かやることがあればこんな馬のように走っている。

ここれを受けて谷口さん、

「これを見たときに、皆さんが「馬は槇さんなのか、施主なのか、スタッフなのか、どれだ」と言っていました（笑）。

慶應建築の系譜をどうつなげるか

慶應の建築は、これからも時代に合わせて更新されていかなければならない。またこれからの社会の要請に対して空間教育とはどのような役割を果たすべきなのか。私たちはどんなことを考え、建築の思考を深めていけばいいのか。これからの慶應に期待する、あるいは慶應がやらなければいけない建築あるいは建築教育について最後に二人から言葉をいただいた。

谷口さんから、

「いろいろなご縁から、私は慶應の建築に関わらせていただきました。最初に父が幼稚舎を設計するきっかけになったのは、槇先生のおじさんの槇智雄さんが父の事務所にいらしたことです。当時、槇智雄さんが父に一言だけおっしゃったのは、「慶應の建築には福澤先生の建学の精神が宿っている。それをぜひつないでほしい」ということだったそうです。その話が私の記憶に非常に残っています。」

槇さんは、

「人生にはいろいろなご縁というものがあり、いま言ったように幼稚舎を私も存分に使わせていただきましたし、その後、谷口吉生さんがハーバードに行ったときに初めてお目にかかりました。非常に

楽しい出会いであったと言えます。それをやはり大事にしていきたいという気持ちは今でも非常に思います。」

慶應でも建築教育というものが少しずつ始まってきている。慶應の建築の系譜というものが、どのような未来になっていってほしいと思うか聞いた。

谷口さんからは、

「慶應には建築学科はないのですが、父から聞いた話では、過去にいろいろな試みはあったらしいですね。日本の場合、建築学科というのは、最初から地震に耐える建築、火事に強い建築という要請からエンジニアリング、工学部に多くは属している。でも、そうするとデザインという分野からは離れていく。

エンジニアリングを求めるのか、それともデザインを指向するのか、両方のバランスがうまく取れた新しい学科がもし慶應にできれば、非常にユニークなものになるのではないかと思います。」

慶應義塾ではまさに今、エンジニアリングとデザインの融合に向けたチャレンジをしようとしており、どういう教育をすれば、そこを育った人たちが社会で活躍でき、社会のためになれるのかを模索しているところである。理工学部でやってきたこと、そしてSFCでやってきたことを、これから両輪にして共同して新しい空間創造のための教育・研究を行なっていくことが重要であり、そこにまた新しい教育分野が入ってくることを目指していきたいと改めて感じた。

今回の対談の内容で特筆すべきことの一つは、一つ一つの建築の作品が、実はそれを取り巻く人と人との縁によって時間をかけて少しずつ紡ぎ出されてきたということである。時代を超えて引き継がれていく人同士の関係を大事にしてきたことが現在の慶應の建築の歴史を作ってきたということができよう。私たちが次の世代に引き継ぐべきは慶應義塾が始まったときに思い描いた理想の教育を心に、その時々に与えられた使命を一つ一つ丁寧に人の繋がりを大切にして果たしていくことにある。そこからこれからの空間創造のあり方を探求していきたい。

この対談において、槇文彦さん、谷口吉生さん二人から慶應建築との関わりについて話しを聞いたが、この歴史を辿りよくその意味を考えることで、私たちにはこれから先に求めるべき未来が見えるのではないかと考えるところである。

（本稿は、2019年7月19日、日吉キャンパス協生館藤原洋記念ホールにて、理工学部創立八〇年・藤原銀次郎翁生誕150周年記念イベントおよび慶應アーキテクチャプロジェクトの一環として行われた、対談「慶應建築の系譜」を編集したものである。司会は小林博人が務めた。）

⑬湘南藤沢キャンパス

⑮湘南藤沢中高等部教室

⑭湘南藤沢中高等部

⑯谷口吉郎・吉生記念　金沢建築館

⑰槇先生の絵

日吉図書館

F

The snapshots from production
of Keio Architecture

FURNITURE1

Mamushi-room Shelf & CDW Exhibition Stand
蝮ルームシェルフとCDW展示会スタンド

All shelves and tables in the exhibition hall are handmade by students. At the same time we also proposed and constructed a sustainable shelf that could also be used for interior decoration of the mamushi room. We did not rely on off-the-shelf ready-made products but designed and produced them by using the facilities in the university.

展示会場の棚や台はすべて学生による手作りのものである。同時にまむし部屋の内装にも使えるようなサステナブルな棚の提案と施工も行った。提案から設計、施工まで外注の既製品に頼ることなく大学内の設備を使用して加工し、試行錯誤しながら製作した。

1 Study by model of room 　　　　　部屋の模型による検討
2 Cutting machine of SFC campus 　　SFC キャンパスの切削加工機
3 Mock-up production 　　　　　　　モックアップ製作風景
4 Sanding of section 　　　　　　　　切断面のサンディング
5 Examination of the size of the stand 　ボードを展示する台の大きさの検討
6 Processing at the Yagami Campus 　矢上キャンパスでの加工
7 Examination of display shelves of books 　本の展示棚の検討
8 Student meeting 　　　　　　　　　学生ミーティングの様子
9 Critique by Mr. Kobayashi of SFC 　SFC の小林先生によるクリティー
10 Critique by Mr. Radovic 　　　　　ラドヴィッチ先生によるクリテ

第9章　レクチャーシリーズ

One of the pillars of emerging Keio Architecture programme is rich guest lectures programme, the aim of which is to diversity inputs and stimulate creative and critical thinking among staff and students. In the years 2018-19 Comprehensive Design Workshop and support provided by the Faculty of Science and Technology and industrial sponsors helped us achieve a truly extraordinary series of visiting lectures by both Japanese and international speakers, the diversity and richness of which is partially presented at the following pages.

　慶應アーキテクチャの中核として、多くのゲストレクチャープログラムがあります。その目的は、生徒はもちろん、教員やその他スタッフにも、多様性に触れ、刺激的、創造的、時に批判的に考える機会を与えることです。2018-2019年度のCDWプログラムでは、理工学部とスポンサーの皆様方のおかげで、日本と海外から実に多くの講演者を招くことができました。簡単ではありますが、この章では各講演の様子を記載しております。魅力的なレクチャーによってさまざまな分野が取り上げられておりますので、是非お楽しみください。

The fusion of space and environmental design 意匠設計と環境設計の融合	Reporter Lecturer	Daisuke Kobayashi　小林大介 Gabriele Masera
Evaluating human scale design in public space 公共空間におけるヒューマンスケールデザインの評価	Reporter Lecturer	Junpei Kawamoto　川本純平 Leonardo Chiesi
The role of engineering エンジニアリングが担うもの	Reporter Lecturer	Yukie Takasu　高須雪絵 Manuela Grecchi
Realizing a complex / complicated design 複雑なデザインの実現を目指して	Reporter Lecturer	Yang Xuang　楊宣 Matteo Ruta
Harmony between the old and new 古いものと新しいものの調和	Reporter Lecturer	Shinichi Nishibori　西堀槙一 Vladimir Lojanica
Understanding the city through drawings ドローイングによる都市の把握	Reporter Lecturer	Shun Kato　加藤旬 Ray Lucas

Revisiting 'The Rise and Rise of the Culture-Led Urban Regeneration' 繰り返し発展する、文化主導による都市再生	Reporter Lecturer	Masahito Motoyama　元山雅仁 Ronan Paddison	
The atmosphere of the city 都市の空気感	Reporter Lecturer	Motomi Matsubara　松原元実 Alison Young	
The essence of "Roji" space 路地の持つ空間の本質	Reporter Lecturer	Norimi Kinoshita　木下規海 Haide Imai	
VR Urban Morphology VR 都市形態	Reporter Lecturer	Zan Krivec　ジャン・クレヴィック Vuk Radović	
Doing Research リサーチとは	Reporter Lecturer	Manca Kosir　マンカ・コシール Davisi Boontharm	
Lecture review レクチャーシリーズを終えて	Reporter	Akitaka Suzuki　鈴木瑛貴	

165

The fusing of space and environmental design
意匠設計と環境設計の融合

Reporter　　Daisuke Kobayashi　小林大介
Lecturer　　Gabriele Masera

Professor Gabriele Masera conducts research on eco-efficiency of buildings, and at the same time captures buildings from the viewpoint of engineering. The topic was about how to design the intermediary spaces between inside and outside when designing architecture with consideration for the environment and energy consumption.

First of all, he showed that more than a third of the EU's CO2 emissions comes from buildings. I learned once again how important it is for European countries, where there is few resources, to increase building environmental performance. In addition, he was very interested in the Japanese word "Fudo(風土)". Contrary to ideas of globalization, he advocated that it is important to think about the architecture within its local natural environmental context. Like the idea of ZEB, we often see buildings covered with solar panels these days. However, Professor Masera insists that architecture should be designed in a way so that it can survive without much energy.

Professor Masera gave "La Tallera" of Frida Escobedo as a good example. There is buffer zone covered by the shadow in between the outside and inside of the architecture, and that space succeeds in mitigating energy consumption very much. Additionally, this space is not only a simple environmental equipment, but also a place that increases the quality of the entire architecture. Through this lecture, I learned the importance to design from both, space and environment.

　ガブリエル・マゼーラ氏は建物の環境効率に関するリサーチを行うと同時に、エンジニアリングや施工性といった工学デザインの視点からも建築を捉えており、今回の講演では環境やエネルギー消費に配慮した建築において、内部空間と外部空間の中間領域をどう設計するかということに焦点が当てられた。

　まず初めに彼が示したのは、EU の CO_2 排出量の 3 分の 1 以上が建築物に由来しているという事実であり、資源が少ないヨーロッパ諸国において、建物の環境性能を向上させることがいかに社会にとって大切かということを改めて感じた。加えて、彼は日本の「風土」という言葉に非常に関心を抱いており、グローバリズムに反して、地域の自然環境に根付いた建築を考えることが大切だと唱えていた。これは、ZEB 化などという言葉と共に単に太陽光パネルをたくさん設置した建物が増えている状況下で、エネルギーを生み出そうとする前にデザインによってエネルギーを使わない設計をすることが大切であるという彼の主張に基づいている。

　具体例として、フリーダ・エスコベドの「La Tallera」に見られるように、外部空間と室内との接続点が影で覆われ、外部より涼しく感じるような中間領域を設けることで、消費エネルギーを和らげるようなバッファスペースを設計することが重要であると述べていた。この空間は単なる環境装置としてばかりではなく、建築の質をさらに向上させるようなデザイン性も兼ね備えており、意匠デザインと環境設計が融合するような瞬間を設計することの意義と必要性を再認識させられる講演であった。

Evaluating human scale design in public space
公共空間におけるヒューマンスケールデザインの評価

Reporter   Junpei Kawamoto   川本純平
Lecturer   Leonardo Chiesi

Professor Leonardo Chiesi gave a lecture about evaluating the human scale in public space design, which in brief, about the relationship of the physical self (health) and (architecture and urban) design. Physical evaluation is the balance of subjective elements, such as intimacy or oppression, and objective elements, such as temperature or humidity of the surroundings. This signifies, as it is clear from vernacular architecture that the optimal architectural method differs between countries or the culture of that region.

For example, in the experiment of P25 mice, many changes were added to the living environment too see the effects coming from it. As a result, the mice that were living in a good environment had a lower risk of getting ill. And the mice which didn't have the opportunity to exercise had a larger risk of getting severely ill. In the case of human, a similar result was noted according to the Tokyo Gas's research on housing supply, which confirmed that 11 to 24 minutes of walking reduces health risks by 12 to 29 %.

One example of an actual architecture that combines architecture and physical design is the "New School University Center" by SOM. This architecture has a staircase that runs along the façade, encouraging various activities within its space. Through this lecture, I learned the infinite possibility of architecture from the aspect of human activities.

レオナルド・キエーゼ氏は公共空間でのヒューマンスケールデザインの評価という題目で話を展開した。それはつまり、デザイン（建築・都市デザイン）と身体（健康）についてである。身体評価とは親密感や圧迫感といった主観的なものと、温度や湿度といった客観的コンディションのバランスから成立する。つまり、土着的な建築に見られるように、国や地域によって異なる文化に応じ、そこで要求される建築的操作も変化する。

例えば、P25 マウス（脳萎縮マウス）の実験では条件設定としてさまざまな生活条件の変更を加えている。結果としてわかったことは、豊かな住環境を与えることで病気を抑えることができること、肥満および運動不足が健康状態に悪影響を及ぼすことがわかった。実際の人間の事例としては大阪ガスの住宅供給に見ることができる。このプロジェクトの結果として、11～24 分間のウォーキングをすることで 12～29% の健康リスクの低減につながることが示された。

実際に建築デザインと人間の行動のデザインが結びついている建築物としては SOM による『The New School University Center』が挙げられた。このデザインは、階段をファサードに沿わせることによってさまざまなアクティビティが階段を通して生まれるという意匠であった。この講義を通して、人間の活動といった視点による建築の大いなる可能性を見ることができた。

The role of the engineering
エンジニアリングが担うもの

Reporter　　Yukie Takasu　高須雪絵
Lecturer　　Manuela Grecchi

With concrete examples, Manuela Grecchi explained about what we should be careful of when we design something. And also the difficulties and the pleasure of design.

Manuela Grecchi says that it is important to analyze things from different perspectives in order to get an optimal answer. In the field of engineering, designers should not only focus on environmental aspects, but also on the cultural and historical aspect of the area. Of course it is important to find solutions considering the environmental impact, and engineers have the responsibility to consider materials and design that saves energy. But at the same time, one needs to listen to what the user's say. One must protect people's community and to imagine the activities happening there. Dealing with garbage, water, inner and outer spaces, etc. is also important. With subsequent analyses, keeping such things in mind, one can reach a high standard sustainable building.

Although we mainly study architectural design, I felt that we were on the same page. For example, we can reduce transportation time and energy by using local materials. The locals will take care of such building better, so we can expect longer use of the building itself. When designing a sustainable architecture, I understood that the key was to think about design and engineering at the same time, through this lecture.

具体的な例を挙げながら、エンジニアとして設計する時に気をつけたこと、難しさや面白さを語られた。

最適な答えを導くためには違う視点から物事を分析することが大切だと語るマニュエラ・グリッチ氏。エンジニアリングの分野でも環境面のみに着目してデザインするのではなく、与えられた敷地の周辺や、その地域の文化や歴史に対するリスペクトをデザインすることも大切であるという言葉が印象に残っている。もちろん環境面の影響を考えた解決策を考えることも大切であり、エネルギーをなるべく使わないマテリアルやデザインを考えることもエンジニアとしての責任である。しかし、それと同時に大事にしないといけないのは、使う人々のコミュニティを守ることやそこでの過ごし方を考えること、ゴミをどう扱うか、水をどう使うのか、内部と外部の空間をどう使うのかなど、その建物を利用する人々の意見を参考にすることである。その意識を持って分析を行うことが、さらに高いレベルでのサステナブルな建築を実現させる。

私たちは建築の分野の中でも建築デザインを主に学んでいるが、私たちにも同じことが言えると感じた。例えば、その土地で取れる素材を使ったマテリアルを選ぶことによって輸送時間を短縮することができるし、その土地の人々は愛着を持って建築を利用してくれる。サステナブルな建築を設計する時に、意匠とエンジニアリング両方の分野でこの意識が統一されることが、より良いデザインの実現に繋がると感じた。

Realizing a complex / complicated design
複雑なデザインの実現を目指して

Reporter   Xuang Yang   楊宣
Lecturer   Matteo Ruta

The lecture started with explaining two words: "complicated" and "complex". Professor Ruta said that when people deal with complicated problems, it's necessary to unfold it and to solve the problems one by one. Architectural design is often a typical complex problem. Every element ought to be redesigned if one other part changes.

The most typical examples comes from Zaha Hadid. Professor Ruta brought many photos and construction details of her famous works, from "Vitra Fire Station" to the "Shanghai Theater". Since there are many curves in the design, the architecture applies concrete structure combined with space frame and curtain wall system. This helps keeping a smooth and light impression at the same time. Besides Zaha's works, the professor presented some other examples to explain how the complex shapes affect public space. One of them was the "Educatorium" in Utrecht by OMA. The Programmatic, spatial, and social deployment planning were amazing. Such open and flexible places provide several opportunities to the visitors.

Another example was the "Maggie's Centers", which are networks of several drop-in centers. This center was built for people suffering from cancer, and "Architectural Placebo Effect" was expected. These buildings were designed by famous architects like, Frank Gehry, Zaha Hadid and Rem Koolhaas. Each center has an open kitchen where patients can gather for a cup of tea, or rooms where they could enjoy the beautiful landscape and so on. The complex inner space design has the power to make people happy.

　講義は "complicated" と "complex" という、2 つの単語を説明するところから始まった。マッテオ・ルタ氏は、建築デザインというのは 1 つの変更に伴ってすべての要素に再設計が要求されてしまう、複雑な問題であると話した。

　最も典型的な例はザハ・ハディドの作品にある。マッテオ氏 は『Vitra Fire Station』や『Shanghai Theater』といった、彼女の名作の写真や詳細図をたくさん紹介した。これらの設計にはたくさんの曲線が含まれており、形態をなめらかにし、軽やかな印象を与えるためにはカーテンウォールやスペースフレームシステムと組み合わせたコンクリ―ト構造を用いる。ザハの作品に加えて、複雑な形態がどのように公共空間に影響しているかを示すためにさまざまな事例を示した。その中には OMA によるユトレヒトの『Educatorium』もある。プログラムや空間、そして社会的な配置計画が建物の中で展開されており、このように開かれていて適応性のある場所がさまざまな人々に多様な居場所を提供している。

　その他の事例として、一連のドロップインセンターを作るプロジェクトである『Maggie's Centres』が挙げられた。この施設は癌に侵された人々を支援するためのもので、建築によるプラシーボ効果を期待して建てられた。これらの建物は、フランク・ゲーリーやザハ・ハディド、レム・コールハースといった第一線の建築家たちによって設計されている。それぞれの施設は患者がお茶を気軽に飲めるようなキッチンやランドスケープ、美しい眺めを楽しむことができる空間を含んでいる。これらの建物の内部空間における複雑性は、人々の気分を高めてくれる可能性も秘めている。

Reporter   Shinichi Nishibori   西堀槙一
Lecturer   Vladimir Lojanica

Professor Vladimir Lojanica gave a lecture about his involvement in designing a mixed-use building. A "Business-Commercial and Hotel Center Rajićeva", located in the historical commercial district of Belgrade, Serbia, surrounded by buildings of considerable historical buildings. The site was even more unique because it was on the top of the hill too.

"Patience", "persistence" and "hard work" were terms repeated throughout the lecture. The professor expressed how tuff his 20 years of work was to complete this large building. He told us how difficult it was to talk with his clients, all the 17 design ideas he made, starting all over the planning from scratch because of the change in law, and taking care of 2000 detail design. Through his talk, I understood what it means to design such a big facility like this.

One of the most interesting topics of his talk was about the harmony between the old and the new. Due to the historical character of its site, many ancient artifacts, for example a vase from the 7th century, were discovered just by digging a meter. Considering this situation, Professor Lojanica decided to design the building in   order to show the old remains. An old bridge is placed beneath the current courtyard and an old courtyard can be observed through the new glass floor. Also, the glass facade blends in with the existing stone architecture and creates a harmony between the beauty and the history.

Despite all the difficulties, I was very impressed to hear how happy he was when his clients said they were 100% satisfied with the outcome, and to see the many visitors using the architecture after the construction.

ブラディミル・ロジャニカ氏は昨年 7 月に完成したベオグラードを敷地とする文化センター、ホテル、商業を含む複合施設『Business-Commercial and Hotel Centre Rajieva』の設計に携わった話をした。敷地はベオグラードの歴史ある商業地区に位置し、周囲を歴史的建造物に囲まれ、丘の上という地形的特性も相まって非常に特徴がある地域であった。

レクチャーの中では 2"patience" と "persistence" と "hard work" という言葉が繰り返し使われた。クライアントとの交渉、17 ものデザイン案、設計途中での法制度の変更に伴う設計のやり直し、複雑な設計に対する 2000 を超えるディテールの詰め、完成にいたるまでの 20 年間で味わった苦難について語られ、大きな施設の実施設計に関わるということは非常に大変なことであることが伝わった。

レクチャーの中で興味深かったのは、新しいものと古いものの調和の話である。敷地は歴史的な建築物が周囲に残る場所であり、地下を 1m 掘るだけで 17 世紀の壺などを含んだ遺跡が発掘されたという。そこでは、遺跡をあえてさらすような設計をした。現代の広場の下に橋やガラス張りの床を通して、広場の遺跡が見える。また、ガラスでできたファサードを石造の既存建築物とうまく調和させることで、美しさと過去との調和を図ることに成功している。

実務設計の大変さが大いに伝わったレクチャーであったが、最後にクライアントが 100%満足してくれたこと、デザインが実際に人々に利用されていることに非常に喜びを感じていると話していたことが印象に残った。

Understanding the city through drawings
ドローイングによる都市の把握

Reporter   Shun Kato   加藤旬
Lecturer   Ray Lucas

Professor Ray Lucas's lecture was about hand-drawings. With very attractive slides with many beautiful hand drawings, he talked about the meaning of drawings. The first thing he pointed out was the importance of memorizing to draw through your hands, but not through your brain.

Professor Lucas has been doing various experimental attempts with his drawings. For example, he tried to place a frame on one scenery to increase visual sensitivity. Though this kind of experimental attempt, he keeps on trying to expand the range of new expressions.

One of Professor Lucas's purpose of visiting Japan is to conduct an anthropological survey by drawing Sanja Matsuri in Asakusa. At first, he recorded the activities that were performed in public spaces with pictures and videos. Later on, he recorded the surrounding situation and behavior of the people participating in the festival by drawing them. After the drawing, he tried to connect his memory and urban structure by mapping the activities.

Although there are various methods for researching the city, I learned the importance of hand drawing, which is something closely related to our body.

　レイ・ルーカス氏の講演は彼が得意とする手描きドローイングがもたらす意味についての講義であった。たくさんの魅力的なドローイングを随所に散りばめた、視覚的に魅力的なスライドが印象的であった。彼は最初に、実際に手を動かすことで、頭の中で認識するのではなく、筋肉の動きとして描くことを記憶することが大切であると語った。

　彼はドローイングに関してさまざまな実験的な試みを行ってきており、例えば額縁のようなフレームを景色の中でかざすことで、目に見えるものの感度を高める試みを行うなど、常に新しい表現の幅を広げようとしている。

　また彼は、来日の目的の１つとして、浅草の三社祭のドローイングを行い人類学的な調査を行っていることを挙げている。パブリックスペースで行われている活動を写真や動画で記録し、その後、ドローイングによって祭りに参加している人々や神輿、テントなどあらゆるものの活動や状態を記録する。そこからマッピングを行うことで都市と自身のドローイングや記憶を結びつけていた。

　都市のリサーチにはさまざまな手段があるが、手書きドローイングというアナログながら身体に密接に結びついた手法の大切さを認識でき、非常に刺激的な講演であった。

Reporter	Masahito Motoyama 元山雅仁
Lecturer	Ronan Paddison

Mr. Paddison Ronan, a Professor teaching geography in Glasgow University, gave a lecture about the role of culture for regenerating cities. The Professor, who wrote a book titled "Culture-Led Regeneration" in 2007~2008, firstly mentioned about how dramatically culture has become, not just understanding the nature of urban cities, but how to regenerate them in certain ways. About a hundred years ago, culture was only a projection of the city, indicating for instance, music, dance, art, or life style. These days, however, culture has become such an elastic term. It is associated with economy, and effecting the key issues for urban regeneration. Culture is becoming something for defining a rich, shared identity among the citizen, so he encouraged the students to think of culture as an important tool to analyze cities. At the latter half of the lecture, the professor showed how public art, a particular mode of cultural representation that has gained currency in the redesigning of urban spaces, can contribute to place-making, in Glasgow, England. Within several examples, he has explained how a certain "space" can be recognized to people through public art. And he stressed that "Space" becomes a "Place" when it becomes something special for someone. Professor Ronan has focused most of his career on culture-led urban regeneration in European countries, but is sure that this development of culture will and is happening in Asia too. He finished the lecture, by telling future urbanists and architects to re-think what culture is about in urban cities.

地理学者としてイギリス・グラスゴー大学で教授を勤めるローナン・パディソン氏は、都市が再生するうえでの文化の役割について語った。2007 年〜 2008 年にかけて、「文化主導による都市再生」という著書を出版しているローナン氏は近年、文化が都市の性質に通じているだけでなく、さまざまな方法で再生させる存在として益々注目されていると言う。100 年前の歴史をみるに、文化は都市を投影するためだけの存在であり、音楽・ダンス・芸術・生活スタイル等、さまざまな物事を指してきた。しかし近年、文化は経済レベルにまで影響をおよぼす実に多義的な言葉となり、都市再生の鍵を握るまでに力を持つようになった。文化は都市に住む人々の間に、豊かで共有されたアイデンティティーを創出する手段になりつつある。是非文化を、都市を分析する上での重要なポイントとして認識してほしいと語った。講義の後半からは、イギリスの都市グラスゴーを中心に、文化を表現する上で代表的なパブリックアートが、実際にどのようにして都市の再生に貢献してきたか、具体的事例を挙げて紹介された。さまざまな事例の中でローナン氏は、ある「空間」がパブリックアートを通して人々の記憶に残り、「場所」として認識されることを説明した。「空間」は誰かにとって意味あるものとなった時、初めて「場所」となることを強調した。今まで主に西欧諸国に着目してきたローナン氏だが、今後アジアにおいても文化が都市に与える影響はますます大きくなるという。今後の都市創りを担う若い世代に、文化の影響力を再度考えてみてほしいという言葉を残し、講義は終了した。

The atmosphere of the city
都市の空気感

Reporter Motomi Matsubara 松原元実
Lecturer Alison Young

At first, Ms. Alison explained about how to visualize space. The first method was about using diagrams. She stressed that the affinity of those diagrams and the city itself has to be strong in order to show the space clear enough. The second method was about maps. For this method, she mentioned that it is the difficult to draw without any prejudice. In many cases, the power of the authority comes in, so the information is biased in way. A good example of this is where we decide the middle of the world. This is a problem that differs from country to country. Moreover, the earth itself has an ellipse shape, so drawing the earth on a rectangle paper doesn't make any sense geometrically and geographically. And the biggest flaw of making a map is that it can never express the details, affection of human scale and the atmosphere that drifts around the city.

Than the lecture moved on to another theme which was about affection. Affection, in this lecture, referred to the exact moment when a person perceives something. To put it in other words, it is the action of associating things or encouraging emotional feelings, and she has explained that some cities address to public design by using this power of affection. Next she mentioned about atmosphere, which in her words, is a collective product of several experience. She said that this is one of the most important theme for future city / architectural designers to tackle. Should designers keep the city's atmosphere as it is or completely change it? It's really up to them. In any case, it is important that the atmosphere itself has to exist in the context of social and economic backgrounds.

まず、アリソン・ヤング氏はいかにして空間というものを可視化させるのかを説明した。一つ目の方法は、ダイアグラム的な表示形式を取ることである。ダイアグラムの元となるモデルと都市自体の親和性があるかどうか、そこについては熟考する必要があることを強調した。次に地図を書くことを挙げたが、平坦であることを短所としている。そして地図自体にはその製作者、往々にして権力当局の誘導したい方向にバイアスがかかってしまう、つまり情報の選別が起こってしまう。例えば、世界地図の中心をどこに据えるのかは国によって異なることなどが挙げられる。そして地球は楕円であり、世界地図が長方形で表されること自体が幾何学的にも地理学的にも正確ではない。そして最も大事なのは人間レベルの細かいディテール、アフェクション、そして都市に漂う空気感、これらが表象されないことだ。

なお、アフェクションは人が何かに気づく瞬間のことを指している。そのように、物事を連想させたり、情動を促したりするアフェクションの作用を利用して、一部の都市ではさまざまなパブリックデザインに取り組んでいる。次に空気感について語ったヤング氏は、これを集団的な経験の産物であるとしている。この空気感を演出、デザインすることは、都市・建築デザイナーにとって重要なテーマの一つとなる。都市の既存の空気感を果たして変えるのか、それともそれを保つのか、それ自体も大きな命題の一つとなっている。そして何よりも重要なのは空気感そのものが、社会的、経済的なコンテクストを背景として存在し得るものであることだ。

The essence of "Roji" space
路地の持つ空間の本質

Reporter   Norimi Kinoshita   木下規海
Lecturer   Haide Imai

Ms. Haide's lecture was about "Roji" space. By showing several examples in Japan, she explained about how Roji is recognized by people and how much influence it has to Japanese cities. Roji space arises from plans to make city blocks for the "Nagaya" style houses typical for Japanese residences. Roji functioned as private and public space at the same time, creating a common space peculiar in Japan. Things like outdoor units, tables and chairs from the café called "Afuredashi", produces its own atmosphere. The special definition of Roji has changed from time to time, especially between Showa Era and Heisei Era, since big development business or apartments appeared. Unfortunately, Roji space has shrunk with these new types of urban planning. The social definition of Roji is a space for daily life and productive activities that changes with the time zone, and even for Matsuri events too. She gave some examples like "Taninaka Ginza" and "Kagura-Zaka" by showing many photos of how several activities were mixed up in Roji space. At the Q&A session, one student asked about the strongest characteristic of "Roji". She said the answer was hidden in the mixture of several activities, such as everyday life of the neighbors. But at the same time, she mentioned that this wonderful mixture is disappearing recently. All the activities that use to happen at the Roji, is now being replaced by SNS. When names or words become commercialized, it becomes really difficult for the power of Roji to appear in real space. Is Roji just going to be something for us to remember our history? Maybe it's time for us to re-think about the space and value that Roji has.

法政大学にて指導しているハイデ・イマイ氏の講義では、"路地"の存在が日本都市に対してどのような立場にあり、都市社会にどのような影響を与えているのかを事例を元に紐解いていった。"路地"は元々長屋による街区計画から生じており、住居地区ではプライベートとして使われ、時には公共空間のように住民で共有され、日本特有のコモンスペースとして機能していた。道にはみ出す室外機や居酒屋のテーブルなどいわゆる"あふれだし"が路地の空間を特異な空間に仕立て上げる。路地の空間的定義は時代を超えて変化しており、特に昭和から平成にかけて開発事業やアパート建設により"路地"の規模が小さくなっている。社会的定義の要素としては時間帯によって変わる日常生活と生産的活動の場、時には祭りなどの町のイベントとしての空間となる点が挙げられる。イマイ・ハイデ氏は谷中銀座や神楽坂などの事例を挙げ、さまざまな活動が路地空間において交ざり合う様子を紹介した。質疑応答では"路地"の一番の特徴は何かという質問に対し、"路地"というのはコマーシャルだけでなく住民やカフェなどさまざまな要素が交わってできる空間であって日本都市の良い点であるが、現代ではそのような混在が減っていると答えるイマイ・ハイデ氏。路地でさまざまな活動が広がりそれ自体が世間に活動を示すものだったが、今となってはその活動が消え、SNSを通じて社会に発信されるようになったのだ。名前や字だけが商品化し世間にあふれ出ていく現代では実際の空間に路地のポテンシャルは生かされていない。路地は昔の活動の記憶のためだけにあるのか、私たちは路地のもつある種特別な空間とその価値について再度考えていかなければいけない。

VR Urban Morphology
VR 都市形態

Reporter   Zan Krivec   ジャン・クレヴィック
Lecturer   Vuk Radović

A lecture on the topic of Urban Morphology was conducted by Vuk Radović, who is researching architecture and urban design at Keio University in Kanagawa. With his expertise and experience, he explained what is Urban morphology, how to approach it, and the main elements of Urban morphology. Urban morphology is a term that combines the concept of urban with the study of morphology. "urban" means city, and "morphology" which is also a combination of morphe and logia, so urban morphology means general sense of shape, form, external structure of arrangement. Several approaches to urban morphology has been conducted in many countries since the old days. In Aristotle's metaphysics, from which the Italian school derives its theory, there are four stages of causality; reading, projecting, building, and dwelling. The projecting part can be understood as the concept of a unique design of an architect, designer, craftsman. The building process is the physical construction of a house through material. Dwelling part is the process of the house as object, the completed articles. Through dwelling the object enters the social conscience of a culture. Most important thing in this part is the dwelling must be fit for purpose. Then reading part is understood as the priori notion of a thing. Through building of objective buildings, this initial stage evolves. Thus in theory every advancement within architecture as building loops back into the cultural reading of a region. As a conclusion, the type-morphology approach to urban morphology is 1) general theory within which further investigation can be undertaken, 2) It follows a techno-deterministic or materialist objectivist logic, 3) The territorial scale, which can be seen as the 'cultural setting' as the all encompassing ultimate scale. Finally, the lecture was concluded with this throw; what if we begin at territory first and work our way down.

　都市形態のトピックに関する講義は、神奈川県の慶應義塾大学で建築と都市デザインを研究しているヴック・ラドヴィッチによって行われた。彼の専門知識と経験をもとに、彼は都市形態とは何か、アプローチ方法、都市形態の主要な要素について説明した。都市の形態は、都市の概念と形態の研究を組み合わせた用語である。「都市」とは街を意味し、「形態」とはモーフィングとロジアを組み合わせたものであるため、都市の形態とは、一般的な形、形態、配置の外部構造を意味する。都市形態へのアプローチは、多くの国で長年にわたって試みられた。イタリアの学校が理論を導き出したアリストテレスの形而上学には、因果関係の４つの段階がある。読書、投影、建築、住居。投影部分は、建築家、デザイナー、職人が心に抱いているユニークなデザインの概念として理解できる。構築プロセスは、材料を介した家の物理的な構築である。住居部分は、対象としての家、完成品のプロセスである。住むことにより、オブジェクトは文化の社会的良心に入る。この部分で最も重要なことは、住居が目的に適合しなければならないことだ。それから、解読部分は事物の先験的な概念として理解される。客観的な建物の構築を通じて、この初期段階は進化する。したがって、理論的には、建築としての建築のあらゆる進歩は、地域の文化的解読にループバックする。結論として、都市形態へのタイプ形態アプローチは、１）さらなる調査を行うことができる一般的な理論、２）テクノ決定論的または唯物論的客観主義の論理に従い、３）領域スケールは「究極の規模をすべて網羅する文化的環境」である。最初に領域から始めて、これまでの作業を遡って行くとどうなりますか？という問いかけで講義は締め括られた。

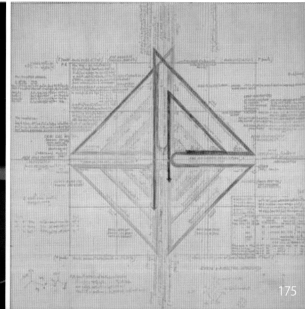

Doing Research
リサーチとは

Reporter   Manca Kosir   マンカ・コシール
Lecturer   Davisi Boontharm

A lecture on the topic of doing research was conducted by prof. Davisi Boontham, who is teaching architecture and urban design at Meji University in Tokyo. With her expertise and experience, she explained what research is, how to approach it and the main elements of developing the theme. The process of doing research starts with asking the research question and formulating the topic in a question form, performing a literature review in order to define the theoretical framework. As she stated, the importance of the second part is designing a research method to answer the research question, by collecting quantitative and qualitative data. And at last, through different kinds of analysis, we need to create a synthesis as well as present the work in a visual and textual way. The professor described the structure not as sequence of steps, yet an interlacement of elements. Setting a goal of research, knowing what are the small questions-hypothesis, the large questions, or problems that the research addresses, knowing to whom the research is important, what can it contribute, the importance of asking quantitative and qualitative questions, ways of analyzing and presenting data are all important aspects of the process of doing research.

明治大学で建築・都市デザインを教えるダビシ・ブンタム氏より、リサーチの仕方に対する講義が行われた。彼女の専門や経験から、リサーチとは何か、どのようにして行うか、そしてテーマを発展させるうえでの主要素について説明があった。リサーチの過程はまず、リサーチ上の疑問を自分に問い正し、質問形式でトピックを定式化し、文献調査から理論的枠組みを決めることから始まる。次に、量が多く質の高いデータを集めることで、リサーチ上の疑問を解決する手法を計画することが大切であるという。そして最後に、多種多様な分析を通して、結果を文章や図・写真等を用いて統合すべきであると説明した。また、これらを連続した段階として捉えるのではなく、折り重なった要素として捉えることが大切であると話した。リサーチの目標を設定すること、細かい質問と仮説を把握すること、大きな疑問や問題が何なのか、誰にとって自分の調査は重要なのか、何に貢献できるのか、量と質の観点から考える重要性、プレゼンするデータの分析方法、全てが大切であるということがわかった。

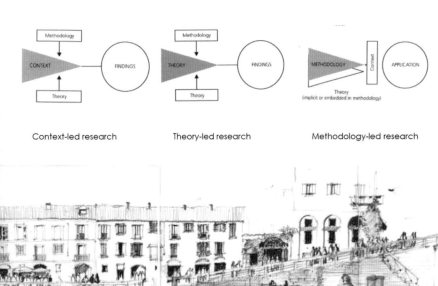

Context-led research   Theory-led research   Methodology-led research

The lecture series by invited lecturers from various discipline, profession, and countries, is becoming one of the core activities in architecture education at Keio University. It is a wonderful how we can discuss various issues coming from home and abroad, free from the division of academic fields and customs, even though Keio doesn't have an Architecture department.

The Lectures for the 2018-19 became a big input for the design activities around Hiyoshi Campus which is familiar for Keio students. 2 Studios, "Seizu III" for Undergraduates and "StudioB" for Master Students were held as a part of 「Comprehensive Design Workshop for the Athletic and Recreational Facilities of the Hiyoshi, Shimoda and Yagami Campuses」. I heard that the lessons were meaningful from many of the students who took part in them. This year, students were provided with an opportunity to acquire knowledge from various disciplines, professions, countries and, particularly in relation to the design studio activities, to interpret and integrate these inputs to concrete proposals for the Hiyoshi Campus and the surrounding area, where students spend their university life, with real, live experiences.

I hope this type of lecture series continues in coming years, becoming an open platform to discuss future architecture and urban spaces, overarching different scales, disciplines and culture. In the end, I would like to thank all the lecturers who gave us these significant lessons.

さまざまな分野・地域で活躍されている講演者の方々を招いてのレクチャーシリーズは、慶應義塾における建築教育の軸の１つとなりつつある。建築学科をもたず、関連する教育の歴史も他大学に比べて短い慶應義塾ではあるが、学問分野の境界や慣習にとらわれず、さまざまな視点を国内外から持ち込んで議論できるという環境は、１つの大きな魅力であると感じている。

2018-19年度のレクチャーは、日吉キャンパスとその周辺という身近な場所を対象とした設計課題へのインプットが鍵となった。「Comprehensive Design Workshop for the Athletic and Recreational Facilities of the Hiyoshi, Shimoda and Yagami Campuses」の一環として、学部４年生の「空間設計製図III」と大学院の「建築設計スタジオB」の２つの設計演習が行われたが、多くの学生から、これらのレクチャーが大いに参考になったと聞く。新しく得た視点や概念なども、それぞれが学生生活を送り具体的な体験を積み重ねた日吉という地域に当てはめて検討することで、よりリアリティをもって理解することできる機会となったのではないかと思う。

このようなレクチャーシリーズはこれからも継続していくと思われるが、理論と実践、さまざまなスケールや分野、地域や文化などを横断しながら、新しい建築・都市空間の在り方がより活発に議論されるプラットフォームとなることを期待している。最後に、有意義なレクチャーをしていただいた講演者の皆様にお礼を申し上げます。

F

The snapshots from production
of Keio Architecture

FURNITURE2

CDW Exhibition Stand
CDW展示会スタンド

All shelves and tables in the exhibition hall are handmade by students. Designed and produced on a human scale, not only the exhibition, but also the visitors and local residents were involved in the exhibition.

展示会場の棚や台はすべて学生による手作りのものである。人のスケールで設計・製作を行い、展示だけでなく、来場者や地域住民を展示に巻き込み賑わいが生まれた。

第 10 章　プロフィール

The list of participants in CDW included (in alphabetic order)

CDW　メンバー

Visiting Lecturers

Shigeru Ban	坂茂
Davisi Boontharm	ダビシ・ブンタム
Motoo Chiba	千葉元生
Leonardo Chiesi	レオナルド・キエーゼ
Tadej Glažar	タデイ・グラザール
Manuela Grecchi	マニュエラ・グリッチ
Haide Imai	ハイデ・イマイ
Hiroyuki Ito	伊藤博之
Neno Kezić	ネノ・ケジック
Katsuhito Komatsu	小松克仁
Tetsuo Kondo	近藤哲雄
Olena Kopytina	エレーナ・コピティーナ
Kengo Kuma	隈研吾
Vladimir Lojanica	ブラディミル・ロジャニカ
Ray Lucas	レイ・ルーカス
Fumihiko Maki	槇文彦
Yusuke Maruyama	丸山優佑
Gabriele Masera	ガブリエル・マゼーラ
Kazuma Monya	門矢和真
Ronan Paddison	ローナン・パディソン
Renan Prandini Tan	レナン・プランディニータン
Vuk Radović	ヴック・ラドヴィッチ
Estanislau Roca	エスタニスラウ・ロカ
Matteo Ruta	マッテオ・ルタ
Takumi Saikawa	齋川拓未
Toshiaki Sakai	坂井利彰
Satoshi Sano	佐野哲史
Kazuyo Sejima	妹島和世
Takashi Suo	周防貴之
Yoshio Taniguchi	谷口吉生
Narumi Waki	脇成実
Alison Young	アリソン・ヤング

Keio Professors

Jorge Almaźan	アルマザン・ホルヘ
Akira Haseyama	長谷山彰
Kohei Itoh	伊藤公平
Tatsuya Kishimoto	岸本達也
Hiroto Kobayashi	小林博人
Akira Mita	三田彰
Eiji Okada	岡田英史
Darko Radović	ダルコ・ラドヴィッチ

Keio General Staff, led by

Yuri Kajihara	梶原佑理
Kenichiro Kuryu	栗生賢一郎

Students

Gabriel Chatel	ガブリエル・チャテル	Keitaro Onishi	大西慶太郎
Alice Covatta	アリーチェ・コヴァタ	Yusuke Ono	小野裕介
Mannon Ellie	マノン・エリー	Ilham Ras	イルハム・ラス
Ivan Filipović	イヴァン・フィリポヴィッチ	Takuomi Samejima	鮫島卓臣
Akari Hara	原明里	Satoshi Sano	佐野哲史
Maroya Harigaya	針谷円	Daiki Sekiguchi	関口大樹
Ryota Ibaraki	茨木亮太	Hiroki Shigemura	重村浩槻
Yumi Ishii	石井結実	Shunsuke Shimizu	清水俊祐
Kyoko Ito	伊藤京子	Kyoko Suganuma	菅沼響子
Itaru Iwasaki	岩崎達	Akitaka Suzuki	鈴木瑛貴
Amami Iwata	岩田あま美	Koki Suzuki	鈴木浩貴
Francisco Javier Celaya Maron	フランシスコ・ハヴィエール・セレヤ・モロン	Yukie Takasu	高須雪絵
Shun Kato	加藤旬	Yuna Takeda	武田有菜
Junpei Kawamoto	川本純平	Yuichi Tatsumi	巽祐一
Norimi Kinoshita	木下規海	Yuki Wada	和田雄樹
Daisuke Kobayashi	小林大介	Shohei Yamashita	山下翔平
Manca Kosir	マンカ・コシール	Yuko Yamashita	山下裕子
Zan Krivec	ジャン・クレヴィック	Muxi　Yang	楊沐渓
Deric Low Seong Hee	デレク・ロウ・セオウ・ヒー	Xuang　Yang	楊宣
Daiwei Lyu	ダイウェイ・リュ	Ayano Yasunaga	安永彩乃
Ayumu Magome	馬籠歩	Yoshitomo Yonamoto	要名本義朋
Mayu Masuda	増田真由	Sanja Zonja	サーニャ・ゾーニャ
Motomi Matsubara	松原元実		
Mayuko Mikogami	御子神繭子		
Kousuke Miyano	宮野公輔		
Yuki Mori	森祐樹		
Mei Morimoto	森本芽衣		
Yoshihisa Moriya	守屋嘉久		
Masahito Motoyama	元山雅仁		
Yusuke Nakagawa	中川雄介		
Shinichi Nishibori	西堀槙一		
Hiroshi Ohara	小原寛史		

街をつくる人に未来を描く力を

日本で最も多くの1級建築士を輩出し続けている学校です。

We are the school which continuing to produce
the largest first-class architectures in Japan.

令和元年度 1級建築士
学科・設計製図試験
全国 合格者占有率

59.9%

合格者数 3,571名中／
当学院現役受講生 2,138名
<2020年2月12日現在>

総合資格学院の合格実績には、模擬試験のみの受験生、教材購入者、
無料の役務提供者、過去受講生は一切含まれておりません。
合格者数は、(公財)建築技術教育普及センターの発表による。

NEWS
建築士法
改正

令和2年度から新しい建築士試験がスタート!

建築士の高齢化などを背景に、建築士法が改正されます。
受験資格や実務経験が見直され、特に若い人の受験機会の増加・早期化を図る内容となっています。

▶実務経験がゼロでも受験可能に!

改正前は受験要件として扱われていた実務経験が、改正後は免許の登録要件となります。つまり、大学、専門学校等において指定科目を修めて卒業すれば、卒業の年に1級建築士を受験できます。合格すれば2年の実務経験で免許登録が可能。実務経験年数は試験前・後で通算できます。

▶学科試験合格の有効期限が3年から5年に伸長!

改正後は、学科試験合格後に引き続いて行われる4回の建築士試験のうち2回(学科試験合格年度の設計製図試験を欠席する場合は3回)において学科試験が免除されます。

▶実務経験の対象実務が拡大!

近年、建築士は単に設計・工事監理を行うだけでなく「建築物の総合的な専門家」として役割を果たすことが求められています。今回、対象実務の考え方に「建築物を調査・評価する」業務が追加されたとともに、対象実務も拡大されました。

[例]指定科目を修めて大学を卒業し、1級建築士の免許を取得する場合

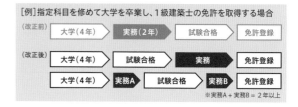

総合資格学院

東京都新宿区西新宿1-26-2　新宿野村ビル22F

22F SHINJUKU NOMURA BLDG.1-26-2,
Nishishinjuku,Shinjuku-ku,Tokyo

School web site :http://www.shikaku.co.jp/
Corporate web site :http://www.sogoshikaku.co.jp/

総合資格 (検索)

KEIO ARCHITECTURE Year Book 2018-2019
慶應アーキテクチャ イヤーブック 2018-2019

発行日　　2020 年 3 月 20 日　初版発行
編著　　　慶應アーキテクチャ編集委員会

発行人　　岸 隆司
発行元　　株式会社 総合資格
　　〒 163-0557　東京都新宿区西新宿 1-26-2 新宿野村ビル 22F
　　TEL 03-3340-6714（出版局）
株式会社 総合資格　　　　http://www.sogoshikaku.co.jp/
総合資格学院　　　　　　https://www.shikaku.co.jp/
総合資格学院　出版サイト　http://www.shikaku-books.jp/
印刷　　　シナノ書籍印刷 株式会社

編集・デザイン　　　慶應アーキテクチャ編集委員会
　　　　　　　　　　ダルコ・ラドヴィッチ（編集責任者）、小林博人、ホルヘ・アルマザン
　　　　　　　　　　佐野哲史、高須雪絵、元山雅仁、鮫島卓臣、木下規海、石井結実、加藤旬、
　　　　　　　　　　岩田あま美、川本純平、西堀槙一、重村浩槻、鈴木浩貴、森祐樹、楊沐渓、
　　　　　　　　　　他多数
編集協力　　　　　　株式会社 総合資格 首都圏統括本部（田中雅弘）
　　　　　　　　　　株式会社 総合資格 川崎支店（増井進之介、一瀬克典、霧生航稀）
　　　　　　　　　　株式会社 総合資格 出版局（新垣宜樹、金城夏水）、牧妙
デザイン協力　　　　株式会社 総合資格 出版局（三宅崇）

Printed in Japan
ISBN 978-4-86417-340-7
Ⓒ 慶應アーキテクチャ編集委員会

First edition　　　3/20/2020
Editor　　　　　　Keio Architecture Editorial Committee

Publisher　　　　Takashi Kishi
Publisher　　　　SOGO SHIKAKU CO.,LTD.
　　　　　　　　　Shinjuku-Nomura Building 22F 1-26-2 Shinjuku-ku, Tokyo, 163-0557, Japan

Japan
+ 81-3-3340-6714
SOGO SHIKAKU CO.,LTD.
http://www.sogoshikaku.co.jp/
SOGO SHIKAKU CO.,LTD. SOGO SHIKAKU Academy
https://www.shikaku.co.jp/
SOGO SHIKAKU CO.,LTD. publishing department
http://www.shikaku-books.jp/

Printing　　　　　Shinano books Printing Co,.Ltd.

Editorial team　　　Keio Architecture Editorial Committee:
　　　　　　　　　　CDW Keio Architecture Core Team:
　　　　　　　　　　　Darko Radović (Responsible Editor), Hiroto Kobayashi, Jorge Almazán
　　　　　　　　　　Technical Editorial Team:
　　　　　　　　　　Satoshi Sano, Yukie Takasu, Masahito Motoyama
　　　　　　　　　　with Takuomi Samejima, Norimi Kinoshita, Yumi Ishii, Shun Kato,
　　　　　　　　　　Amami Iwata, Junpei Kawamoto, Shinichi Nishibori, Hiroki Shigemura,
　　　　　　　　　　Yuki Mori, Koki Suzuki, Muxi Yang and other members of co+labo radović
Editorial Cooperation　SOGO SHIKAKU CO.,LTD. Metropolitan Area Headquarters (Masahiro Tanaka)
　　　　　　　　　　SOGO SHIKAKU CO.,LTD. Kawasaki Branch (Shinnosuke Masui,
　　　　　　　　　　Katsunori Ichise, Kazuki Kiriu)
　　　　　　　　　　SOGO SHIKAKU CO.,LTD. Publishing Department
　　　　　　　　　　(Yoshiki Arakaki,Natsumi Kaneshiro), Tae Maki
Design cooperation　SOGO SHIKAKU CO.,LTD. Publishing Department
　　　　　　　　　　(Takashi Miyake)

Printed in Japan
ISBN 978-4-86417-340-7
Ⓒ Keio Architecture Editorial Committee